I0810425

IMAGES
of America

ALLEGHANY COUNTY

On the Cover: The natural formation of the Falling Spring Falls has been a favorite attraction to local citizens and visitors to the Alleghany County area since the beginning of settlement. This photograph of the falls was taken around 1900 and looks very different from the falls today. Limestone deposits of marl were mined from the face of the falls in the 1930s and were used by local resorts and farms for agricultural purposes. The current view from US Route 220 between Covington and Hot Springs is different because the course of the water flow was altered. (Courtesy of the Alleghany Historical Society.)

IMAGES
of America

Alleghany County

Samuel Hale II and Dr. Paul Linkenhoker
on behalf of the Alleghany Historical Society

ARCADIA
PUBLISHING

ISBN 978-1-4671-2435-5

Published by Arcadia Publishing
Charleston, South Carolina

Printed in the United States of America

Library of Congress Control Number: 2016953607

For all general information, please contact Arcadia Publishing:
Telephone 843-853-2070
Fax 843-853-0044
E-mail sales@arcadiapublishing.com
For customer service and orders:
Toll-Free 1-888-313-2665

Visit us on the Internet at www.arcadiapublishing.com

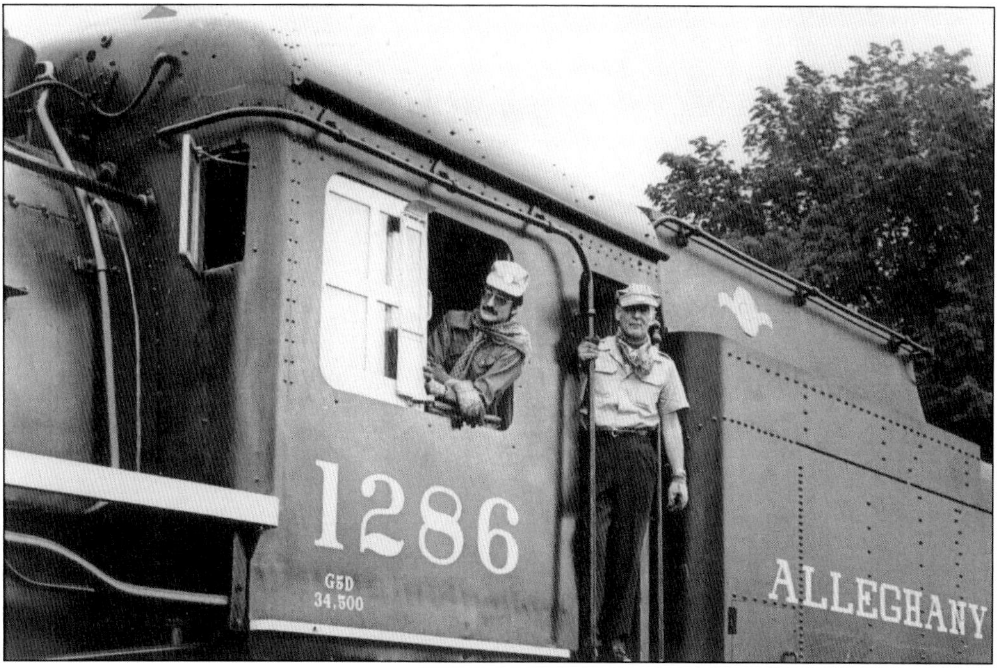

Horton P. Beirne and his father, Richard F. Beirne III, are pictured on Alleghany Central locomotive 1286. This book is respectfully dedicated to Horton, who is daily missed for his work in the newspaper, the historical society, and in the community.

(Courtesy of the Alleghany Historical Society.)

Contents

Acknowledgments

The Alleghany Historical Society (AHS) appreciates the many contributions and the hard work that went into the making of this book. Special thanks go to the entire Beirne family. Three generations of Beirnes have led the *Covington Virginian* and the subsequent *Virginian Review*. Horton and Mary Ann Beirne donated the negatives from the newspaper collections to the society, as well as Horton's collection of early area photographs, without which this book would not have happened. (AHS-VR) is used to identify all of the photographs that came from the Beirnes.

Howard Hammond (HH) graciously allowed the historical society to scan several photographs from his expansive collections, notably on the iron industry. Boys' Home (BH) gave the historical society permission to scan and use some of the early photographs from its collections. The generosity of Derrick Barr (DB) provided the illustration of Dunlap School and Dunlap Tea Room, which had been located on his property. Floyd Harrison and Ed Loiseau provided the society with a donation of early photographs of their home, Milton Hall, a local landmark used often for society events. Anne Wright and Patsy McKinney (AW and PM) provided priceless photographs of the Beaverdam Falls near Earlhurst, in the southern end of the county. The Alleghany Historical Society especially acknowledges the Chesapeake and Ohio Historical Society (COHS) for permitting the use of photographs from its extensive collections in this publication.

While not directly involved in the actual publication, the society would like to recognize other individuals, groups, and organizations whose support ensures our existence and the accomplishment of our mission to preserve the heritage of the Alleghany Highlands and encourage the study of local history. Amy Ray is the hostess of our museum operations and headquarters at the Covington Chesapeake & Ohio Depot Complex. Allen Dressler and Jane Tucker, of the City of Covington Department of Parks and Recreation, provide management and oversight of the depot. Bucky Mottern is an invaluable resource for information about Alleghany County and the significance of local sites of historic interest. Al Kresse has a wealth of knowledge about the local iron industry. Ina Henderson of the Alleghany Highlands Genealogical Society is also a source of local information.

Final recognition goes to the board and members of the Alleghany Historical Society, whose support and encouragement ensured the completion of this project: president Bonnie Keyser, vice president and CEO Paul Linkenhoker, secretary Linda Morrison, treasurer Nancy Tyree, and board members Mary Ann Beirne, Mary Frances Mays-Davis, Floyd Harrison, Garland Jefferson, Vivian Sutphin, and Wynona Crush.

INTRODUCTION

Alleghany County is located in the west-central highlands of Virginia and lies in the midst of the Allegheny Range of the Appalachian Mountains. It borders West Virginia and the Virginia counties of Bath, Botetourt, Craig, and Rockbridge. In his book about place names in Virginia, James Hagemann (1988) has this to say about Alleghany County:

> Formed in 1822 from parts of Bath, Botetourt, and Monroe, this county was named for the Allegheny Mountains that rise to the west. For some reason, the mountains are spelled with an "e" and the county with an "a." The name is an Indian word meaning "endless," and so they must have seemed to the early pioneers.

The two largest communities are Covington and Clifton Forge. Covington emerged as a settlement in 1746, when Joseph Carpenter and Peter Wright settled on the banks of the Jackson River. It was established in 1819, when James and Samuel Merry laid out lots, and it became a town in 1833. It became a city in 1953 and has always served as the county seat.

Clifton Forge was originally known as Williamson Station when it was established in 1861. The terminus of the Virginia Central Railroad had reached the Jackson River depot near Selma prior to the Civil War. When it was established as a town in 1884, the community took on the name Clifton Forge from a nearby iron operation. It became a city in 1906 but reverted to a town in 2001.

There were other prominent settlements that generally appeared due to the mining of iron ore and the smelting furnaces throughout the county. Longdale, Iron Gate, Selma, Low Moor, Rich Patch, Boiling Spring, Jordan Mines, Callaghan, Falling Spring, Stack Mines, Hematite, Earlhurst, Sweet Chalybeate, and Alleghany are smaller communities today that are reminders of the iron era in the county.

There are a number of mountain streams that feed two main rivers, both of which enter into Alleghany from its northern neighbor, Bath County. These two rivers, the Jackson and Cowpasture, flow together just south of the town of Iron Gate and form the James River. Two other streams, Dunlap and Potts Creeks, are nearly large enough to be called rivers and flow into the Jackson at two locations in Covington. In short, a stranger to Alleghany County should envision a mountainous region with clear streams flowing into and through several river valleys.

While some settlers came from eastern Virginia and represented the Anglican heritage, other immigrants found their way into the Valley of Virginia and the trans-Allegheny region by way of Pennsylvania. Germans, Scots, and Scots-Irish were the dominant European settlers. Of course, Native Americans and African Americans were also among the settlers in the region. Today, diverse Alleghany County includes people from most of the world's regions and representatives of many races, creeds, and religions.

Extensive rail shops and yards were located in Clifton Forge, which served as an important terminus of the Chesapeake & Ohio Railway (C&O) and its successor, the Chessie System. When the CSX Corporation took over rail operations in the early 1980s, most of this activity was transferred to other locations. While this had a significant negative effect on the local economy, the area has rebounded and continues to prosper and capitalize on its railroad heritage.

In the early 1900s, the dominance of the iron industry declined, and a new manufacturing venture became the primary employer in Alleghany County. This was the paper mill located at Covington and owned and operated by the West Virginia Pulp and Paper Company. The company is known today as WestRock, and it continues to be the economic mainstay of the region. Many service jobs also exist as a result of the presence of these industries.

The region today is referred to as the Alleghany Highlands and is emerging as a popular tourist destination for those seeking outdoor adventure and activity. It is also developing as a venue for the arts, with a theater and numerous opportunities for both the creative and performing arts. The region's public schools provide a quality education, and Dabney S. Lancaster Community College offers classes and programs that provide individuals with the knowledge, training, and life skills for future development and success.

While there are four governing bodies, with one county, one city, and two towns, the communities work together on a number of different initiatives to help improve economic opportunities. The Alleghany Highlands Chamber of Commerce and Tourism and the Alleghany Highlands Economic Development Corporation have a strong partnership aimed at economic development. Both Clifton Forge Main Street and Olde Town Covington are working toward downtown revitalization.

When the locally owned and operated Alleghany Regional Hospital was sold to Columbia/Hospital Corporation of America in 1995, the Alleghany Foundation was established, and has since provided significant grant funding to help the area move forward and improve life and welfare in the Alleghany Highlands. This book is a celebration and pictorial documentation of the people, communities, and significant historical events of Alleghany County, Virginia.

One

Early Alleghany County

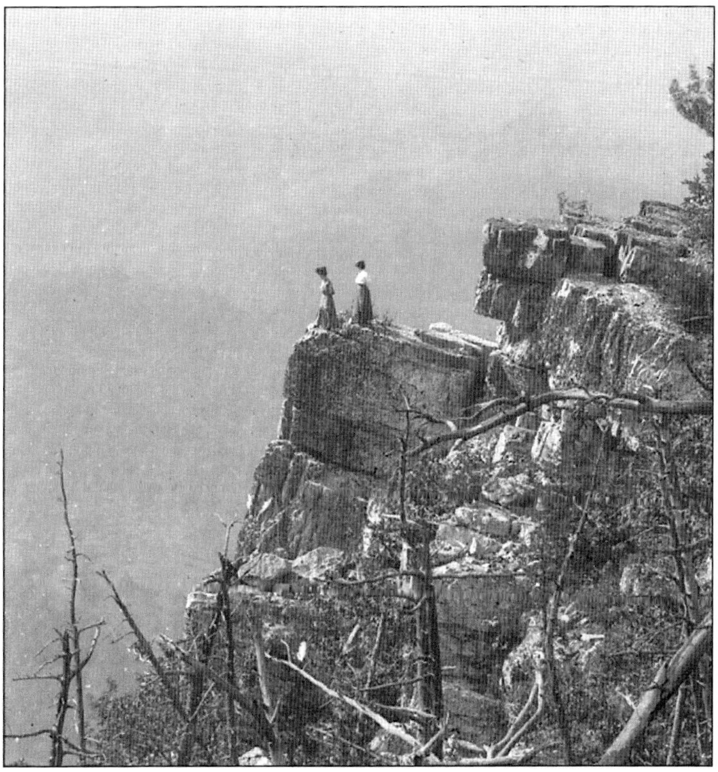

Flag Rock is a well-known landmark on the side of the mountain south of Selma and western Clifton Forge. This should not be confused with a similar feature known as the Devil's Backbone in the Iron Gate Gap. Because of the unimpeded view of the valley from the rock, it was used as a Confederate lookout post. This early-20th-century photograph shows ladies in their long dresses enjoying the view from the rock. (AHS.)

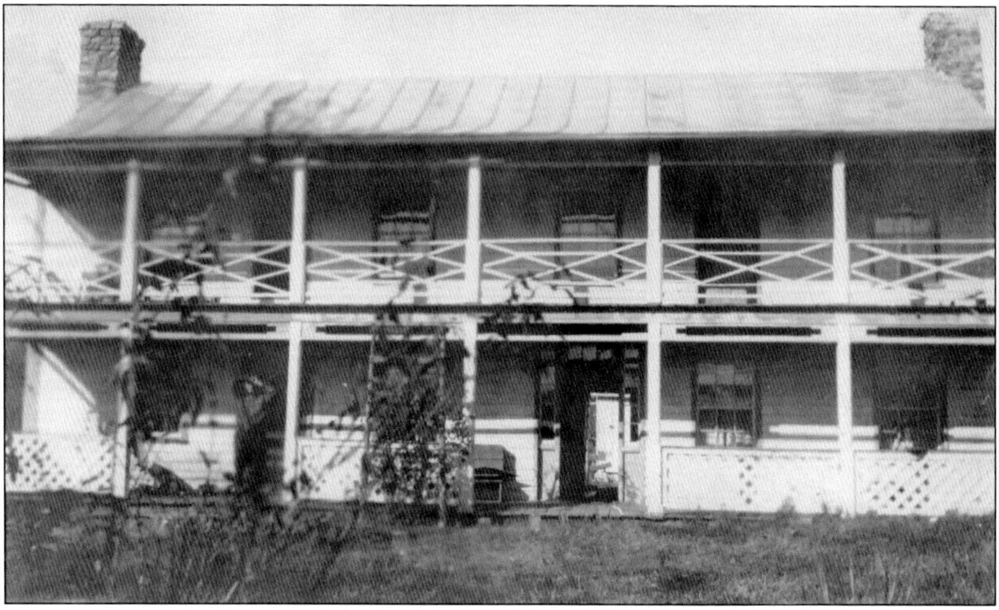

Jacob Persinger Jr. was born about 1752 and was carried off by Native Americans around 1756. He was returned to the region after the French and Indian War and was claimed by Jacob Persinger Sr. He fought in the Revolutionary War in Arbuckle's Virginia Company from September 1775 to November 1776. In 1777, he bought 110 acres of land on Potts Creek, and built this house in 1778. Persinger was a constable from 1809 to 1815 and died in 1840. (AHS.)

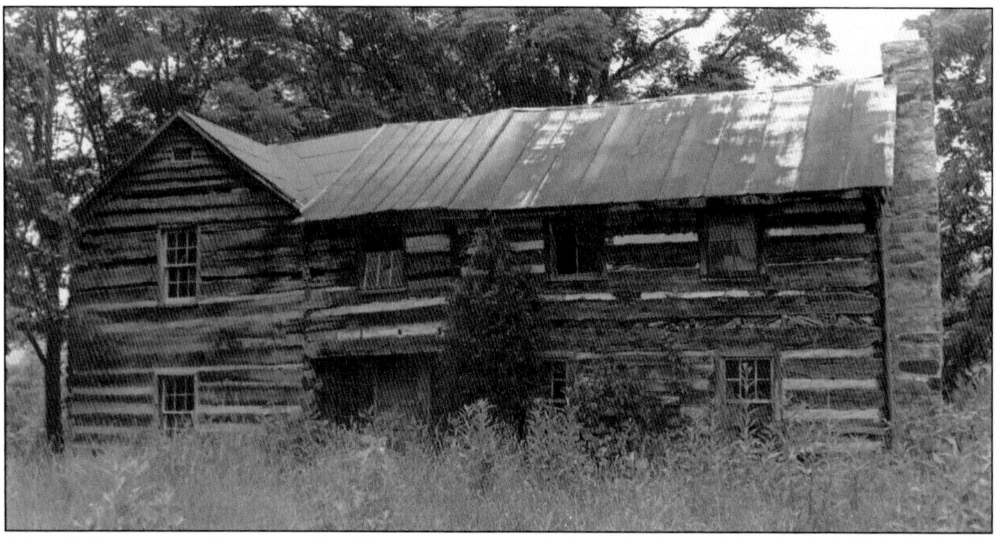

The William Mann house is the oldest surviving structure in the county. Mann was one of the local men who fought at Point Pleasant in 1774. This log house was built by him in 1761 and is located in Falling Spring. It has been partially restored by Rodney Kyle at its original location on Jackson River Road. (AHS.)

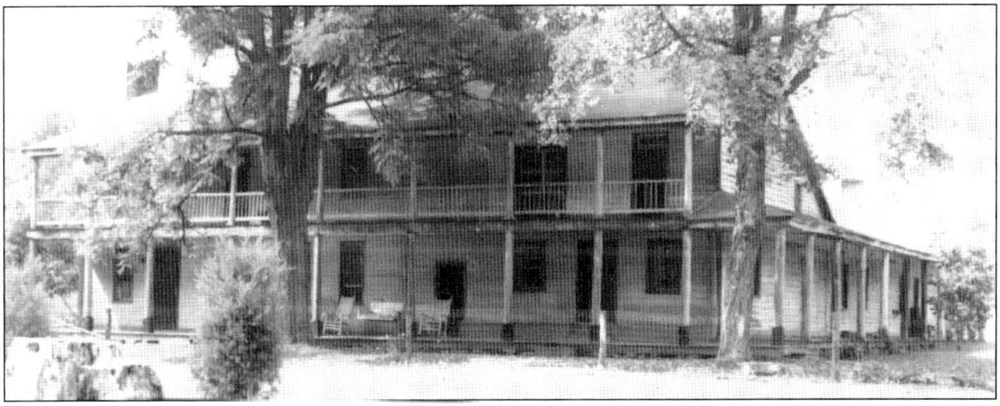

The oldest section of Crow's Tavern was built prior to 1810 by James Crow. His son, Col. John Crow, made the tavern famous. It was an important stop on the road to the various mineral springs and spas. Colonel Crow died in 1861, and the popularity of the tavern went with him, but it continued operating into the 1890s. It was located at the forks of roads leading to Sweet Chalybeate and White Sulphur Springs, now Routes 311 and 159. It burned down in 1969. (AHS.)

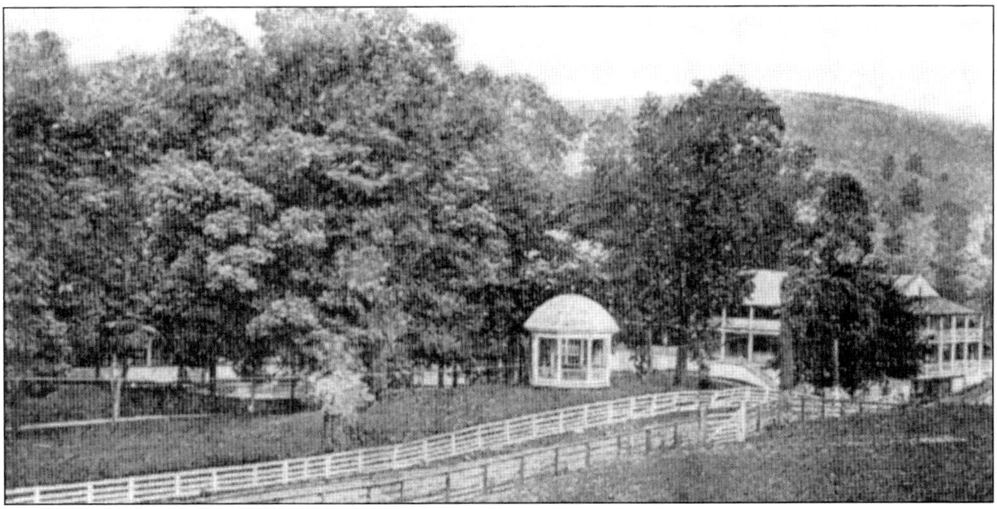

The first recorded use of Sweet Chalybeate Springs was in 1772. It was originally called Red Sweet Springs or just Red Springs. Most of the buildings dated to the early 1800s. The resort, located just a few miles from Sweet Springs, West Virginia, was last used as a spa in 1916. This photograph is from an advertising brochure printed around 1900. (AHS.)

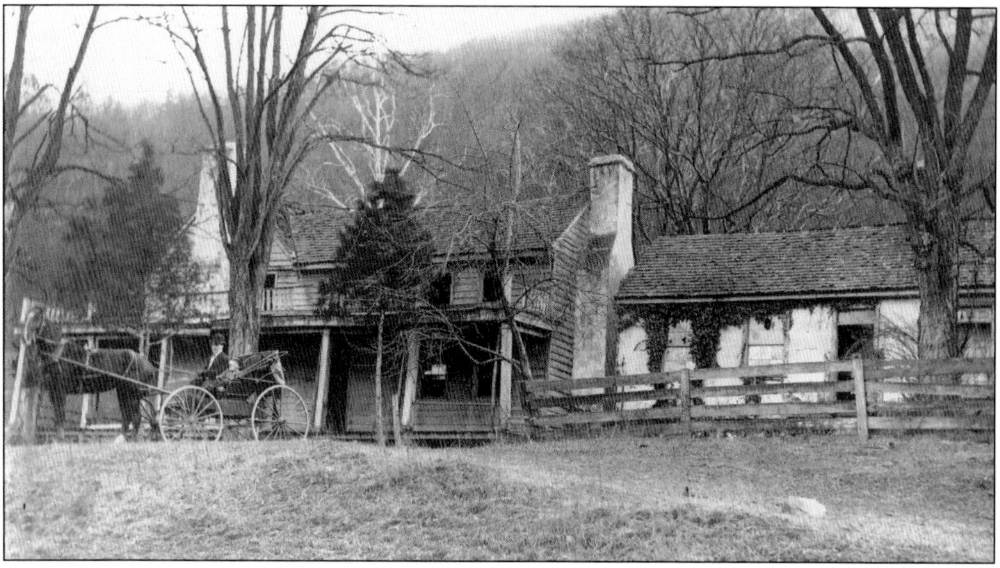

Pence-Steele Tavern was built around 1790 by Peter Pence. It was located on the Lexington-Kanawha Turnpike about a mile west of Low Moor. Peter Pence sold the tavern to Isaac Steele in 1822. The tavern continued to operate until the C&O Railway was built through the area in 1868. It burned down prior to 1937. (AHS-VR.)

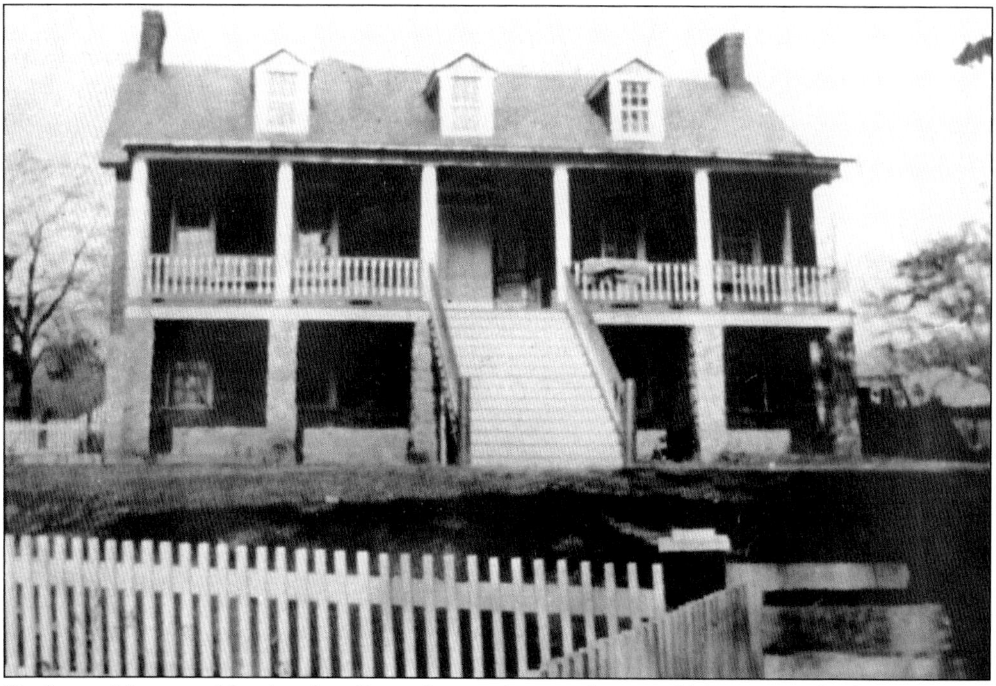

Dr. James Merry and his brother Samuel moved into what would become Alleghany County around 1817 and bought 138 acres that were subsequently divided to create what would become Covington in 1818. This house was built by the Merrys in Low Moor around 1819 and became a working plantation. The land has remained in the Gleason family since the 1890s. Clifton Middle and Mountain View Elementary Schools were built on part of the property, a portion of which was donated by the Gleason heirs. (AHS.)

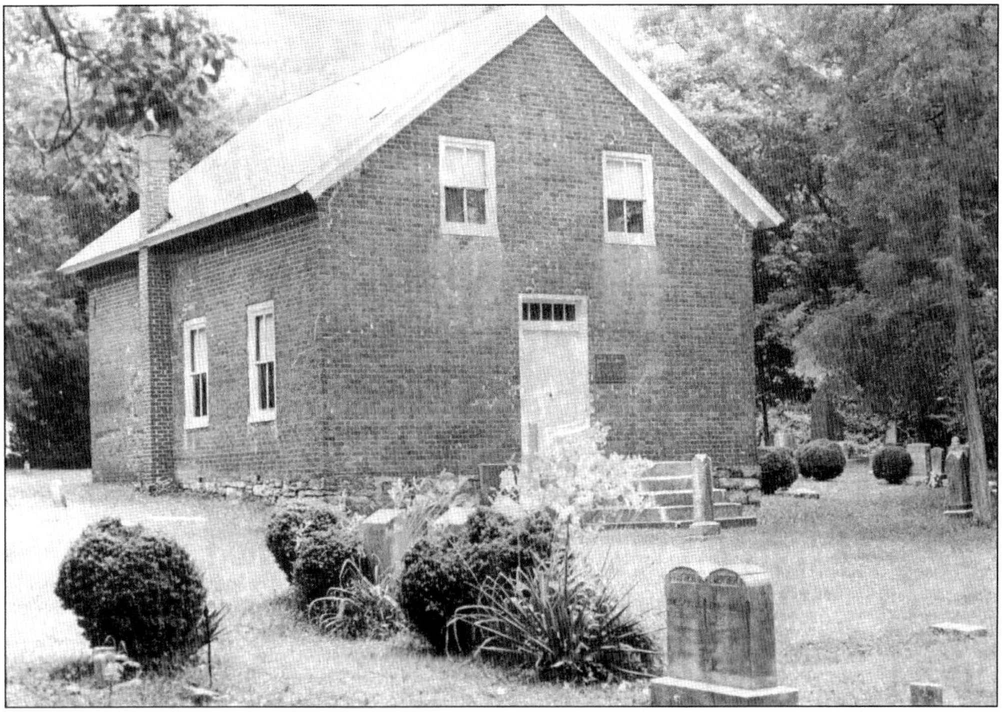

The Oakland Grove Presbyterian Church was built in 1834 utilizing handmade bricks brought from the Merry Farm. There were originally doors on each side of the church for men and women to enter separately. The balcony in the church provided seating for slaves attending services. It was utilized as a hospital during the Civil War. It is still a Presbyterian church and holds an annual worship service. (AHS-VR.)

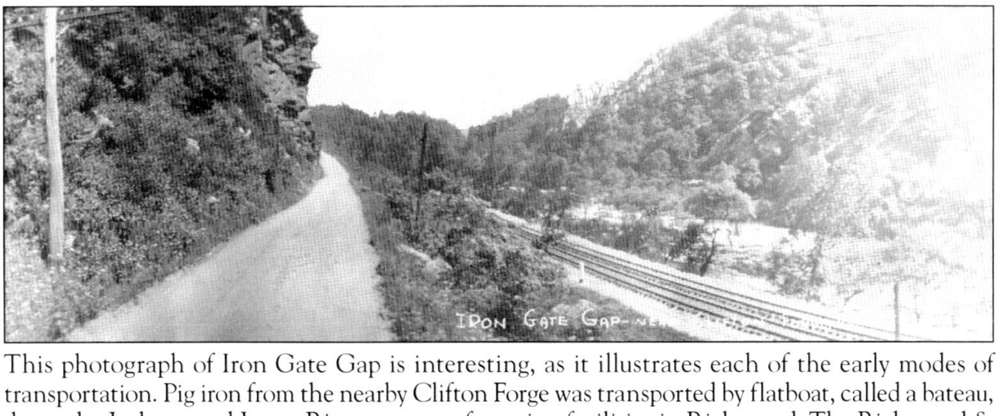

This photograph of Iron Gate Gap is interesting, as it illustrates each of the early modes of transportation. Pig iron from the nearby Clifton Forge was transported by flatboat, called a bateau, down the Jackson and James Rivers to manufacturing facilities in Richmond. The Richmond & Alleghany Railroad built this section of track around 1880; it became part of the C&O in 1890. To make room for the tracks, the old road was relocated above the floor of the gap. (AHS.)

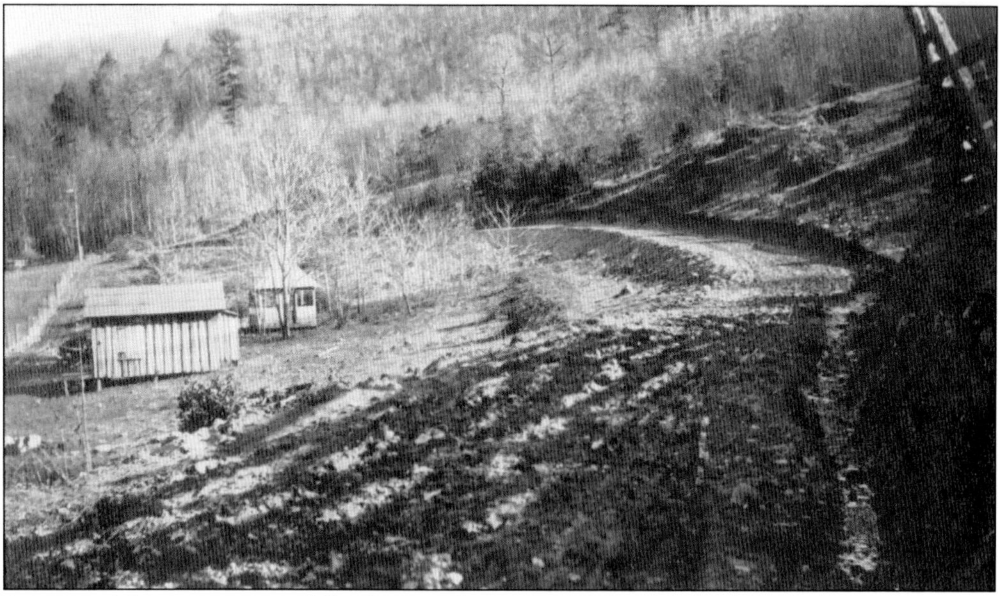

Because of the importance of flood plains for crops, the early roads typically went around the base of the mountains and avoided crossing through prime farm land. This eliminated many river fords and kept the roads from flooding. This photograph from around 1915 shows the road going through Indian Draft to Bath County from Callaghan, near Milton Hall. (AHS.)

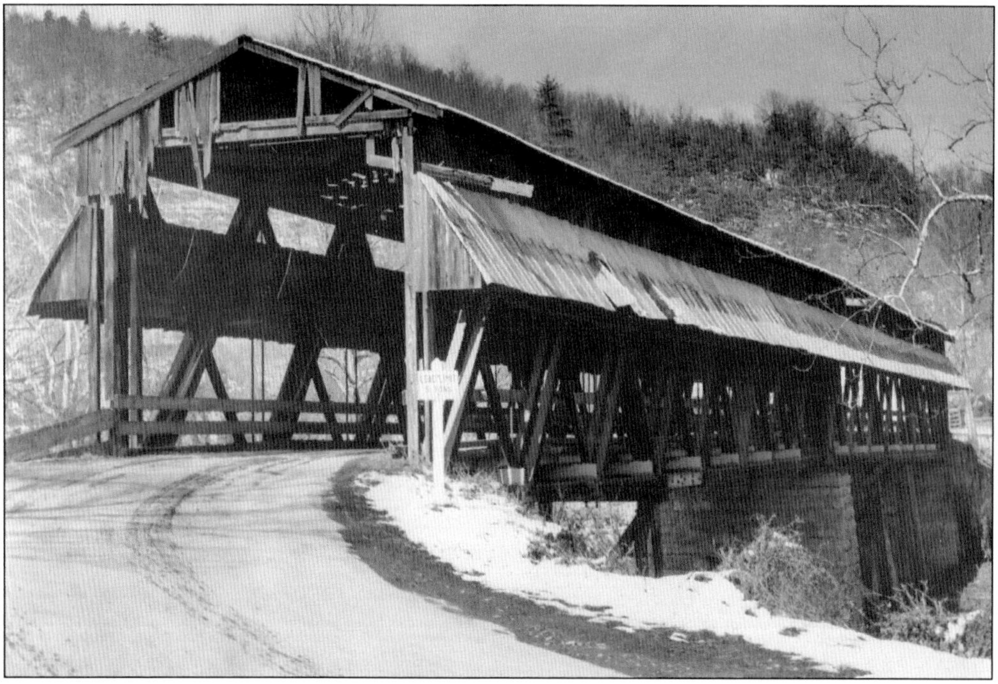

Deep Ford was a ford on the Jackson River dating to the early 1800s. It was deep when the river was low and otherwise impassible, so a bridge was built. This covered wooden bridge is believed to date from the late 1800s and is not the first bridge on the site. This bridge was located at what is known as Petticoat Junction today and was replaced in 1950 with the current concrete bridge. (AHS-VR.)

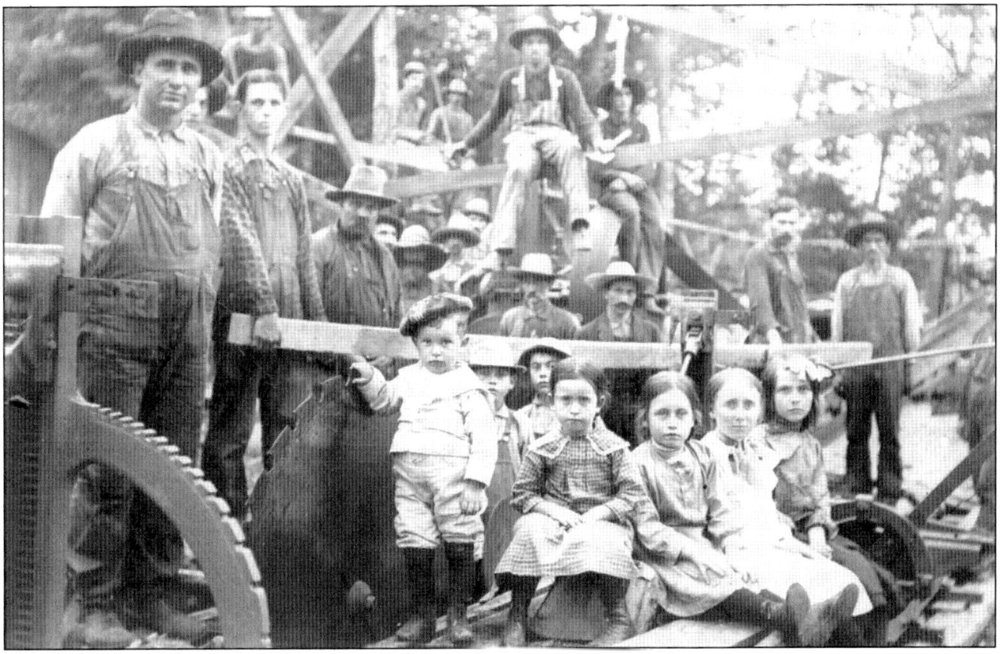

The industrial heritage of Alleghany County developed due to the abundance of several natural resources: timber, iron ore, and water. The wood harvested from local forests was an important commodity for building as well as for making paper and rayon. In this photograph, the Allen Byrd Humphries family is operating their sawmill in the Rich Patch area around 1910. (AHS.)

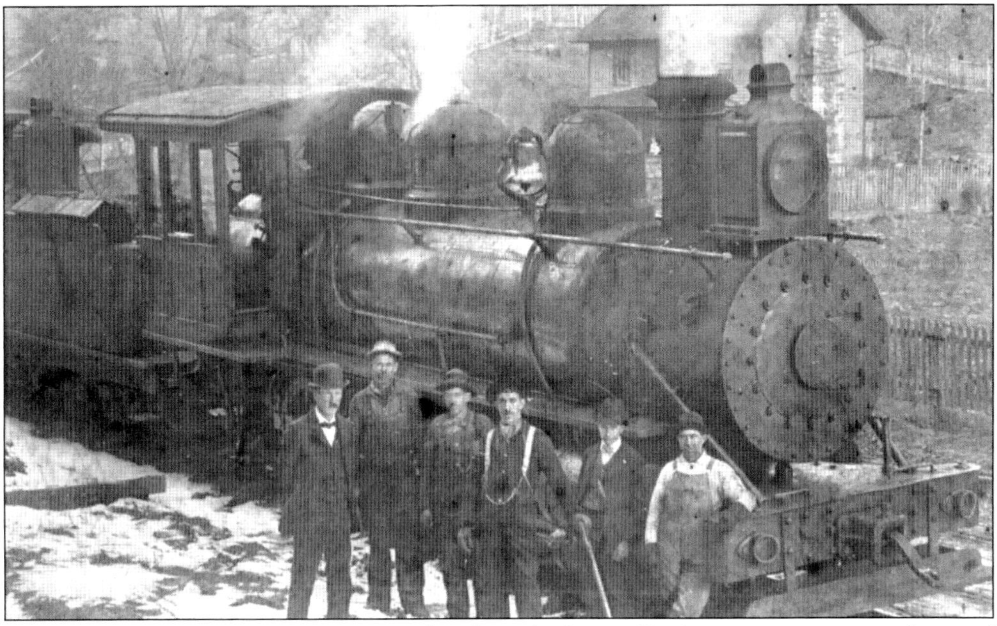

The Longdale Furnace narrow-gauge railroad was built in 1874. It was an instrumental part of community transportation and was utilized to take workers to the mines and iron ore from the mines. Both workers and pig iron were transferred to the C&O Railway. Many workers were carried to the Longdale Station. This locomotive is one of the Longdale dinky steam engines used in the mining operations. (COHS.)

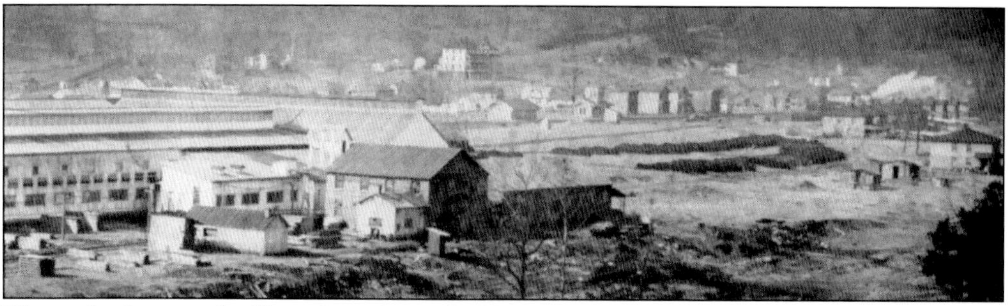

This early photograph of Iron Gate shows the Union Tannery on the left, the Iron Gate Hotel in the middle background, and the Alleghany Furnace on the far right. Farming operations began in the area around 1770, and a trading post was located nearby. The origin of the name is contested, but one legend contends that the town was named for a real iron gate that went across the river. It is the southern gateway to Alleghany County. (AHS.)

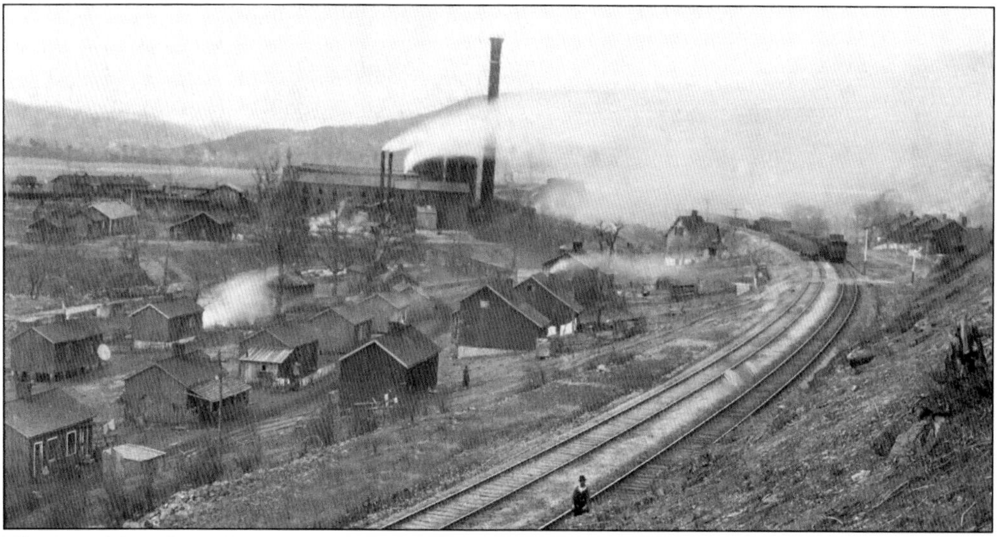

The Low Moor Iron Company was created in 1873 and opened its first blast furnace in 1880. It operated until 1926. The company was in business later than any of the other local iron furnaces. It was primarily located in Low Moor, near the Lewis-Gale Alleghany Hospital and Brian Center, but also had a large blast furnace in the Sunnymeade section of Covington. (AHS.)

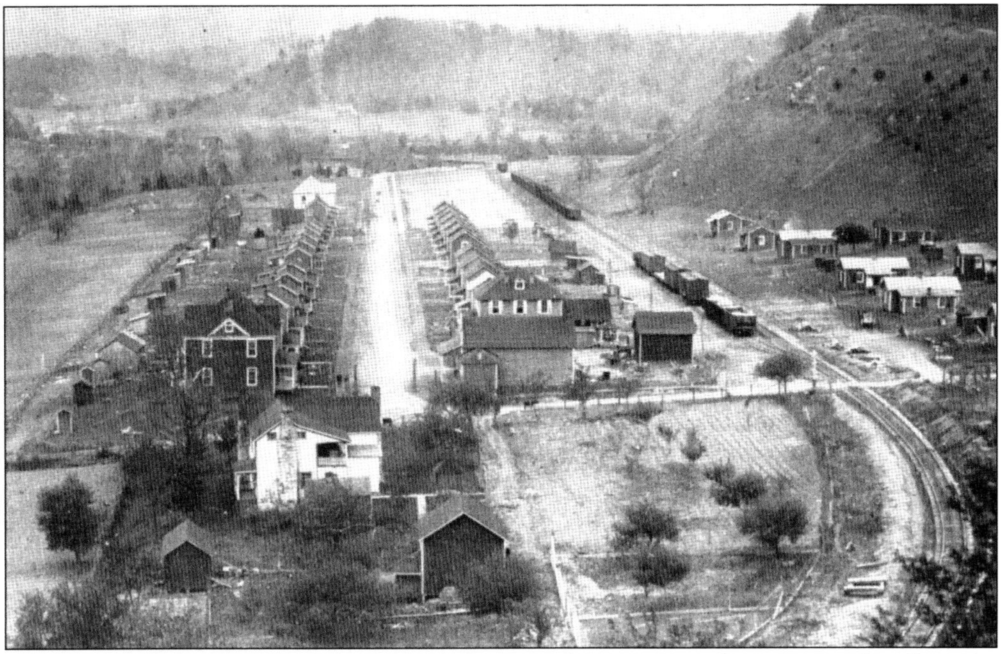

This is the company town of Jordan, located near Jordan Mines in the Potts Creek valley. The Jordan Mines were operated by the Low Moor Iron Company from 1906 to 1920 and produced over 600,000 tons of iron ore. After the mines were shut down, the town was largely abandoned; today, only two of these houses remain. The large white house in the foreground was the doctor's residence, and the large house to its left was the home of the commissary. (AHS.)

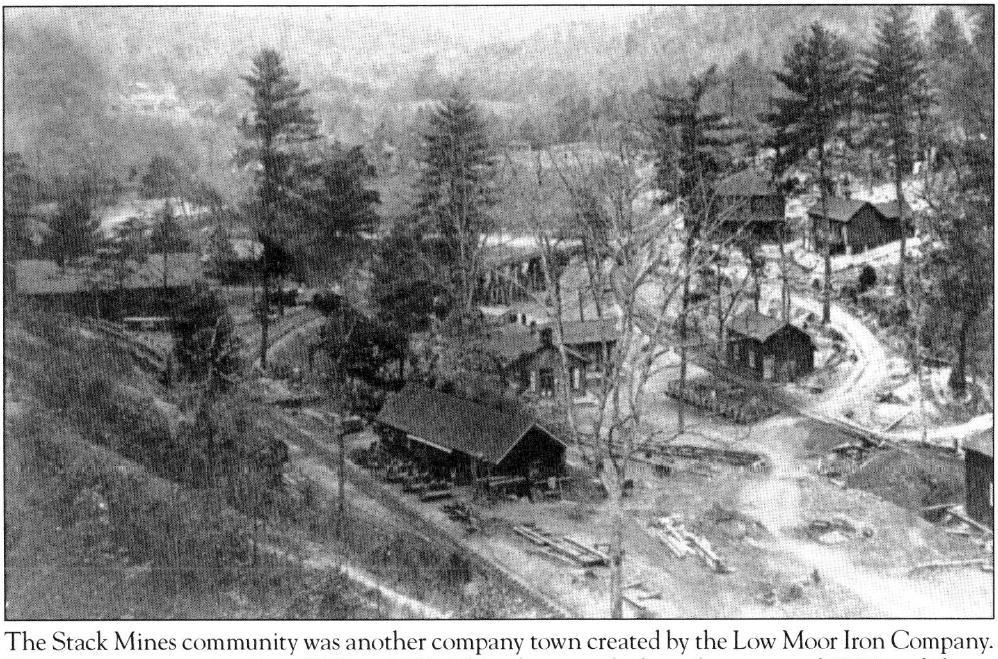

The Stack Mines community was another company town created by the Low Moor Iron Company. The mines were active from 1893 to 1910. This photograph dates from around 1900 and shows some of the equipment houses for mining operations on the narrow-gauge railroad. There are also company houses visible on the right and in the far distance. (HH.)

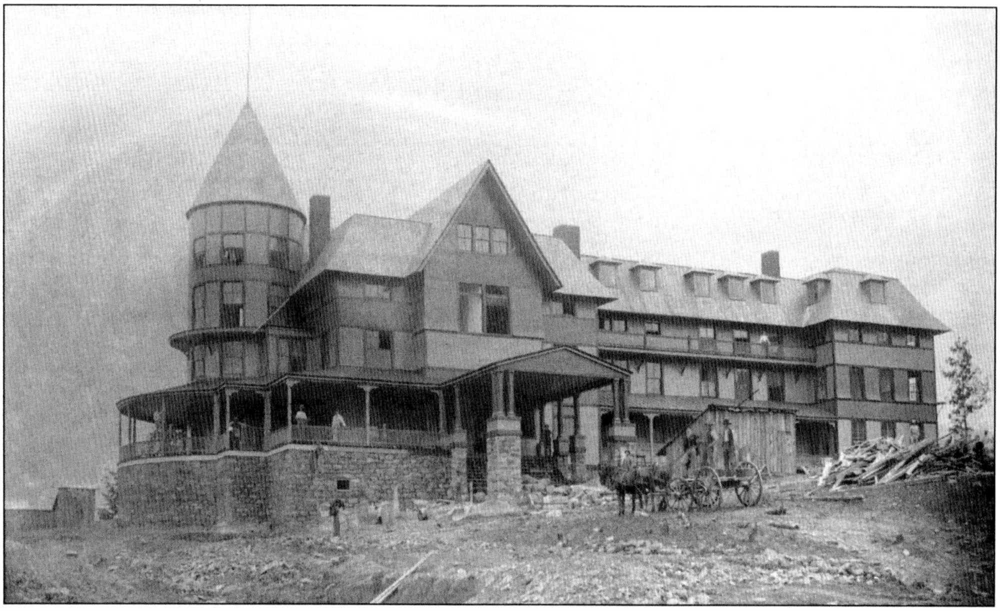

This picture shows the Gladys Inn in Clifton Forge while under construction in 1894. It was built to accommodate the high volume of visitors traveling by rail. Unfortunately, the inn was too far from the tracks, so a new Gladys Inn and depot were built in 1896. This building became the C&O Hospital in 1897 but was razed and replaced with a brick structure in 1917. (AHS.)

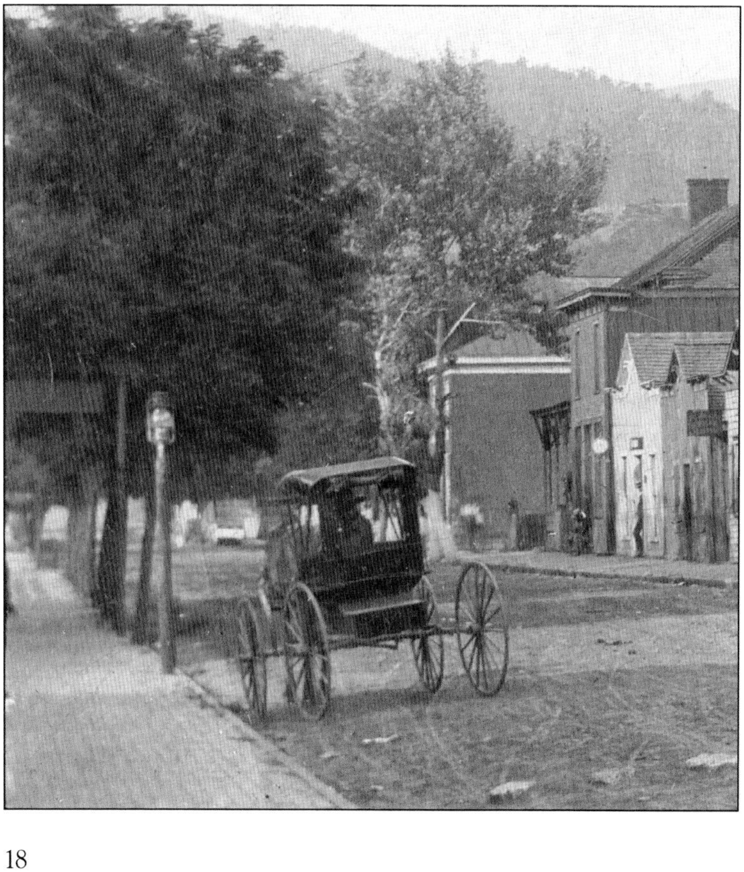

The streets of Covington were designed with the creation of the town in 1818, but they changed names over the years. Maps in 1872 identified this as Main Street, but by 1890, it was called Bath Street. At that point, either name was appropriate. Today it is simply known as Main Street. This picture was taken around 1900. Notice the street light and the step-stone cross walk. (AHS-VR.)

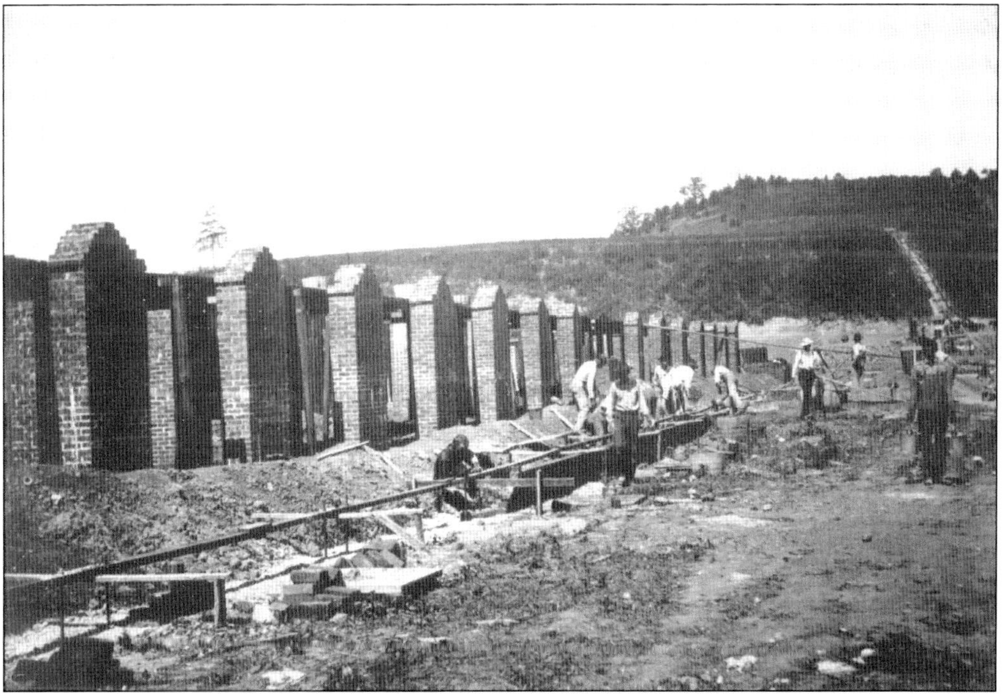

Construction of a paper mill by West Virginia Pulp and Paper began in 1899 on the banks of Dunlap Creek and on the opposite side of the Jackson River from Covington. The area offered everything the mill needed: water, pulpwood forests, and access to the railway. After more than 100 years of operation, expansion, and developing technology, the mill is now the largest of its kind in the world and is the economic mainstay of the community. (AHS-VR.)

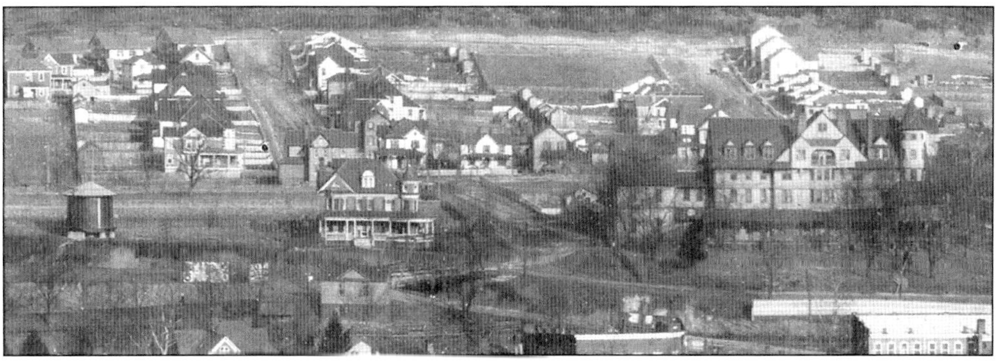

The Covington Improvement Company sold land for the development of the community and encouraged businesses to come into the area. A large hotel was built to accommodate businessmen and travelers on the C&O Railway. The Intermont was built in 1891 with hot and cold water and electricity. It was billed as the finest hotel between Washington and Cincinnati, but competition from the Homestead, Greenbrier, and others resulted in a lack of business, and it was torn down in 1913. (AHS.)

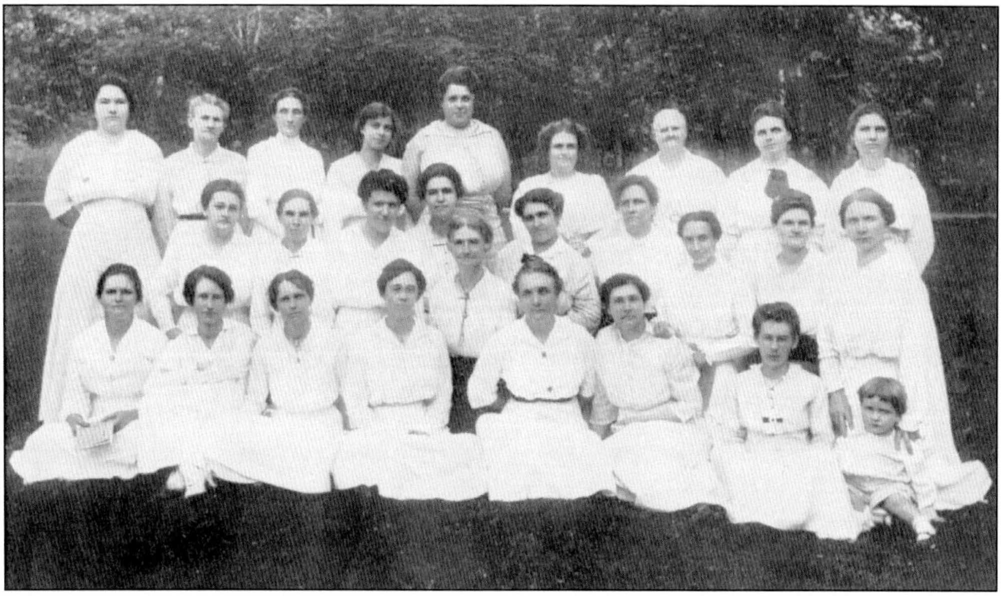

The Low Moor Homekeepers Club was started in 1915. It was a home demonstration club that was devoted to exploring new technology and labor-saving devices to make life easier. This picture shows all the original members. Margaret King was the home demonstration agent for the county at that time. (AHS.)

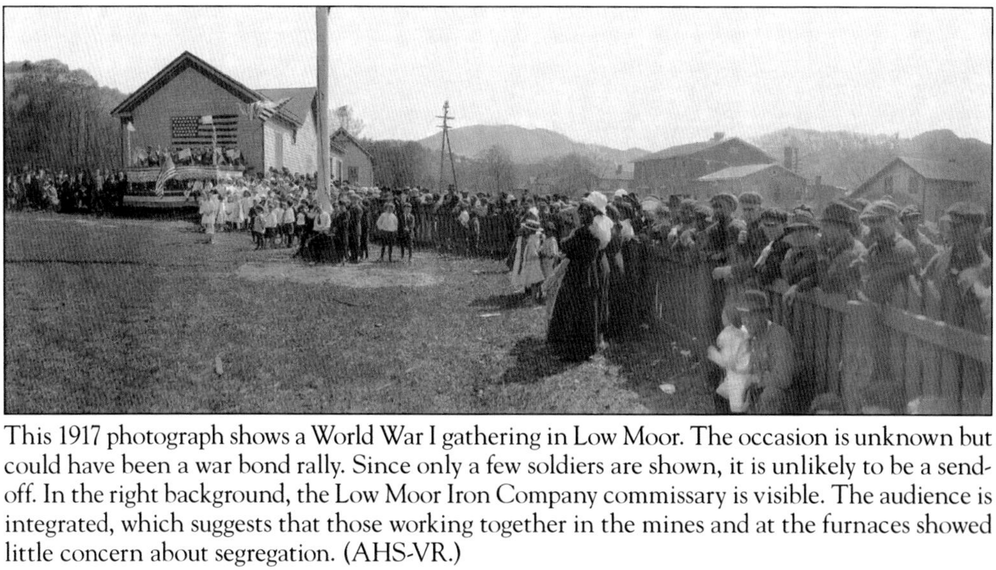

This 1917 photograph shows a World War I gathering in Low Moor. The occasion is unknown but could have been a war bond rally. Since only a few soldiers are shown, it is unlikely to be a send-off. In the right background, the Low Moor Iron Company commissary is visible. The audience is integrated, which suggests that those working together in the mines and at the furnaces showed little concern about segregation. (AHS-VR.)

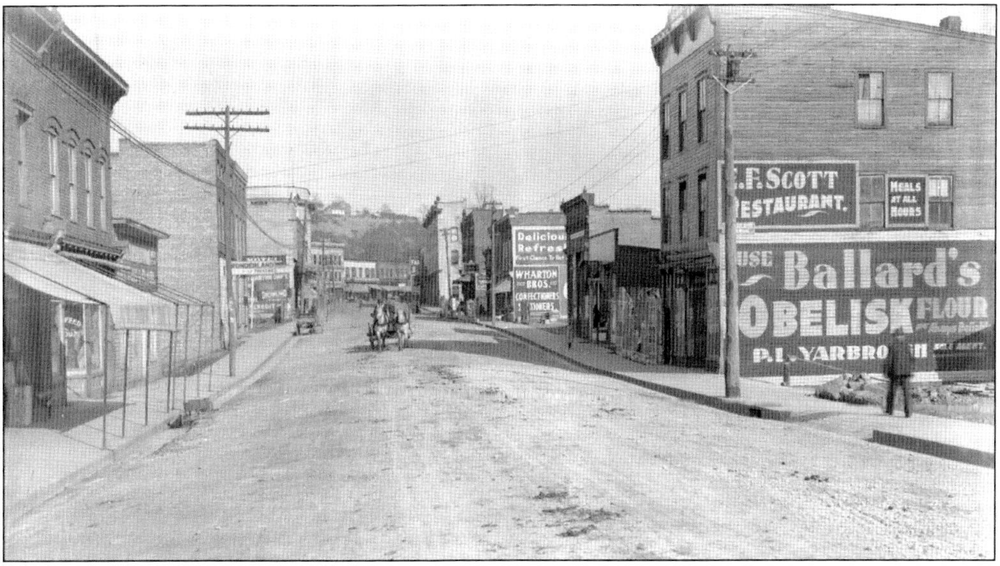

Clifton Forge has changed surprisingly little in the last 110 years or so. This picture was taken looking northeast on Ridgeway Street between 1900 and 1910. Signs painted on the sides of buildings were a prime form of advertising during the period. Wharton Brothers, at center, made early postcards of the area. The Scott building, on the far right, still stands and is next to the taxi building on the corner. (AHS.)

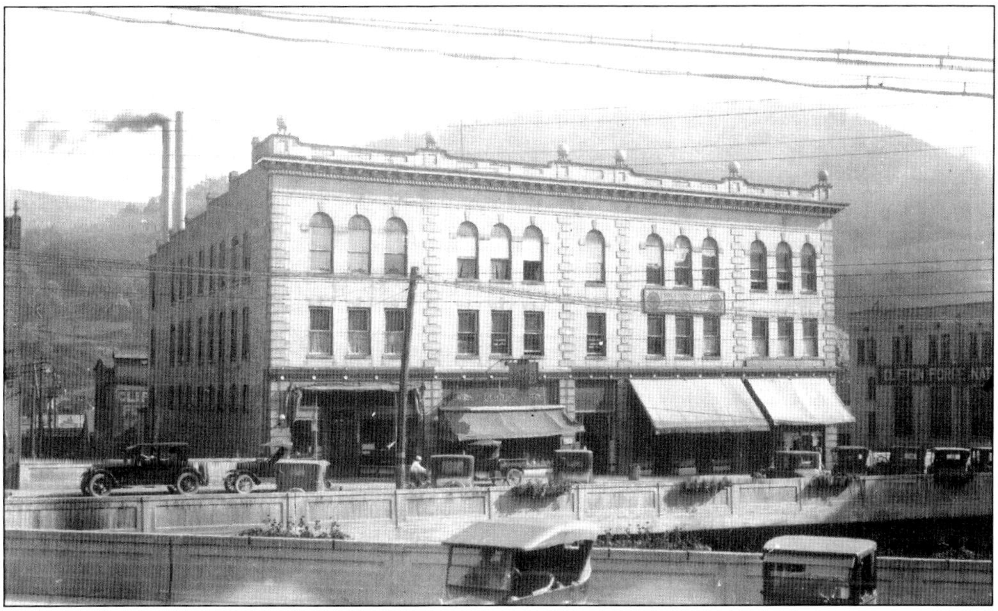

Clifton Forge is known for being "Scenic, Busy, Friendly." The Alleghany Building was constructed in 1910. At the time this picture was taken around 1920, it housed the American Legion and Groves Drug store. Buildings of the Clifton Forge Ice and Bottle Works were behind the Alleghany Building and housed facilities for making ice and ice cream. The large number of vehicles seen here supports the fact that Clifton Forge was busy. (AHS-VR.)

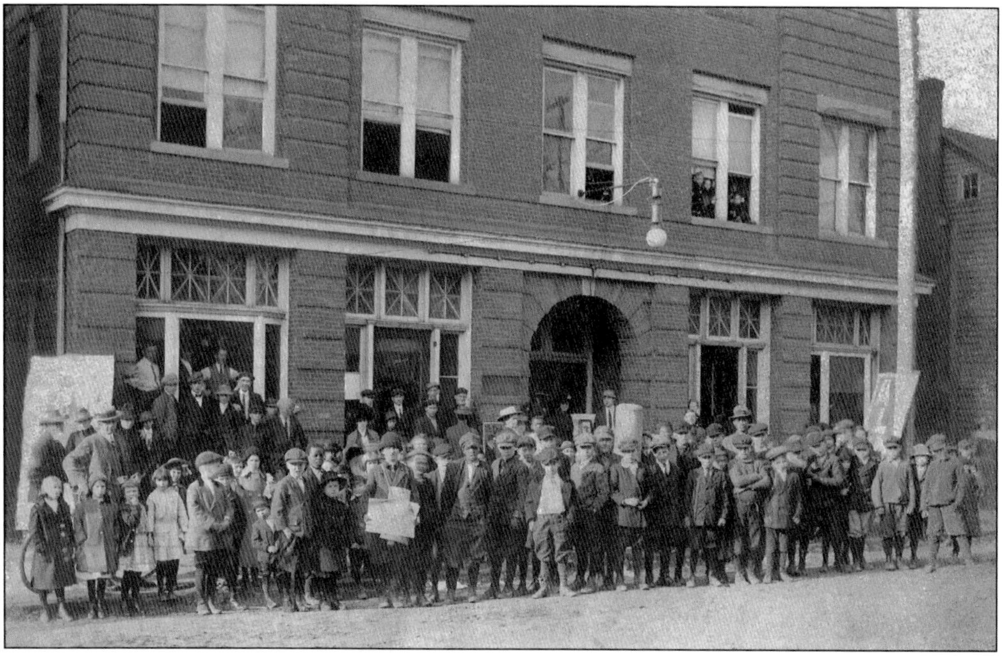

The *Covington Virginian* newspaper started in 1914 as a daily (except Sunday) paper to cover World War I. This is an early picture of the news carriers who hand-delivered each of the papers. The photograph reveals an integrated workforce, as the paper was delivered to every neighborhood in the town. (AHS-VR.)

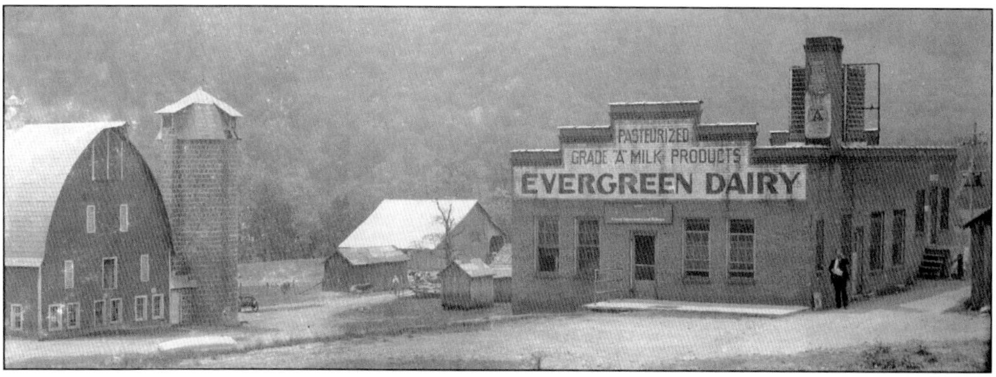

Evergreen Dairy was located in Intervale, just north of Covington. It was managed by Lee Dressler. After it closed, the Covington Women's Club bought the property and used it for meetings. The barn has since burned down, but the office still stands. (AHS-VR.)

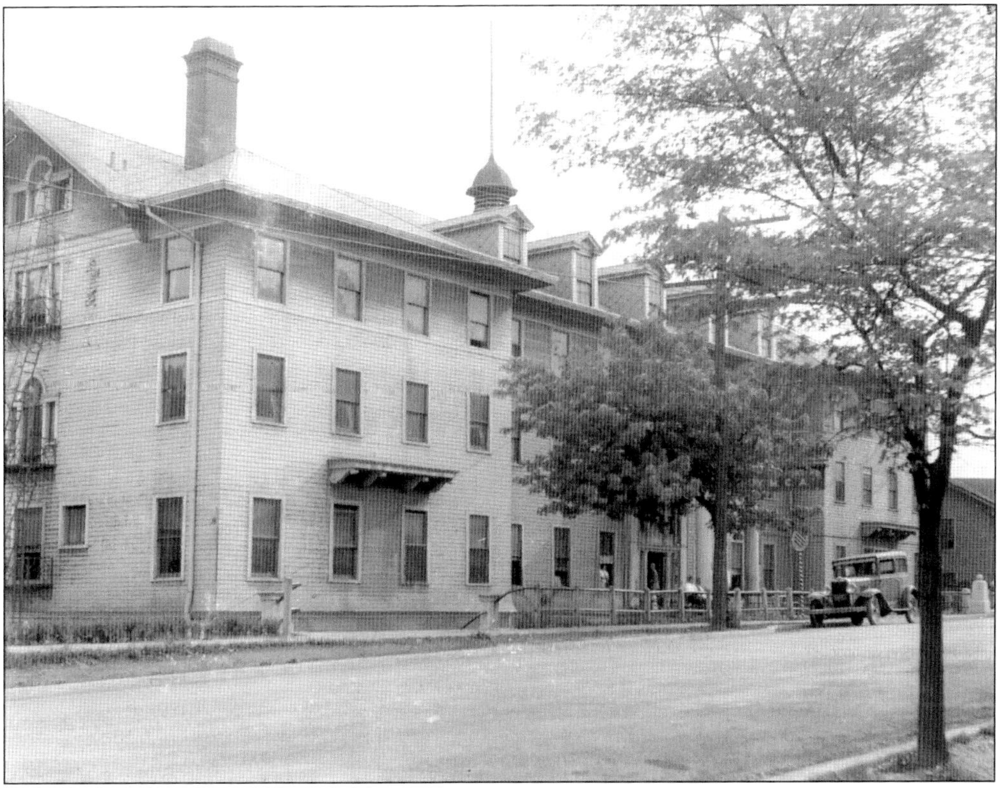

This photograph of the Gladys Inn and YMCA in Clifton Forge dates to the early 1930s. Gladys Inn was the hotel and depot built by the C&O Railway in 1896 to replace the earlier Gladys Inn, built up on the hill. The YMCA was added in 1923 and was torn down in May 1975. (AHS-VR.)

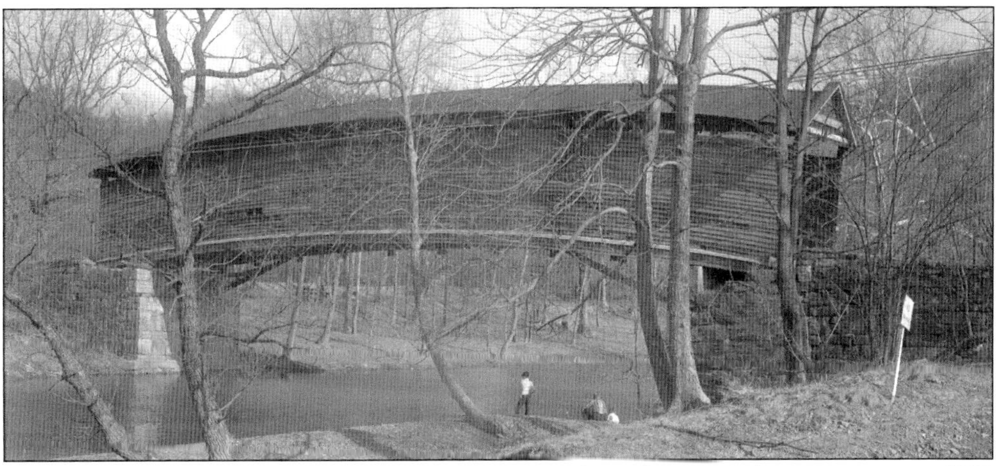

Humpback Bridge was built by the James River & Kanawha Valley Turnpike Corporation in 1857. It was the third bridge built on this site; the previous two washed away in floods. The arched construction of this bridge with no center support protected it from flooding. It was used as a highway bridge until 1929. It was neglected and used as a hay barn until it was restored in 1953 due to the efforts of the Covington Business and Professional Women's Club. It is now maintained by the Virginia Department of Transportation as a wayside park. (AHS-VR.)

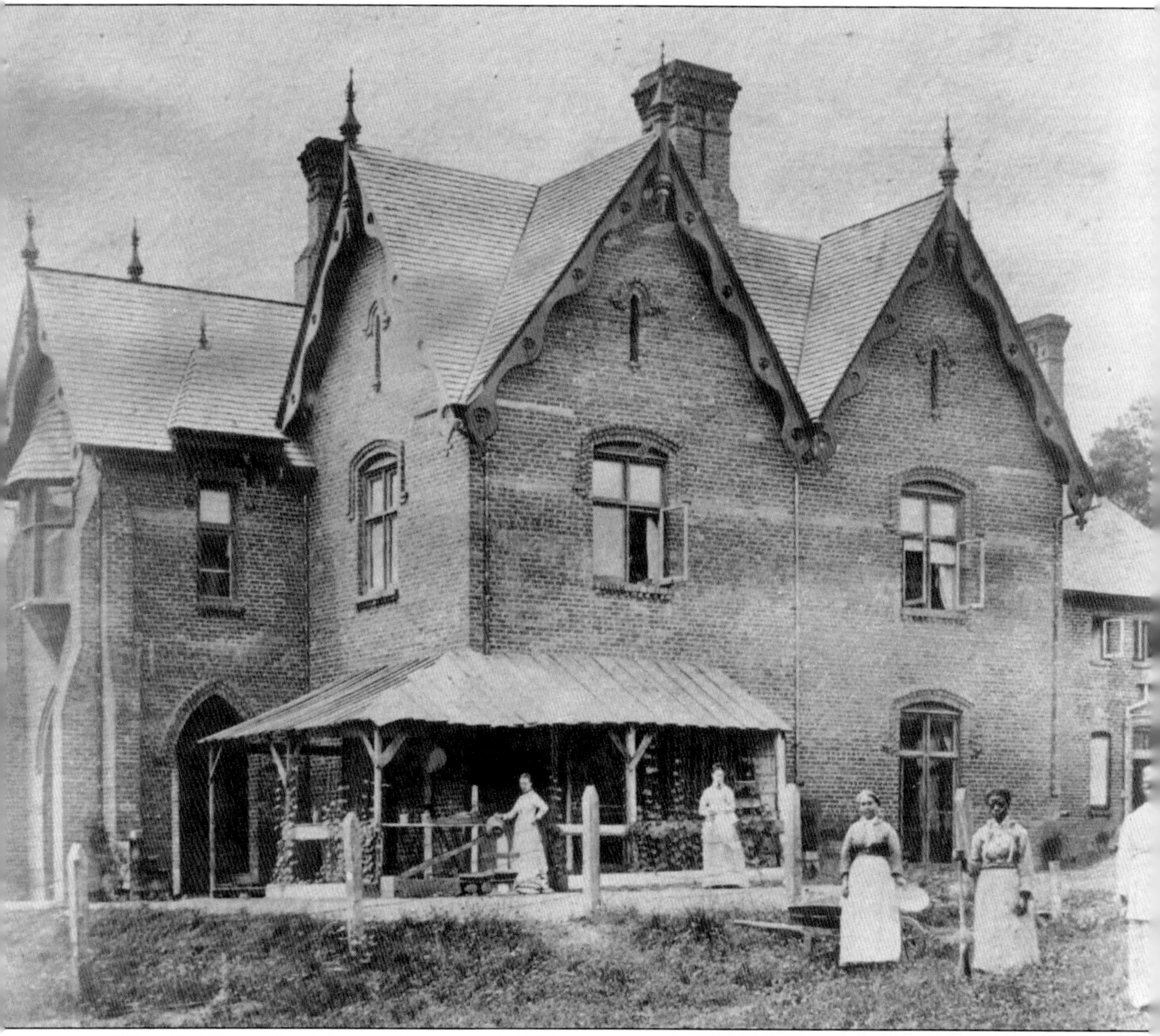

Wood Hall was built by Lord and Lady Milton in the early 1870s. It was built on the land of the old Callaghan Tavern, which burned shortly after the Miltons arrived. The brick for the house was handmade on the Marshall Farm. Hugh McAllister renamed the house Milton Hall. It remains a private residence today. This photograph of Wood Hall is from the late 1800s. (AHS.)

Two

COMMUNITY DEVELOPMENT

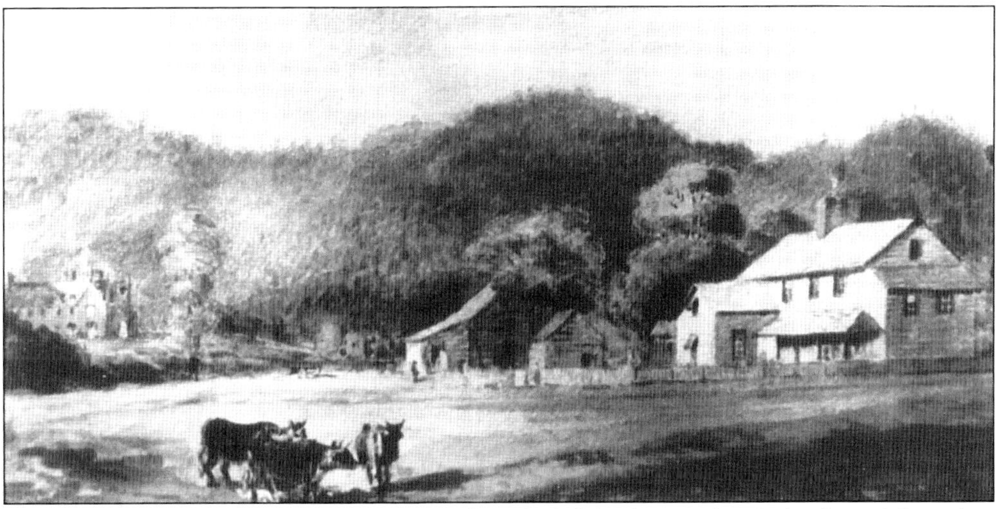

This painting shows Wood Hall (Milton Hall) in the left background with the doctor's log cabin at center and Callaghan Tavern on the right. Callaghan Tavern was opened in 1792 by Dennis Callaghan. The Great Road, later called the Staunton & Kanawha Turnpike, passed near the tavern. The Alleghany Roughs stayed here on their way to fight in the Civil War. It burned down in 1873. (HH.)

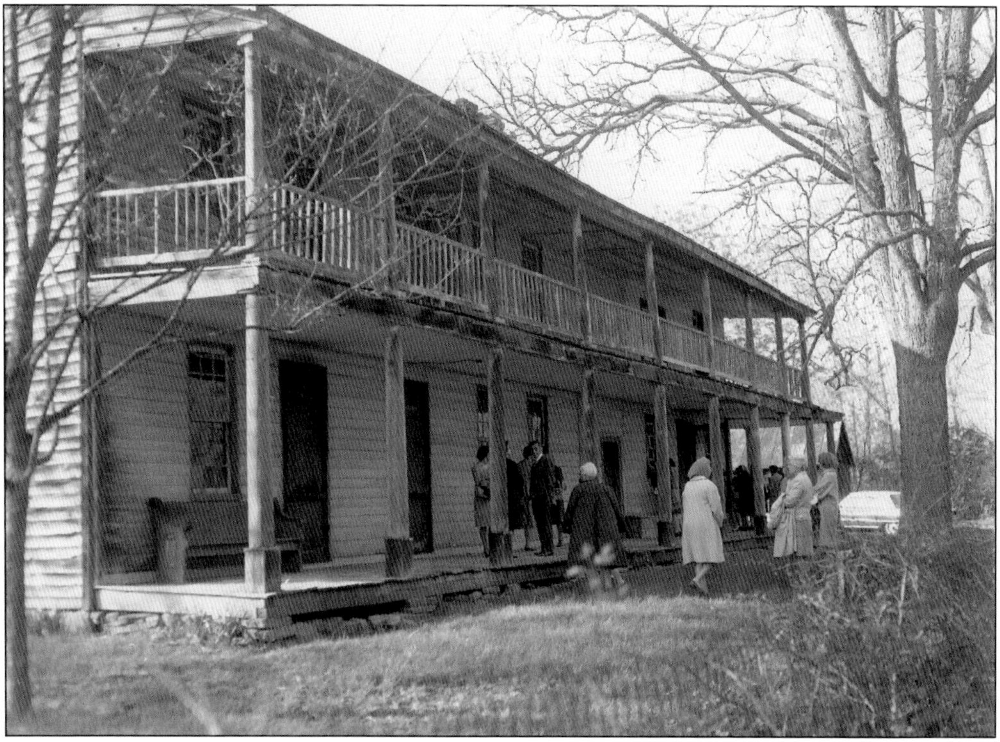

This photograph of Crow's Tavern was taken in 1969 when the Alleghany Historical Society visited the tavern just a few months before it burned down. Taverns were an important aspect of early travel. The roads were poor and horse travel tiresome, so travelers stopped at taverns for a night, for breakfast, or just for a break. Crow's Tavern's colorful owner, Col. John Crow, made it a favorite stop on the way to the popular mineral springs in the region. (AHS-VR.)

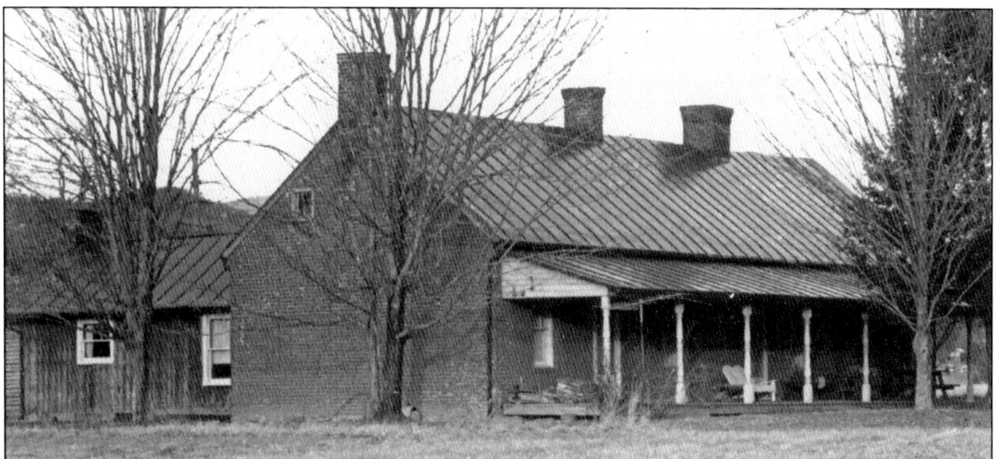

The Armentrout-King Tavern was another one of the wayside stops on the old road between Covington and Lexington. It predates 1824, when George Armentrout purchased the land. In 1871, the tavern was sold to Mansfield King. The tavern still stands on old Route 60 between Clifton Forge and Longdale. (AHS-VR.)

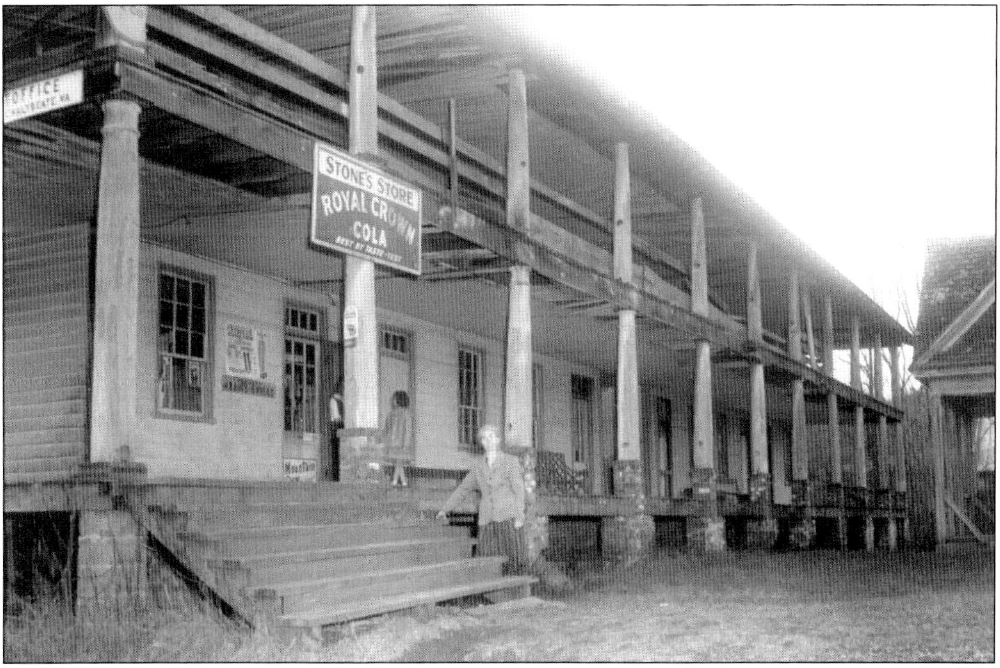

Sweet Chalybeate Hotel was a community center that housed not only resort lodging but also a general store and post office. Mary Stone continued to run the store and post office long after the resort closed. She retired in 1966 after working there for more than 50 years. (AHS-VR.)

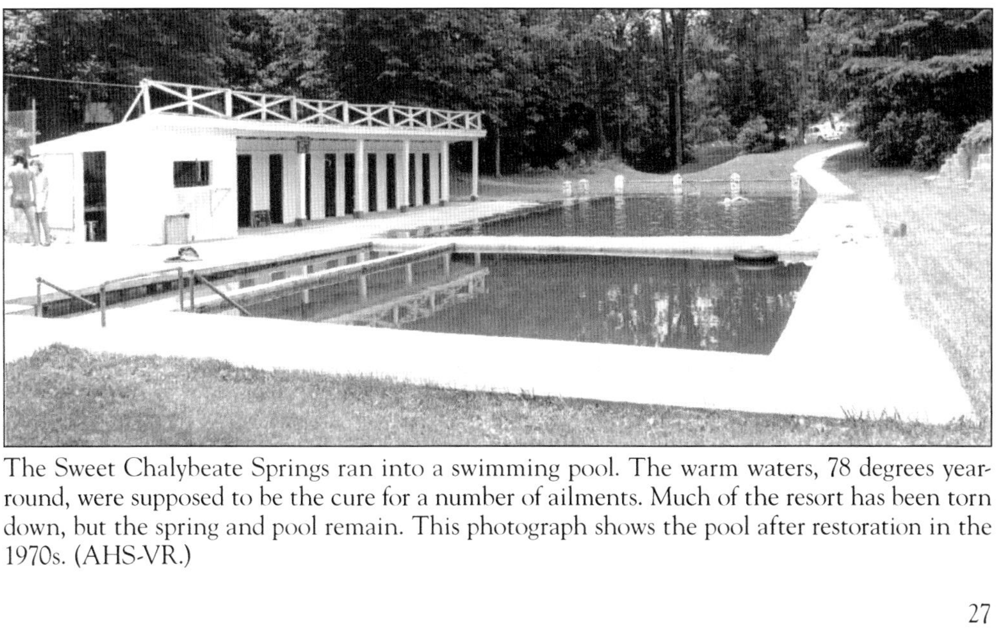

The Sweet Chalybeate Springs ran into a swimming pool. The warm waters, 78 degrees year-round, were supposed to be the cure for a number of ailments. Much of the resort has been torn down, but the spring and pool remain. This photograph shows the pool after restoration in the 1970s. (AHS-VR.)

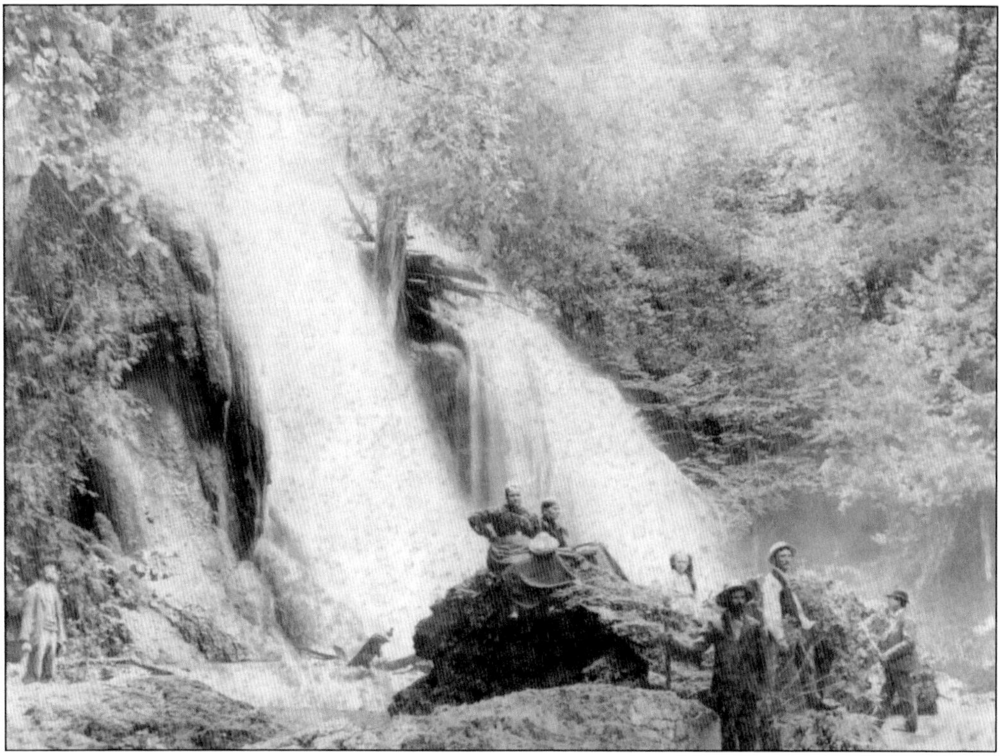

While staying at the various resorts, such as Sweet Chalybeate and nearby Sweet Springs in West Virginia, visitors often went on daytrips in stagecoaches. One of the local attractions for these visitors was the Beaverdam Falls on Cove Creek near Earlhurst. This photograph shows falls visitors in the late 1800s or early 1900s. (AW and PM.)

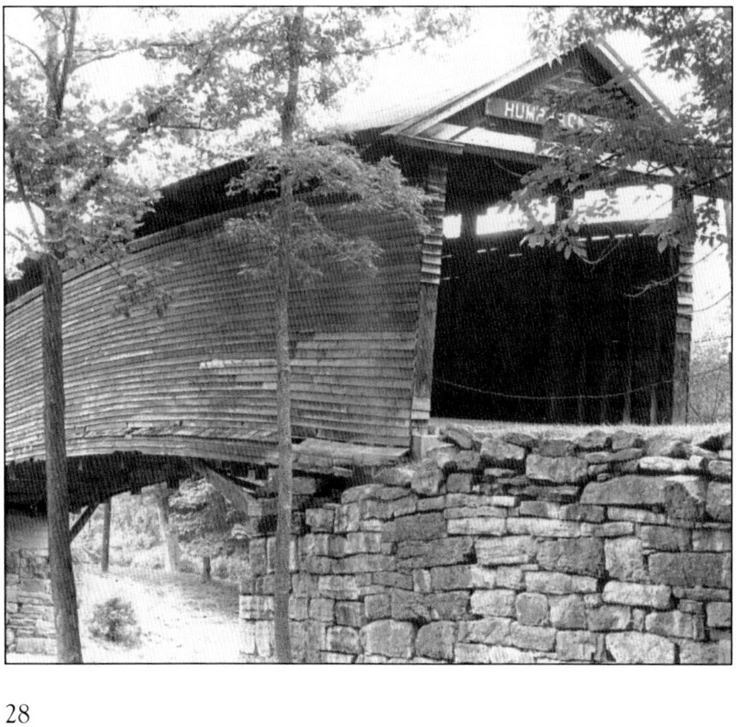

The James River & Kanawha Canal Company was initially created as the James River Company in 1785. It built canals and locks to enable navigation on the James River above the fall line. Its boats came from as far west as Covington. A turnpike road known as the Midland Trail was used for transportation farther west. A number of wooden bridges existed on the trail, including the Humpback Bridge. (AHS-VR.)

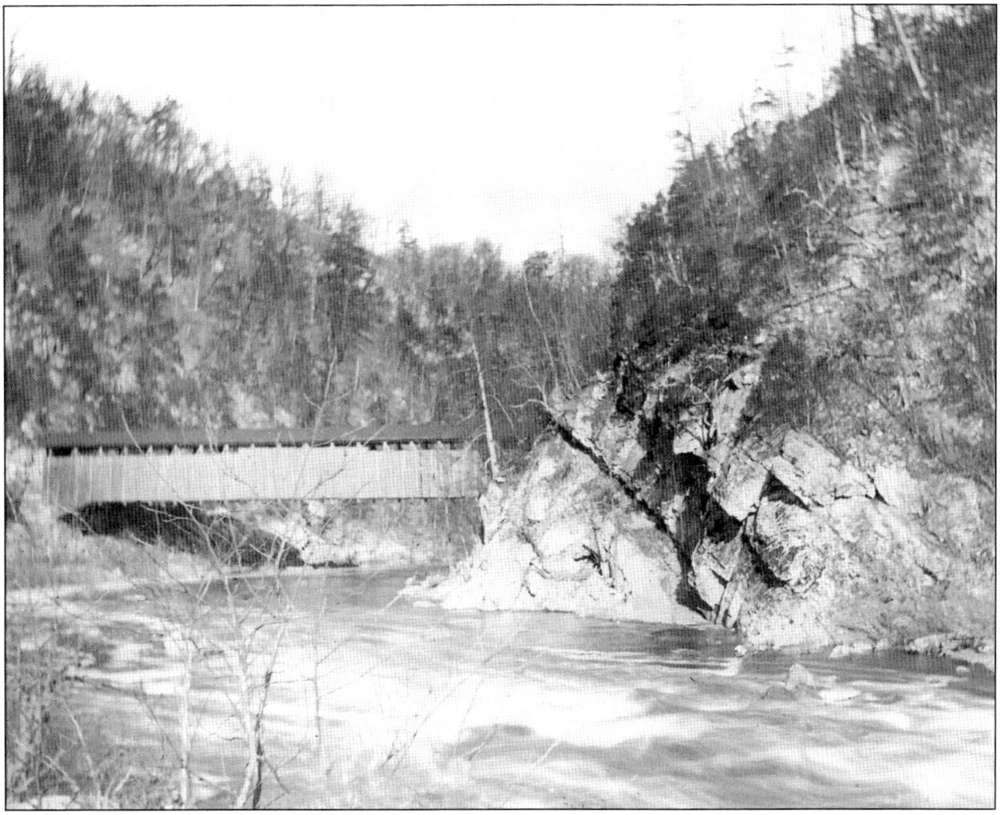

Island Ford was a crossing point on the Jackson River between Clifton Forge and Covington as early as the 1820s. It was a dangerous ford with fast-moving water on either side of the island, so a bridge had been built by the 1850s. The first bridge was burned by Union general William Averell's raiders in 1863 during the Civil War, and was replaced by this bridge in 1886. (AHS.)

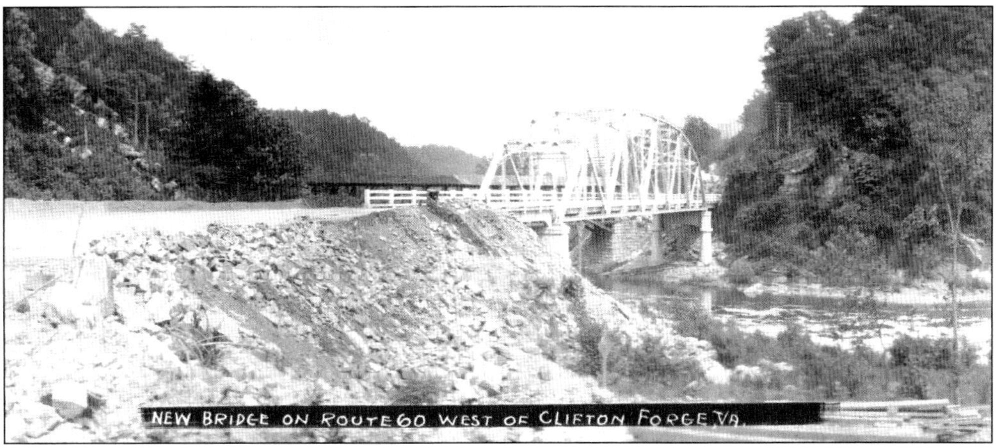

The second Island Ford Bridge was replaced by a steel truss bridge in 1929. The second bridge can be seen in the background during the construction of the new bridge. The cut-stone foundation from the second bridge is visible. This stone remained in place into the 1950s. Whether it was repurposed or washed away is unknown. (AHS-VR.)

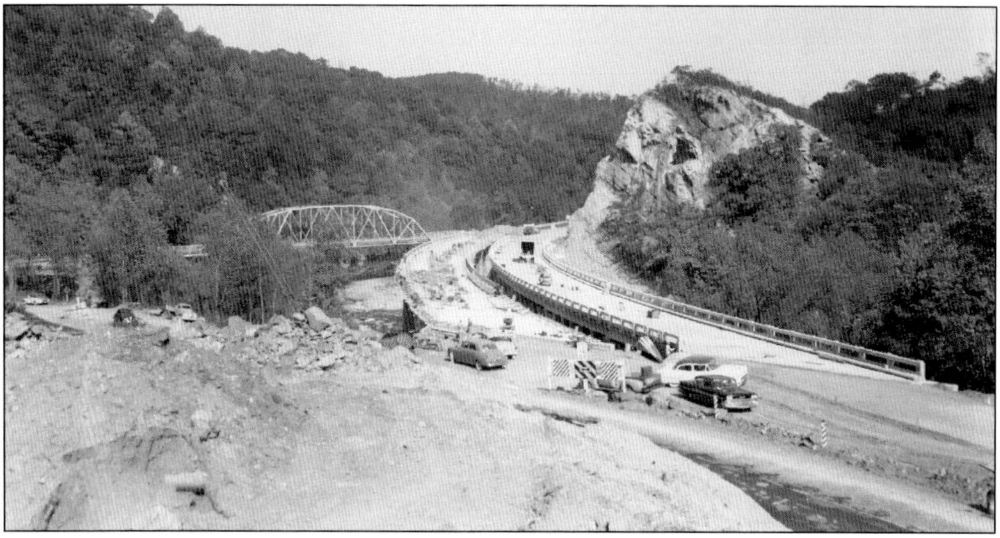

The third Island Ford Bridge was replaced in the late 1950s by the twin bridges of the divided highway. This photograph was taken in 1958. The bridges were originally built for Route 60 but are now part of Interstate 64. The old road had more curves than the modern highway. The steel truss bridge was removed in 1962. (AHS-VR.)

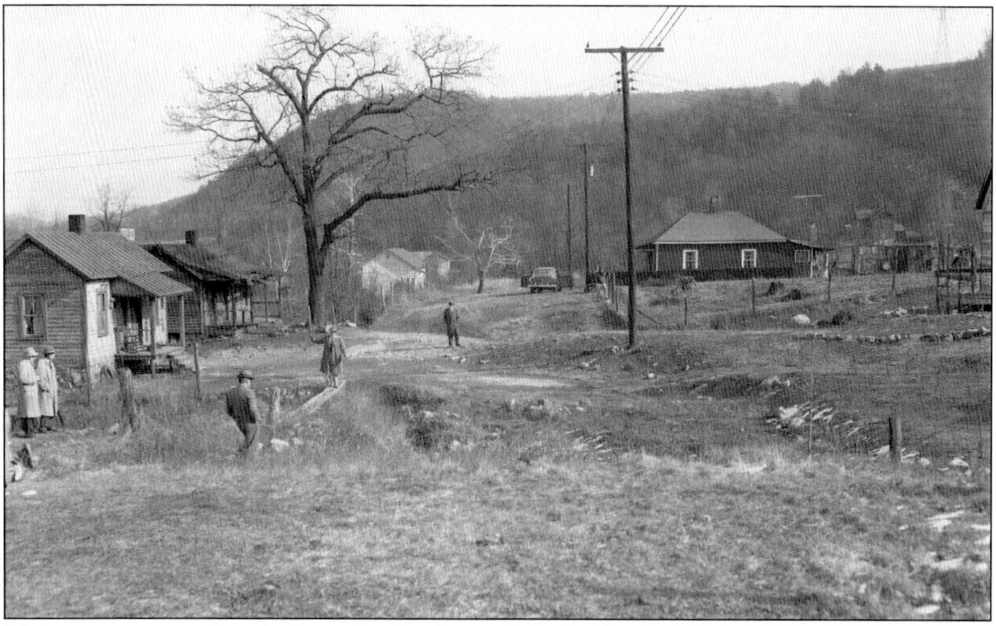

The improvement of roads dramatically changed the landscape. This is Malden Street in Low Moor before the culvert was put in over Kerns Creek. The street was only accessed from one side and allowed only foot traffic over the creek. This photograph was taken in the 1950s; the tree and the mountain are the most easily recognizable features today. (AHS-VR.)

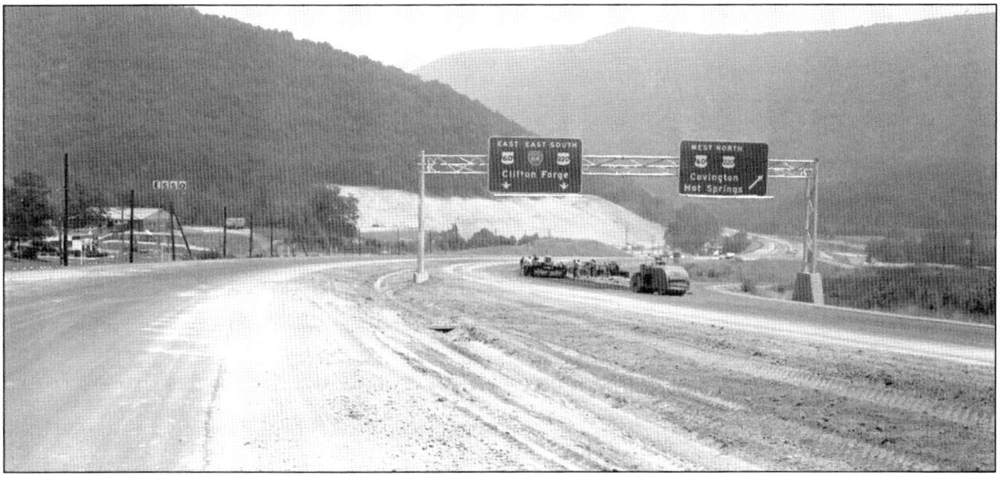

This photograph shows the building of Interstate 64 east of Covington near Mallow and Wrightsville around 1964. The interstate initially opened in sections as improvements for Route 60. After the opening of I-64, US Routes 60 and 220 continued on their original paths through Covington. (AHS-VR.)

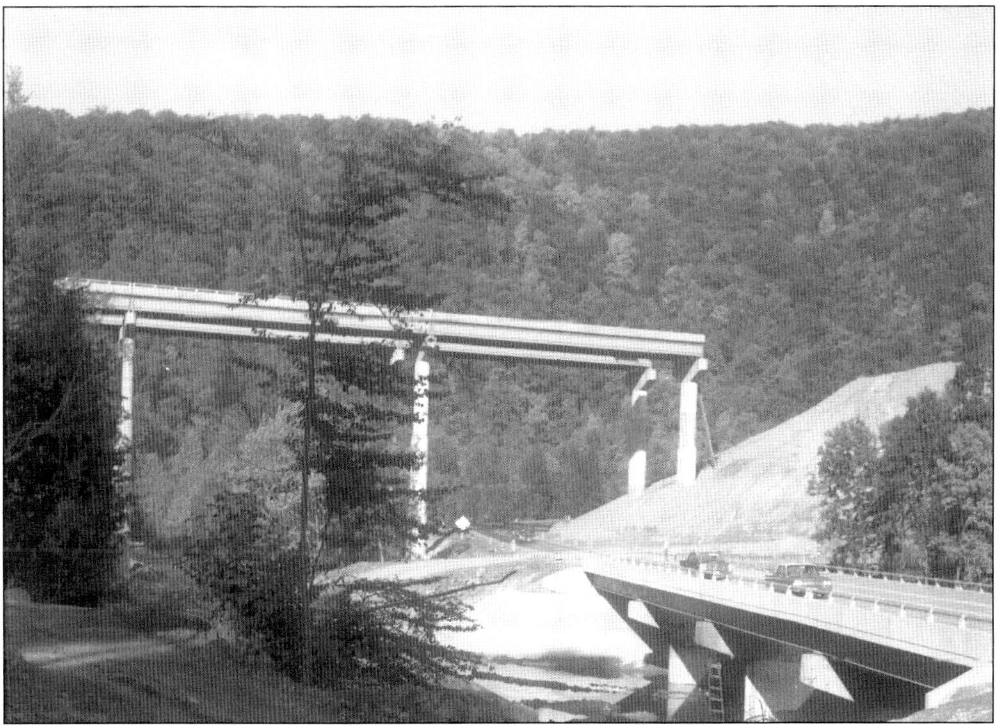

Constructing interstate highways through the mountains took years because of the need to move massive amounts of earth and build bridges. One of the most impressive bridges built on I-64 is pictured here during its construction near Callaghan in 1964. The bridge spans US Route 60, and the picture shows another new bridge over Dunlap Creek. (AHS-VR.)

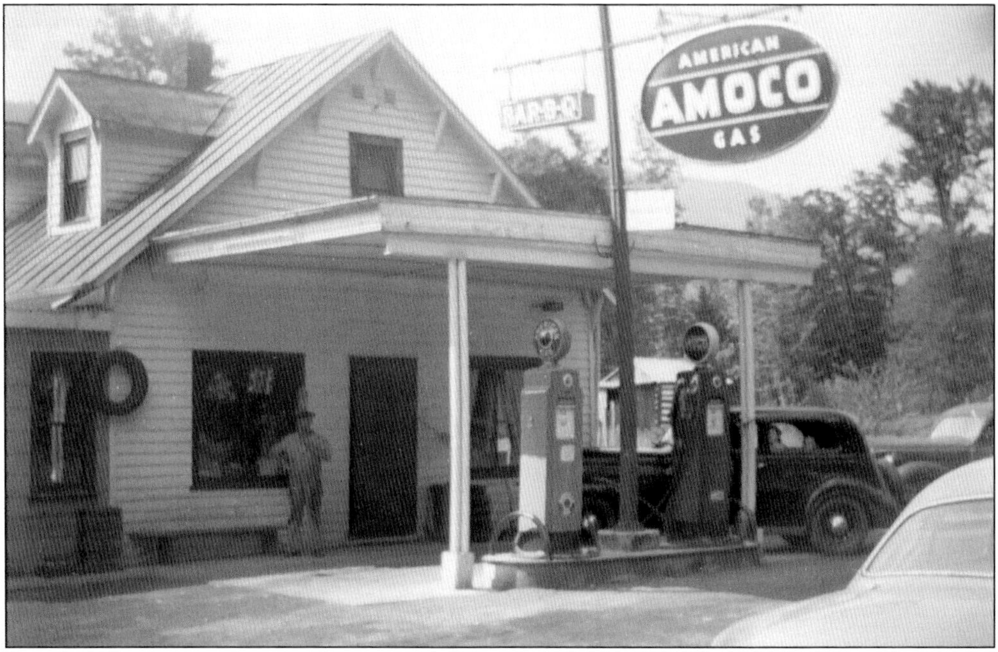

Cold Springs Service Station was located on Route 60 near Longdale Furnace at the foot of North Mountain. It was run by Lowell and Myrna Arritt. Lowell is standing by the entrance in this photograph taken around 1935. The log cabin in the background has been moved, and there is a fish pond there today. (AHS-VR.)

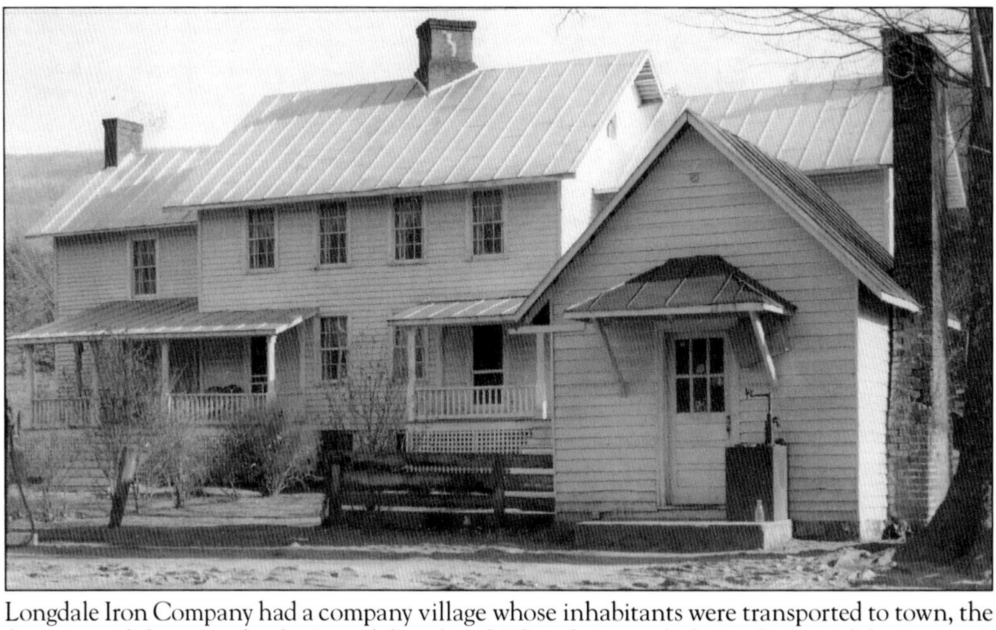

Longdale Iron Company had a company village whose inhabitants were transported to town, the furnace, and the mines by the Longdale railroad. This photograph shows the Longdale manager's office to the left and the company doctor's office to the right. Since mining operations were often nowhere near an established town, company housing was provided to employees as an incentive to work there. The rent was taken out of their wages, along with payment for debt incurred in the company store. (AHS.)

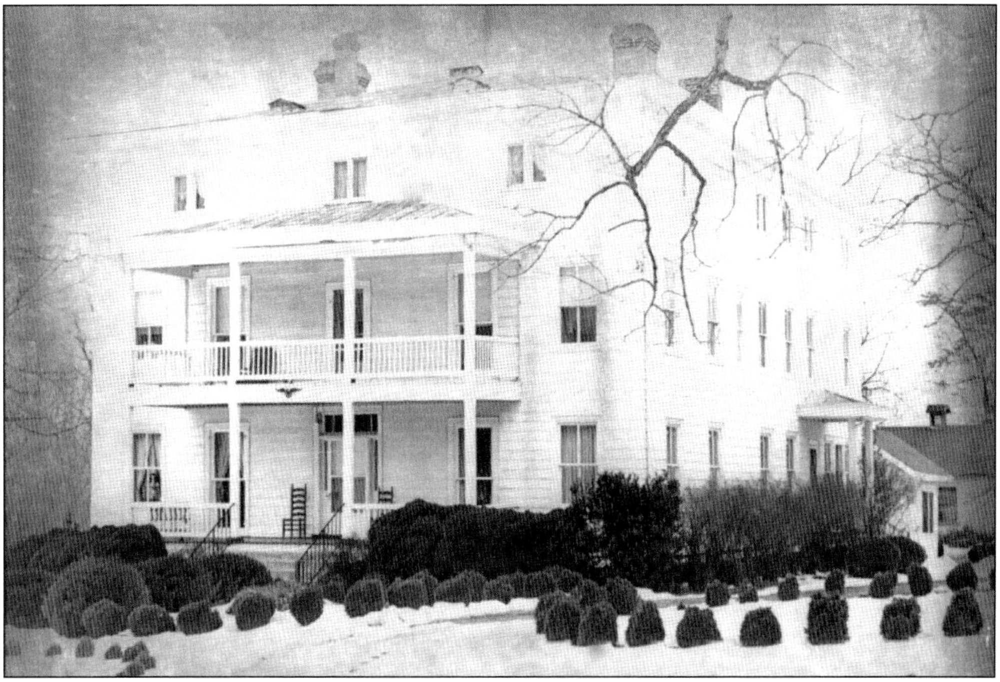

Mennefer was the manager's house of the Low Moor Iron Company. It was built around 1875 and still stands in Low Moor. The name is an Egyptian word meaning "enduring and beautiful." The term is appropriate for the house, but not for the company, which closed in the 1920s. (AHS.)

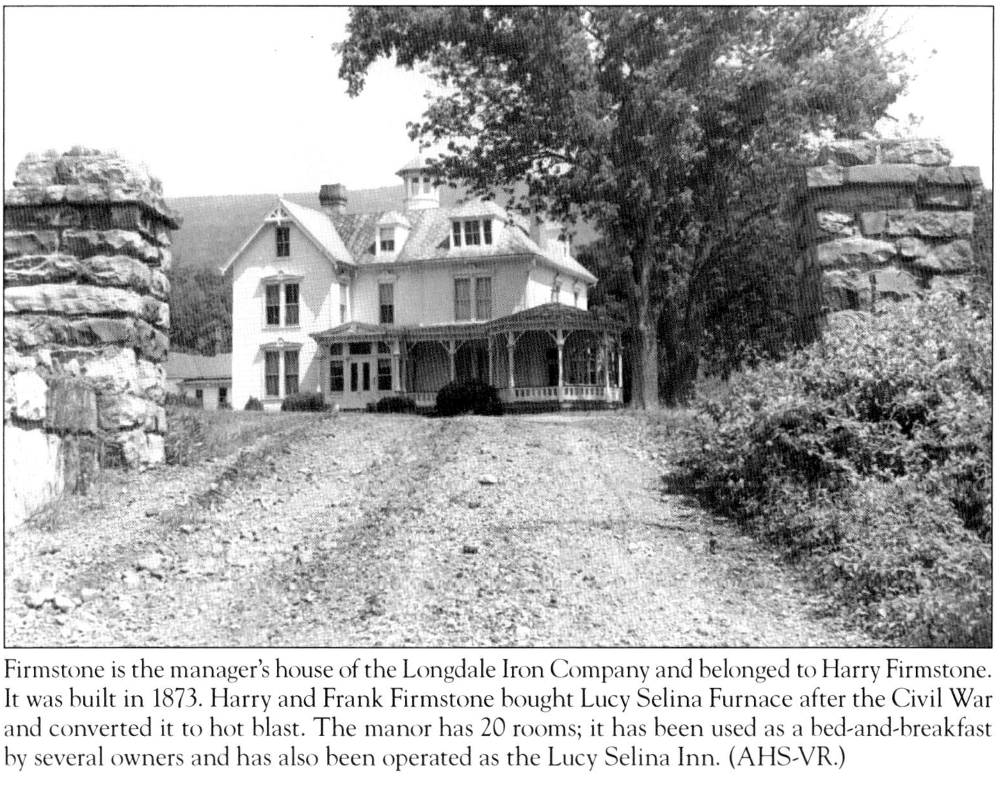

Firmstone is the manager's house of the Longdale Iron Company and belonged to Harry Firmstone. It was built in 1873. Harry and Frank Firmstone bought Lucy Selina Furnace after the Civil War and converted it to hot blast. The manor has 20 rooms; it has been used as a bed-and-breakfast by several owners and has also been operated as the Lucy Selina Inn. (AHS-VR.)

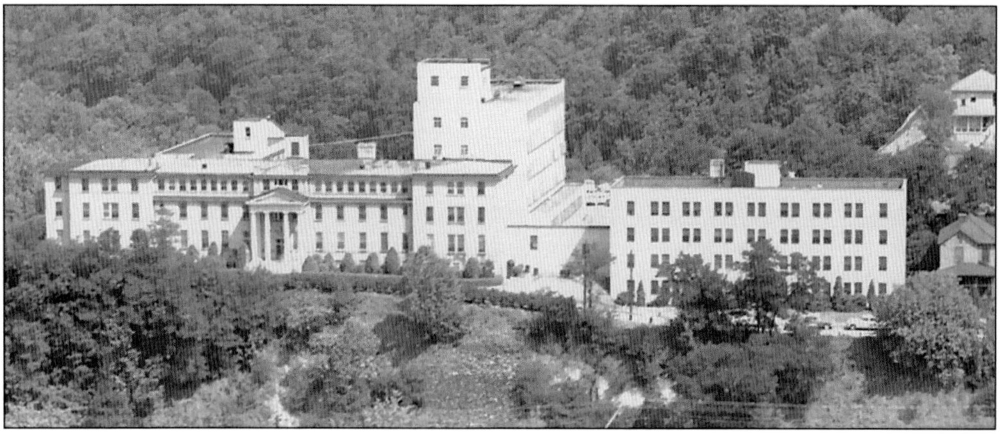

The old Gladys Inn became the C&O Hospital in 1897 and had a capacity of 50 beds. As it was not built to be a hospital, it soon proved inadequate. It was razed in 1917, and a new 90-bed brick hospital was built. The hospital offered up-to-date facilities and in later years had its own school of nursing. (COHS.)

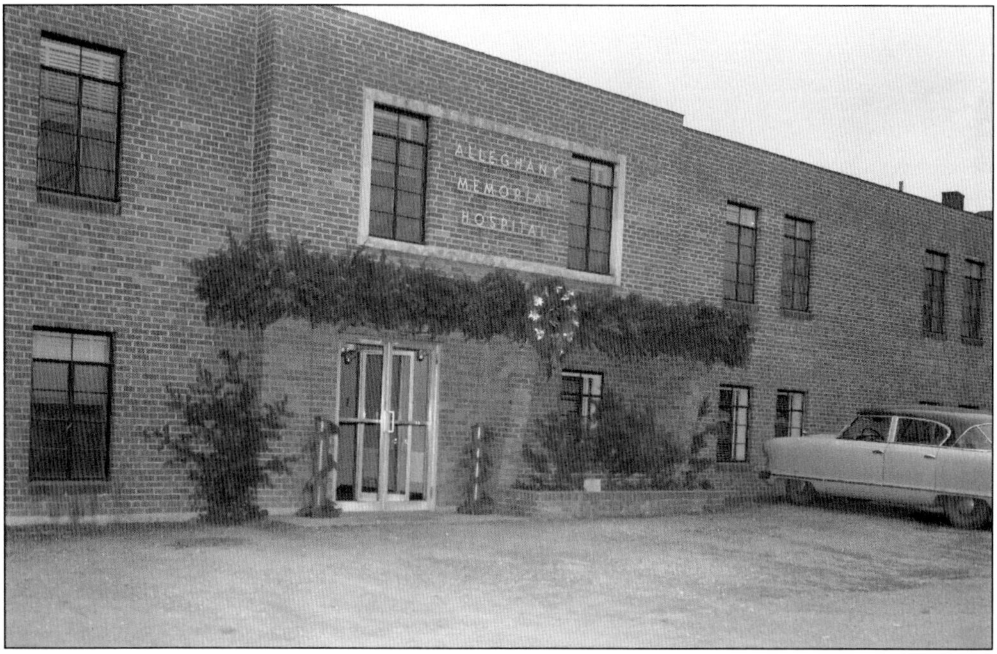

Alleghany Memorial Hospital was created in the 1940s to serve the people around Covington and the western part of Alleghany County. It was located in Rosedale. This picture shows the hospital decorated for Christmas in 1959. Alleghany Memorial merged with Emmett Memorial Hospital (former C&O) under the Alleghany Regional Hospital Corporation in 1976. The two hospitals continued in operation until 1979, when Alleghany Regional Hospital opened in Low Moor. (AHS-VR.)

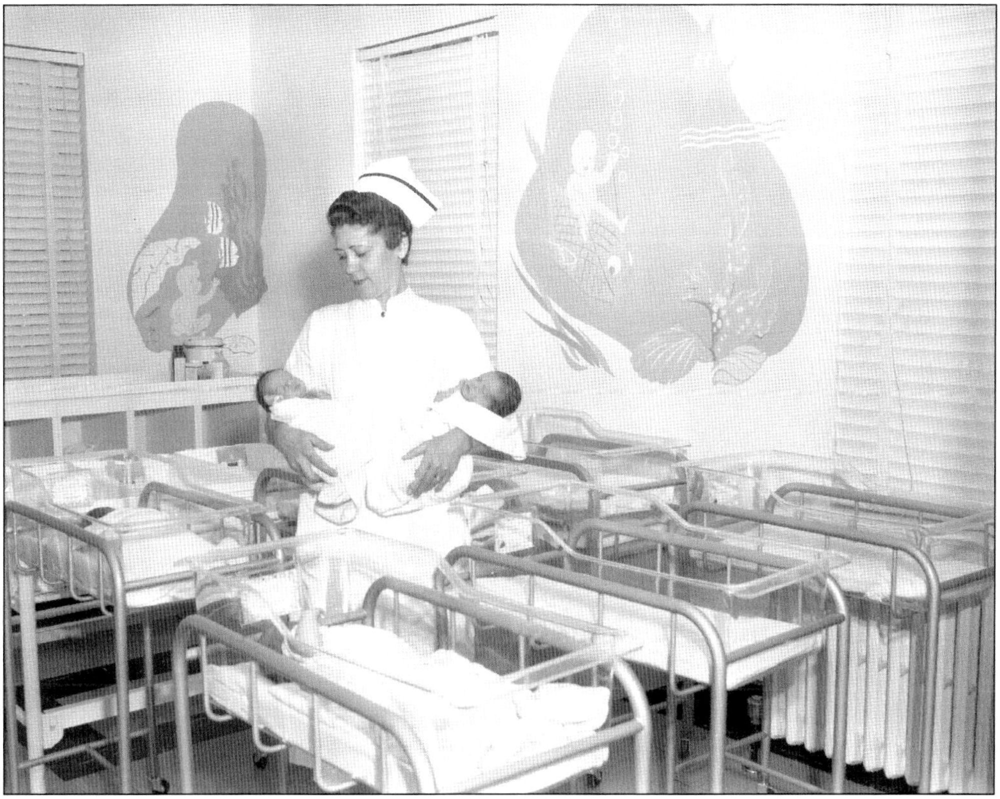

The new nursery at Alleghany Memorial Hospital is seen in this newspaper photograph from December 2, 1958. The caption reads: "new nursery, new twins, Mrs. Sue Angell holds twins Peggy Sue and Betty Lou, daughters of Mrs. Clayton Miller. The murals were painted by Mrs. Paul B. Lacy Jr. and Mrs. Harold G. Bell." (AHS-VR.)

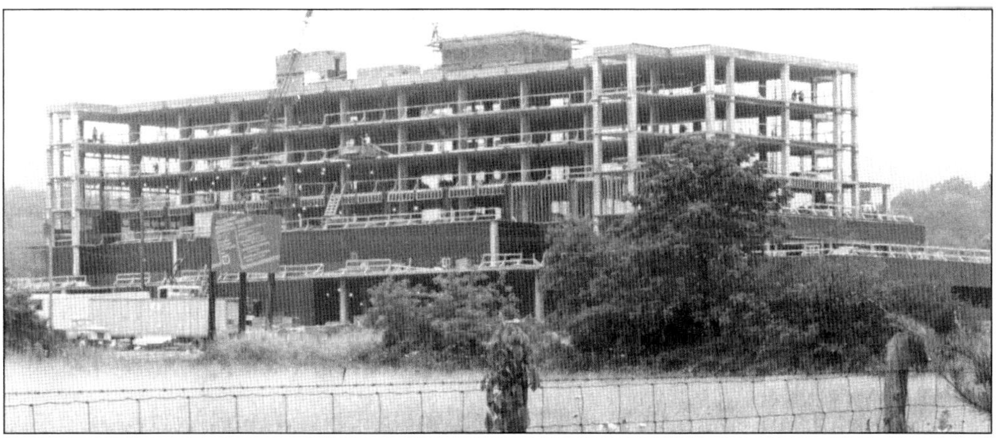

This photograph shows the building of Alleghany Regional Hospital in Low Moor in 1978 or 1979. The hospital is on the site of the old Low Moor Iron Company. Alleghany Regional Hospital is now Lewis Gale Hospital–Alleghany. (AHS-VR.)

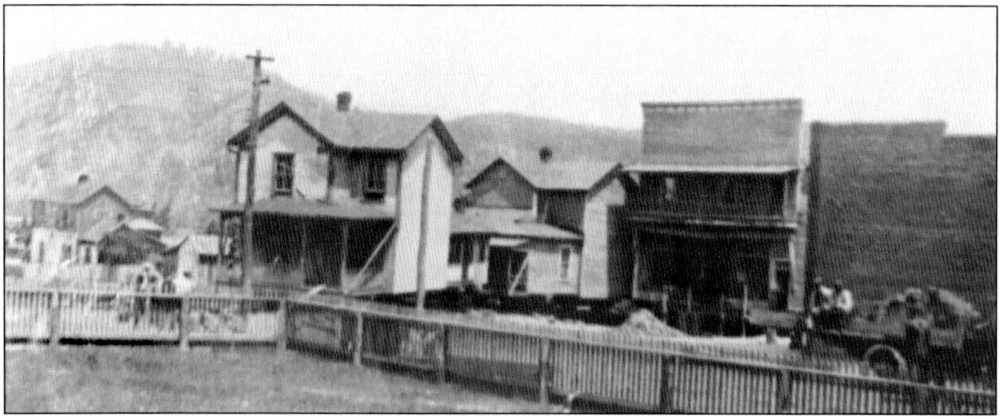

This is an early photograph of the community of Selma, located just across the Jackson River from Clifton Forge. The most notable building pictured is Carter's Store, to the right of the houses. When this picture was taken, the store was located in the flats of Selma, but it was subsequently moved to higher ground after the flood of 1913. (AHS-VR.)

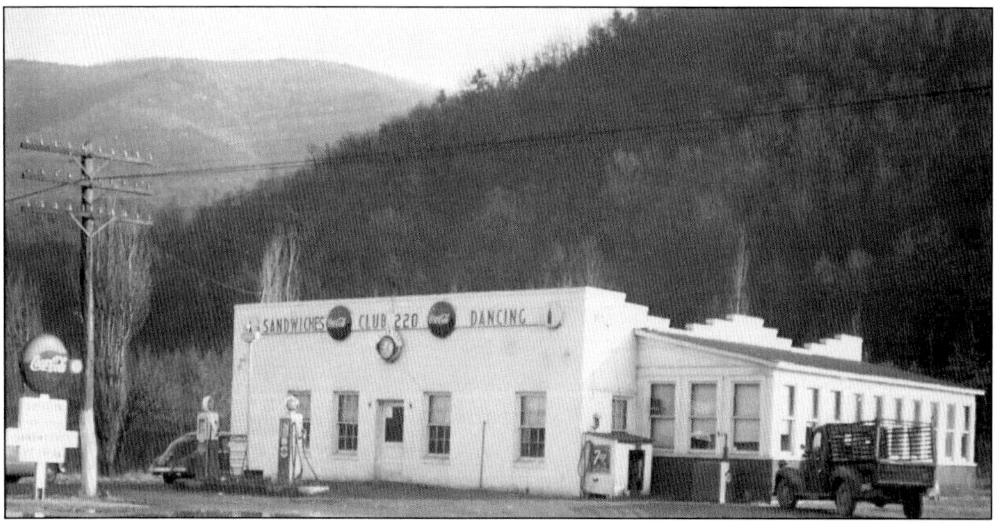

The 220 Club was located on old Route 60 between Selma and Low Moor near Pikes Pond. It went by several different names over the years, but perhaps the most memorable, due to its rough reputation, was the Bloody Bucket. This photograph dates from about 1930. (AHS-VR.)

The Clifton Forge Grocery Store, located on Church Street, was a wholesale grocery store opened in the 1890s. The building still stands and is currently used by the Clifton Forge School of the Arts as a pottery workshop and stained-glass classroom. This photograph was taken around 1930 and shows the C&O Railway siding beside the store. (AHS-VR.)

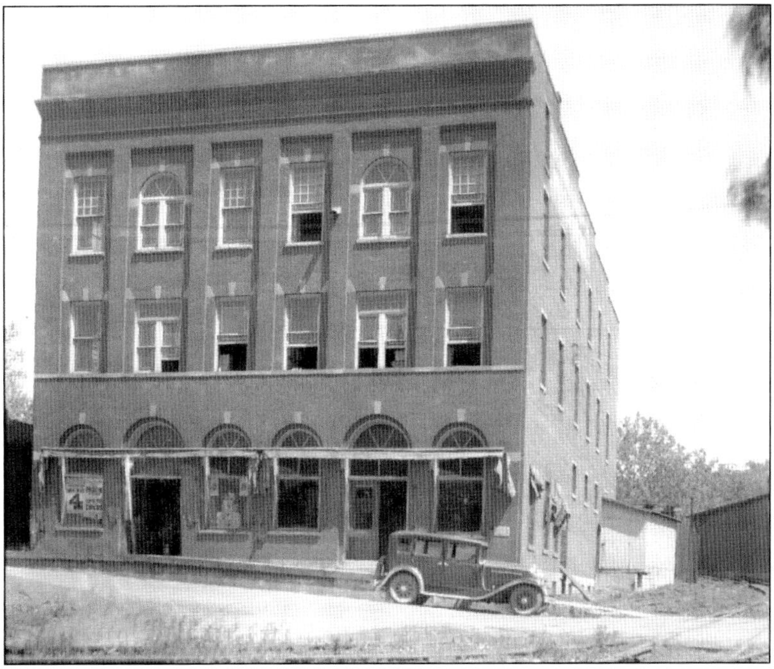

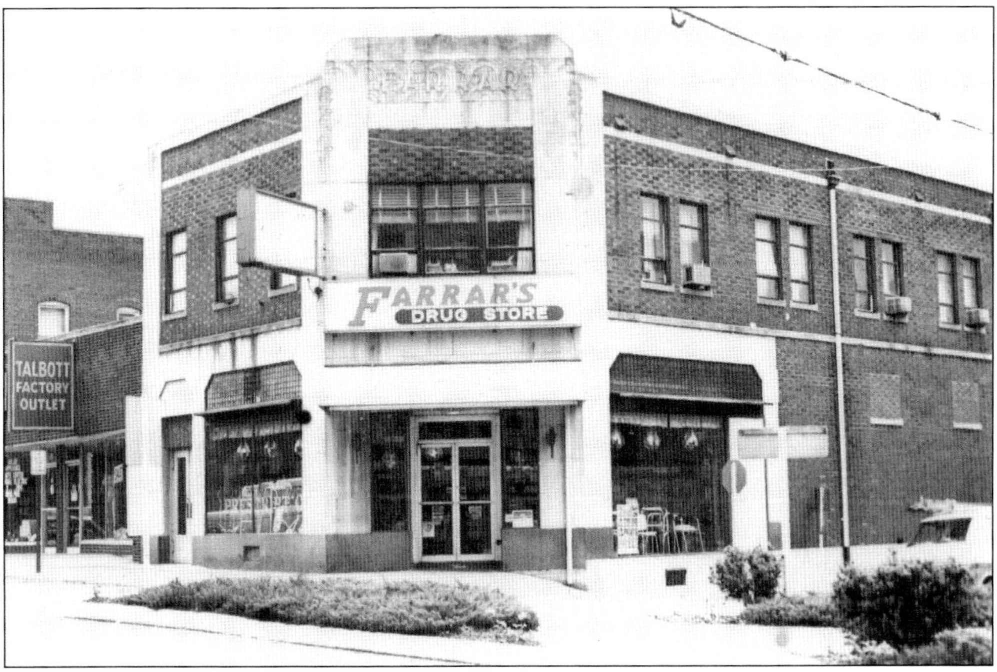

Farrar's Drug Store in Clifton Forge was located on the corner of Ridgeway and Main Streets. Farrar's was a well-known pharmacy and also had a popular soda fountain. The Club Car Restaurant now resides in the drugstore and retains some of the old signage from previous years. (AHS-VR.)

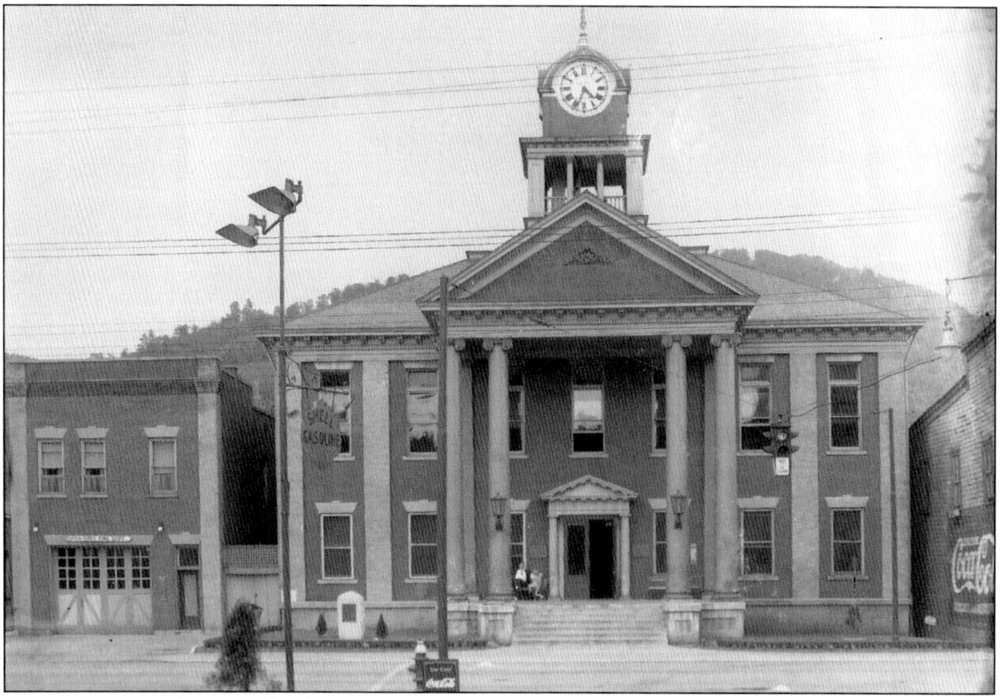

This is a 1930s photograph of Clifton Forge City Hall and the fire department. These buildings survived a major fire in 1944 that burned much of this section and badly damaged city hall. The wooden structure at right was destroyed by the fire. (AHS-VR.)

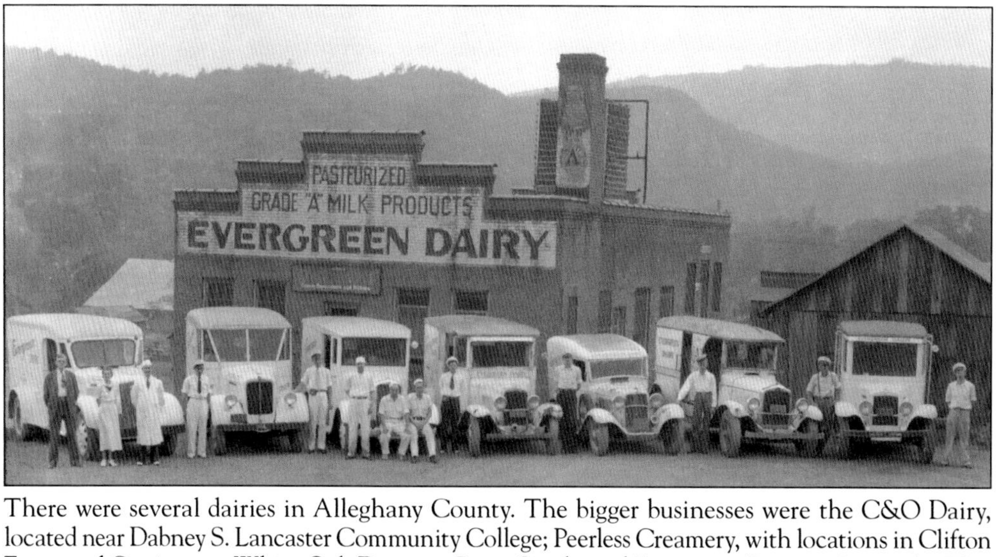

There were several dairies in Alleghany County. The bigger businesses were the C&O Dairy, located near Dabney S. Lancaster Community College; Peerless Creamery, with locations in Clifton Forge and Covington; White Oak Dairy on Potts Creek; and Evergreen Dairy in Intervale. This 1934 photograph shows delivery drivers for Evergreen Dairy. (AHS-VR.)

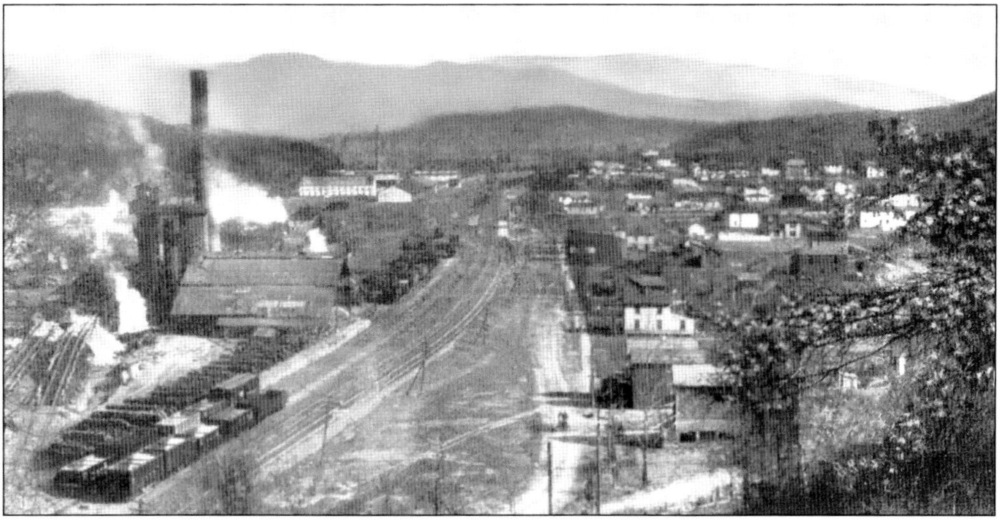

This early postcard of Iron Gate is from around 1900. On the left is Alleghany Furnace, with Union Tannery in the left background. The C&O Railway runs through the middle of the picture, splitting the town, with most of the residential section on the right. (AHS.)

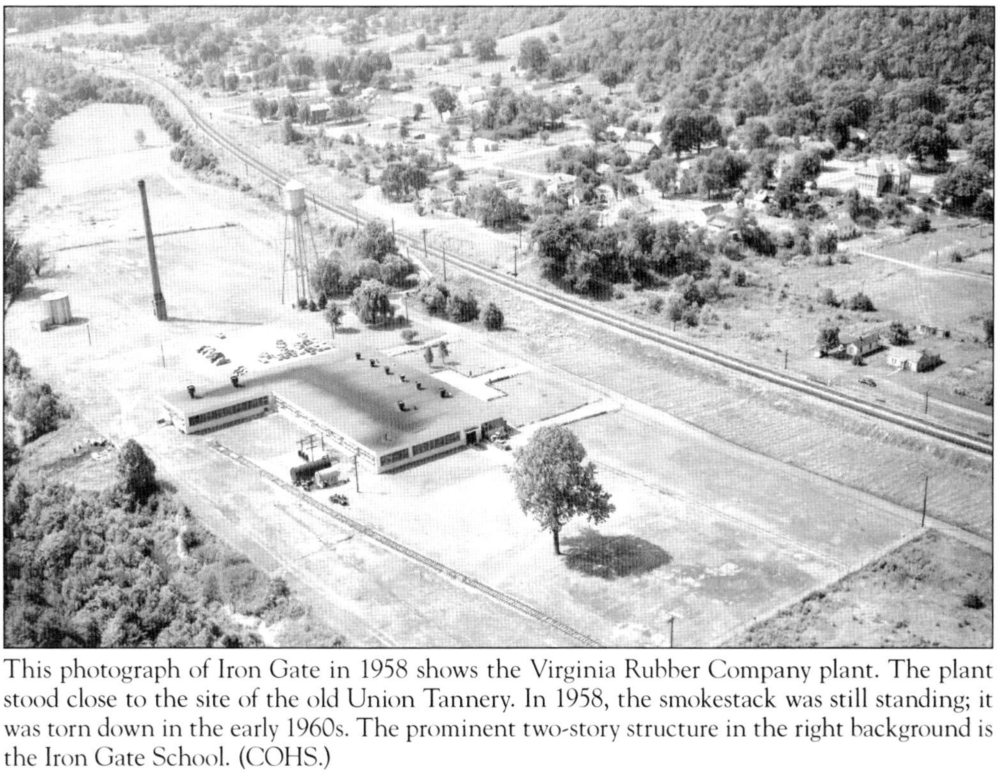

This photograph of Iron Gate in 1958 shows the Virginia Rubber Company plant. The plant stood close to the site of the old Union Tannery. In 1958, the smokestack was still standing; it was torn down in the early 1960s. The prominent two-story structure in the right background is the Iron Gate School. (COHS.)

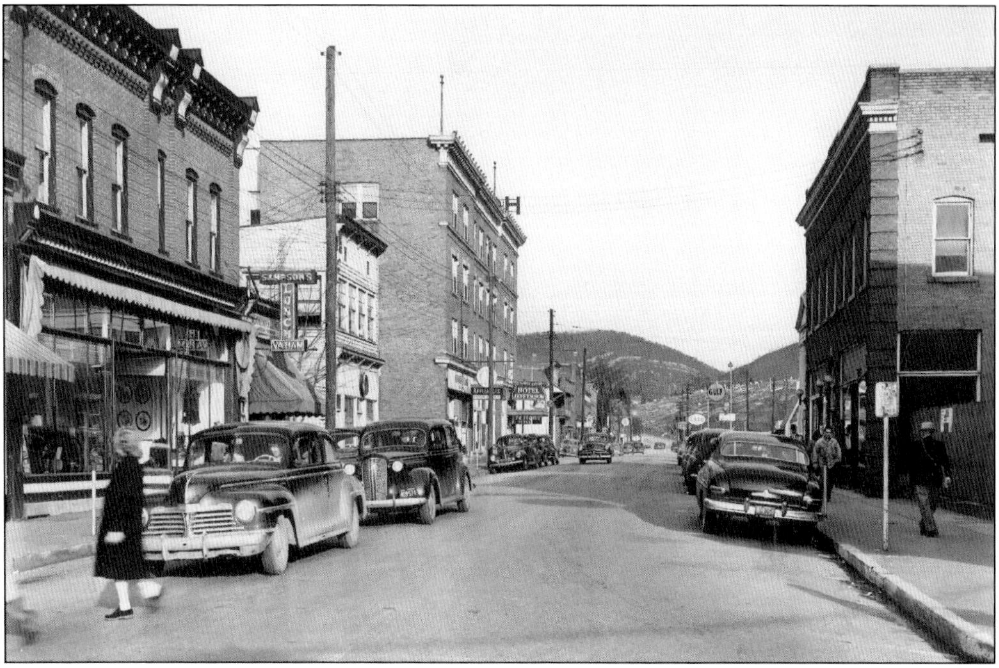

This 1948 photograph shows Main Street of Clifton Forge looking east. Notice Rainbow Rock in the background, as well as Cedar Hill Cemetery. Gasoline stations offering Shell, Texaco, Amoco, Esso, and Gulf products lined the street as travelers neared the edge of town. (AHS-VR.)

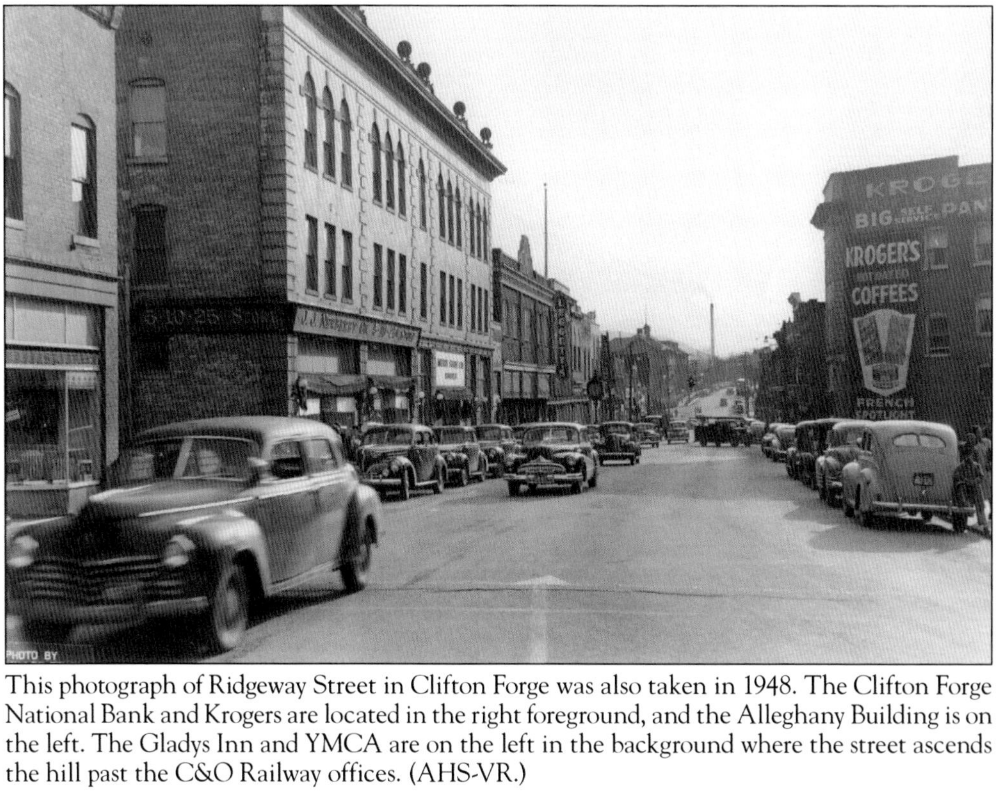

This photograph of Ridgeway Street in Clifton Forge was also taken in 1948. The Clifton Forge National Bank and Krogers are located in the right foreground, and the Alleghany Building is on the left. The Gladys Inn and YMCA are on the left in the background where the street ascends the hill past the C&O Railway offices. (AHS-VR.)

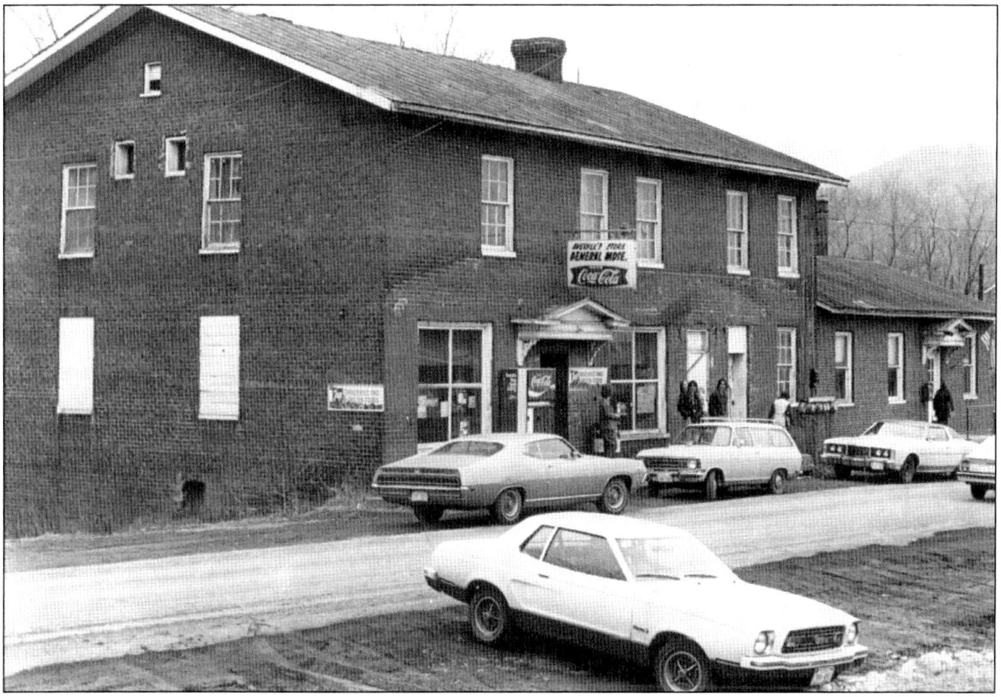

The Low Moor Iron Company paid employees in scrip that could be used in company stores. The company store in Low Moor still stands and was run by the Averill family starting in the 1920s. After the 1920s, Alva "Granny" Averill, matriarch of the family, operated the store and restaurant until it closed in April 2007. Granny died at the age of 109 in February 2016. (AHS-VR.)

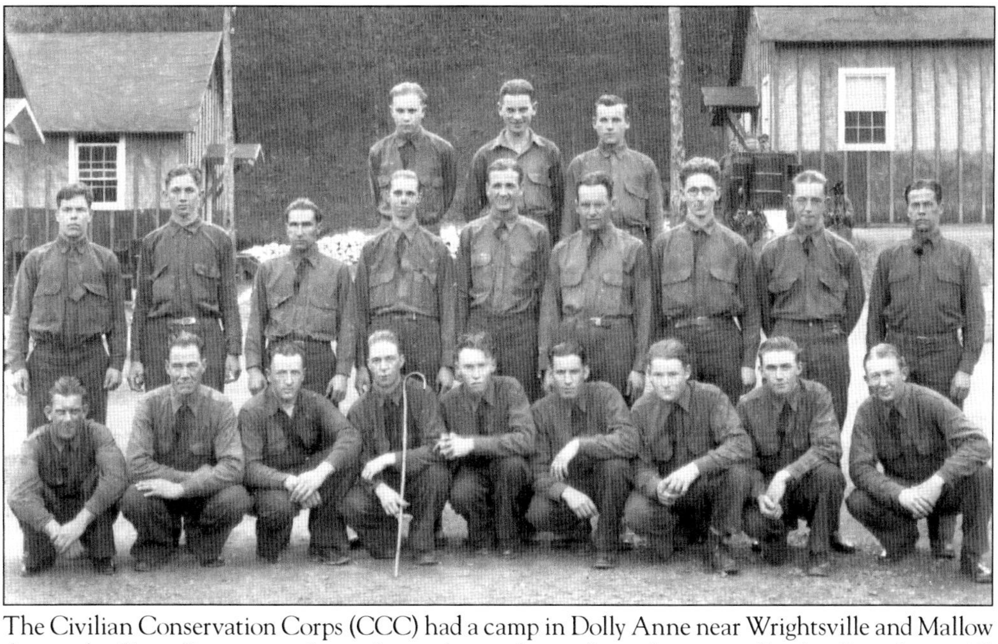

The Civilian Conservation Corps (CCC) had a camp in Dolly Anne near Wrightsville and Mallow during the Great Depression. It was located near the road now known as Smokey Bear Lane. All of the camp buildings are gone except for a dynamite storage house. The CCC built trails and parks in the area, most notably Douthat State Park, which opened in 1936. (AHS-VR.)

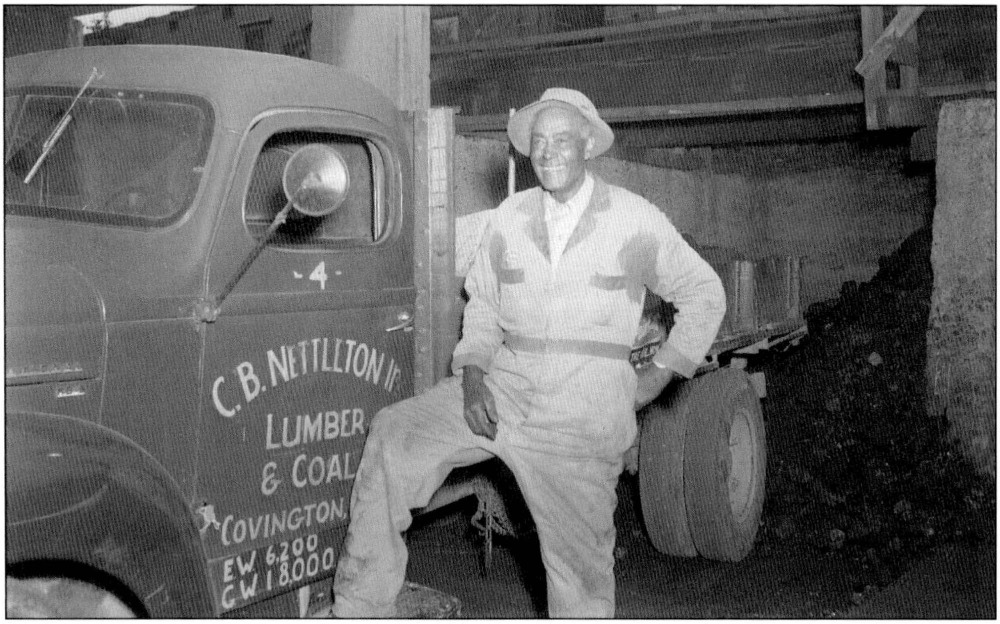

The C.B. Nettleton Company was located on the opposite side of the street from Covington High School. It subsequently became a True Value store but is now owned by the City of Covington. This photograph shows Jesse Wooden delivering coal for Nettleton in 1958. The business was located next to the main line of the C&O Railway and had its own rail siding. Notice the camp cars in the background at top. (AHS-VR.)

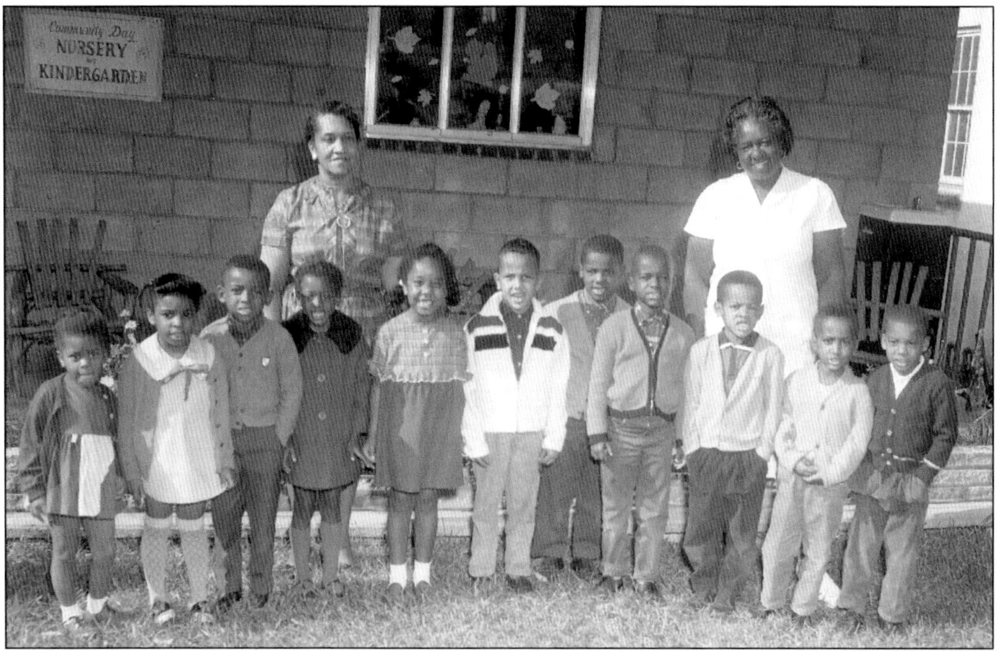

This 1966 photograph is of the Community Day Nursery and Kindergarten on Mercer Street in Covington. It was run by Gladys Smith and Mary Grey. The children have on the proper attire expected at that time, as the girls wore dresses and the boys donned long slacks and sweaters. (AHS-VR.)

Three

INDUSTRY AND RAILROADS

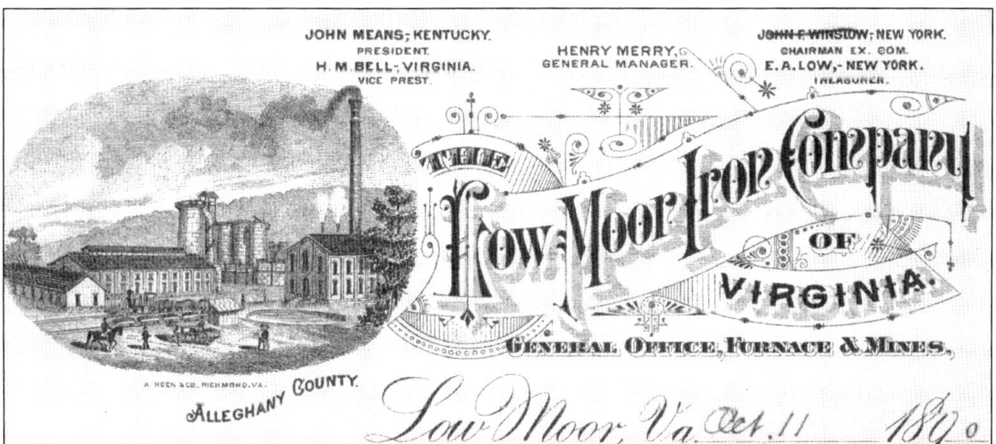

This Low Moor Iron Company letterhead from 1890 includes an engraving of the iron company that only shows the original furnace. A second furnace was built a few years later. Once the furnaces shut down, most of the buildings were torn down, but there are still some remains in the area. (AHS.)

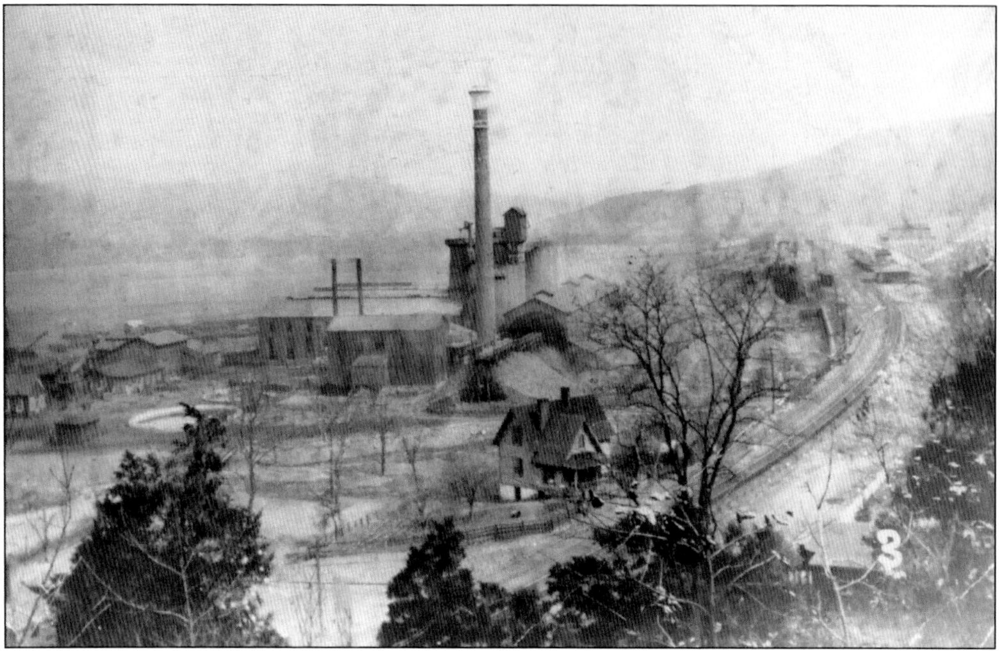

This late 1800s photograph of Low Moor Iron Company shows the covered, elevated railroad beside the smokestack. The covered section housed the coke for the furnaces, while the iron ore sat outside. The circular objects are reservoirs that housed water pumped from the Jackson River for the steam operations. (AHS.)

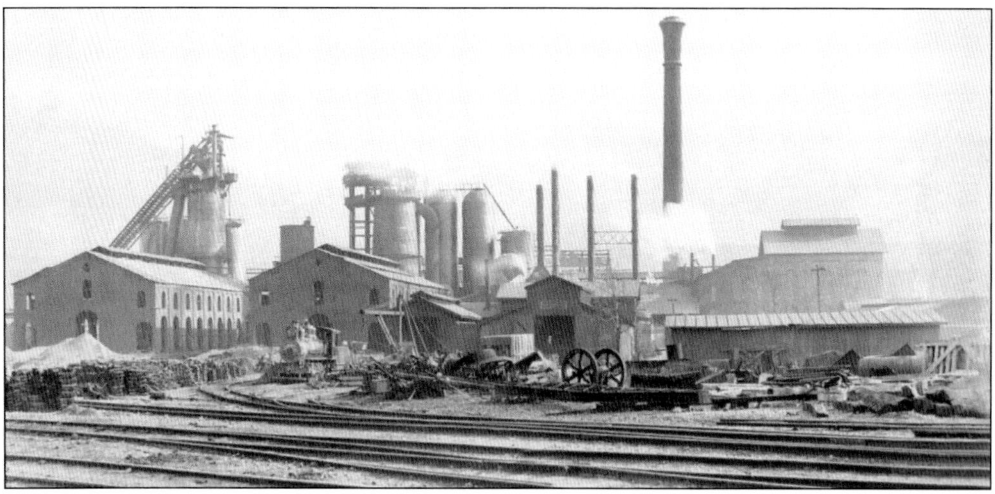

This early 1900s photograph shows Furnace A on the right and Furnace B on the left. The locomotive engine house is directly behind the engine, and to the right is the casting house. The four smaller smokestacks are from the steam plant. Notice the stacks of pig iron in the left foreground and the white pile of limestone used in the iron purification process. (COHS.)

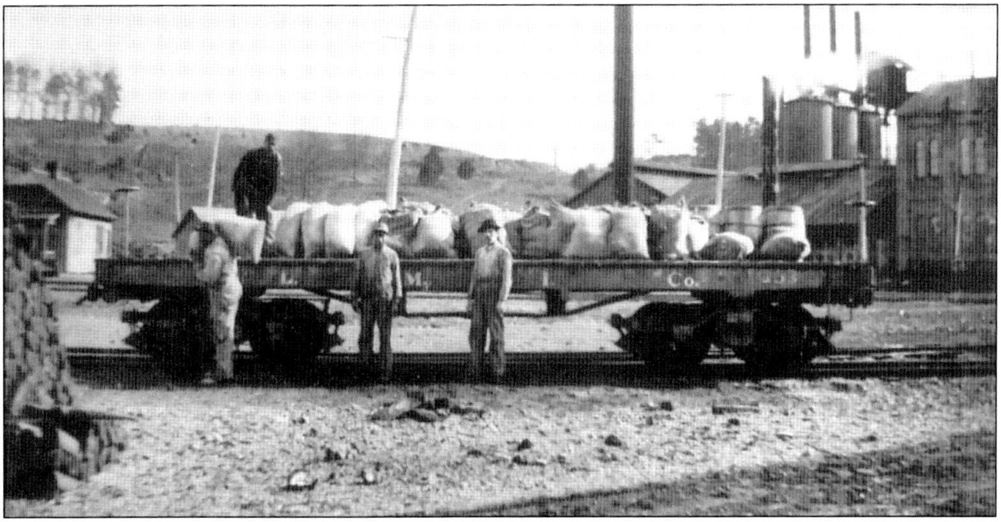

This photograph from the 1890s shows the Low Moor Iron Company operations in the Sunnymeade section of Covington. Notice Town Hill in the background, where a railway cut connects the Dolly Anne Railway to the Covington Furnace and the C&O Railway. The flatcar contains bags of limestone shipped to Covington from the Low Moor mines. (HH.)

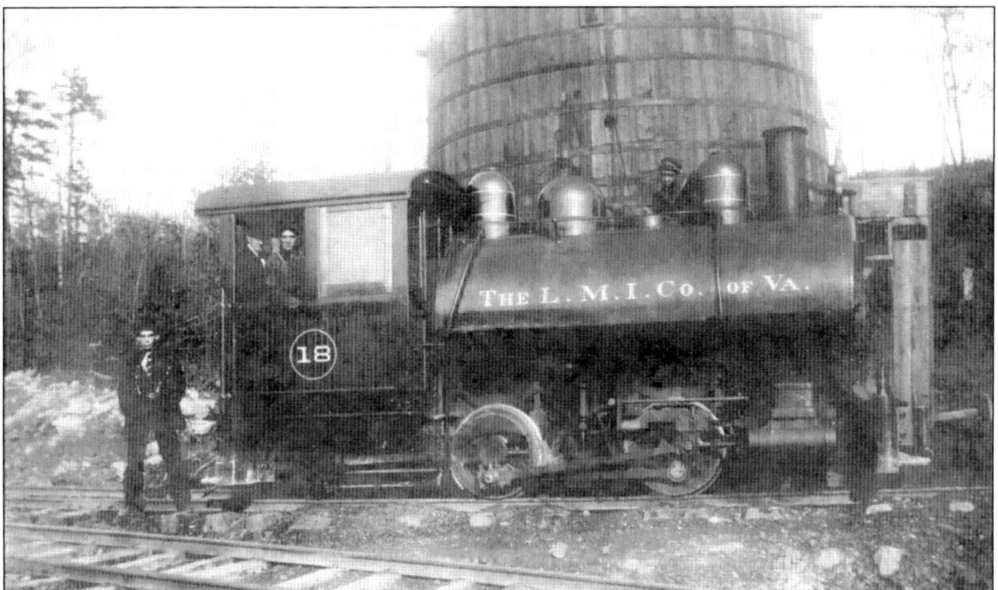

Low Moor Iron Company had a number of different mines in the community with railroads linking them. Several types of locomotives were used in the mine and furnace operations. This standard-gauge dinky engine would have been used to ferry ore to the furnaces and transport pig iron to the Chesapeake & Ohio. (AHS.)

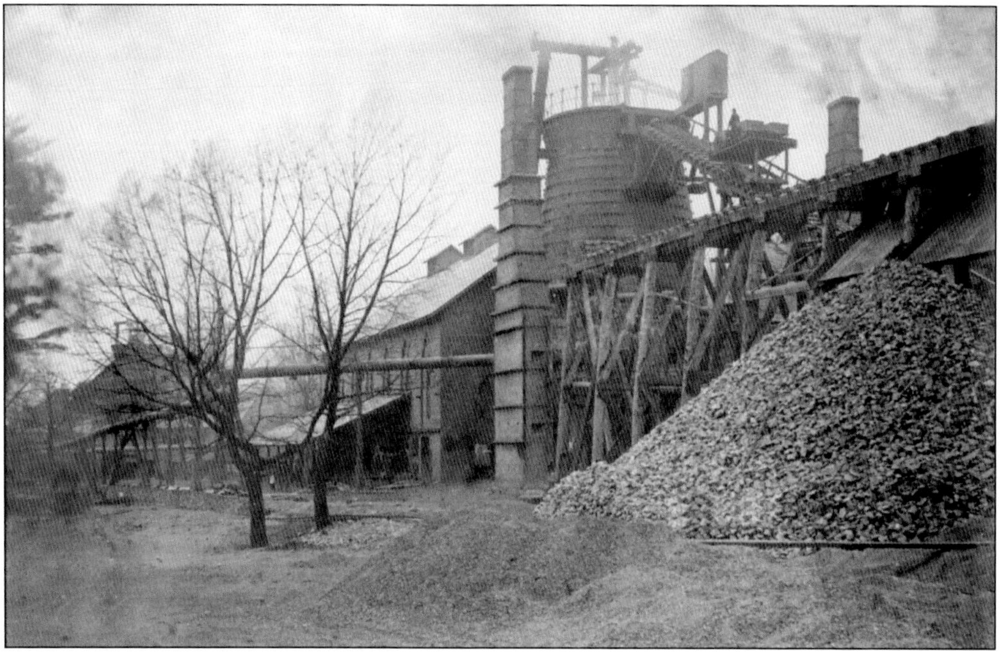

Lucy Selina Furnace was first built as a cold-blast furnace in 1827 by Col. Edwin Jordan. It provided iron for cannons and cannonballs for the Confederacy. After the war, the furnace was bought by Harry and Frank Firmstone, who rebuilt it as a hot-blast furnace and renamed it Longdale. It went out of blast in 1911. (AHS.)

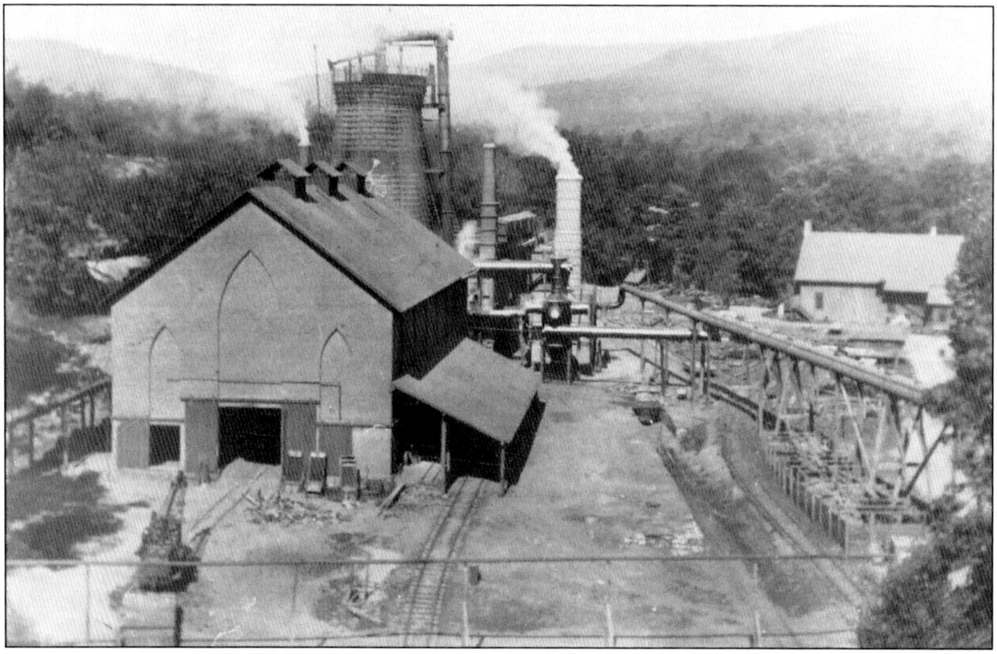

This view of Longdale Furnace from the other side of the furnace shows one of the casting houses. The furnace can be seen behind the casting house. This furnace was originally Lucy Selina and was renamed Longdale 1 after its rebuild. A second furnace was then added to the operation. (AHS.)

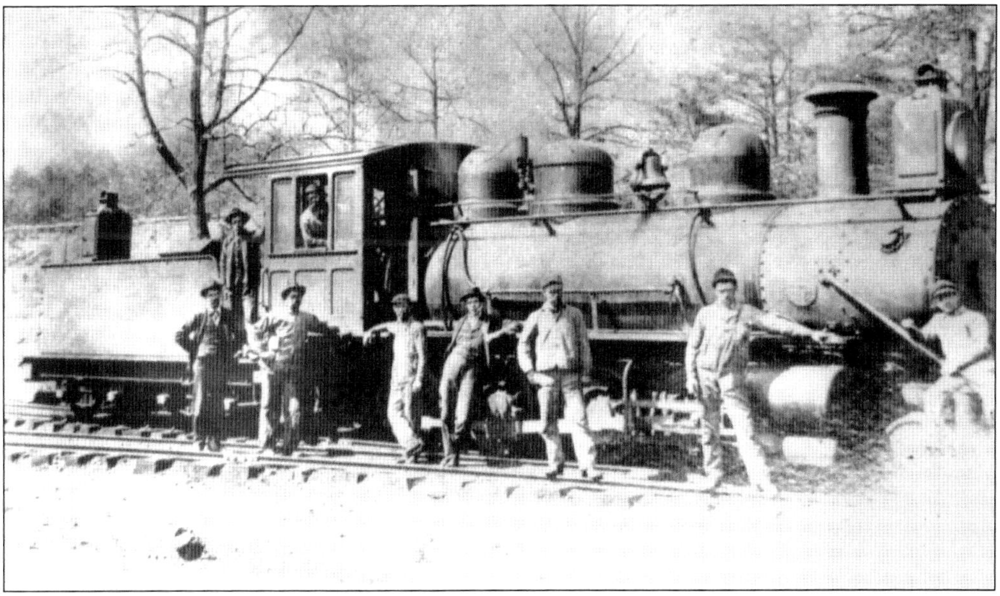

A narrow-gauge railroad was built in Longdale in 1874. It had several small locomotives called dinkies because of their size. As a way of preserving the history of the furnace, dinky No. 1 was called *Lucy* and No. 2 was called *Selina*. This is one of three larger engines from Longdale built by Baldwin Locomotive Works. (COHS.)

This 1958 photograph shows the two stacks at Longdale, which were intentionally left standing as a memorial to Harry Firmstone. The machine shop still stands beside the stacks, and the two buildings in the background are from early Lucy Selina days. Built in the 1820s, the white building was the company commissary, and the log building behind it was the laboratory. (HH.)

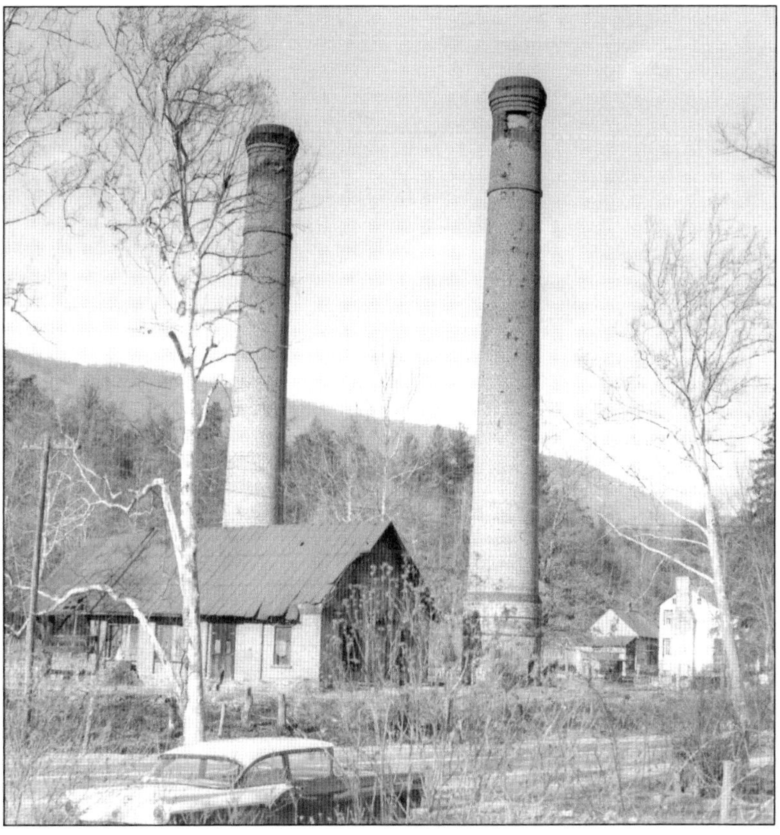

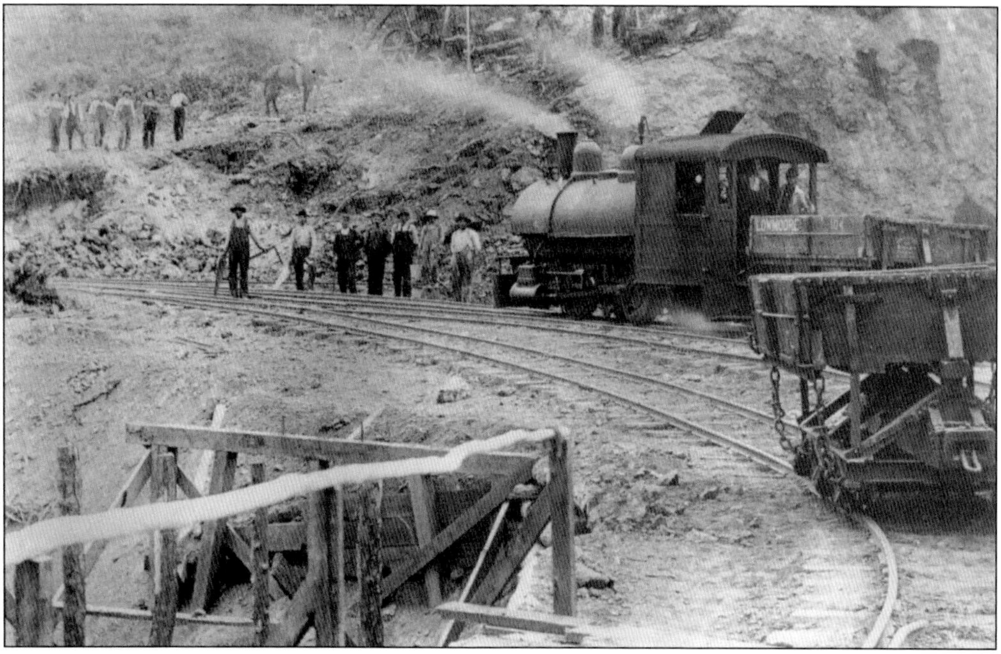

Due to the terrain around the tracks, this photograph from the late 1800s is believed to have been taken at the Stack Mines. Notice the steam drill on the hill in the background and the spelling of "Lowmoore" on the wooden mining car behind the dinky engine. The mining car at right has early link-and-pin couplers. (AHS.)

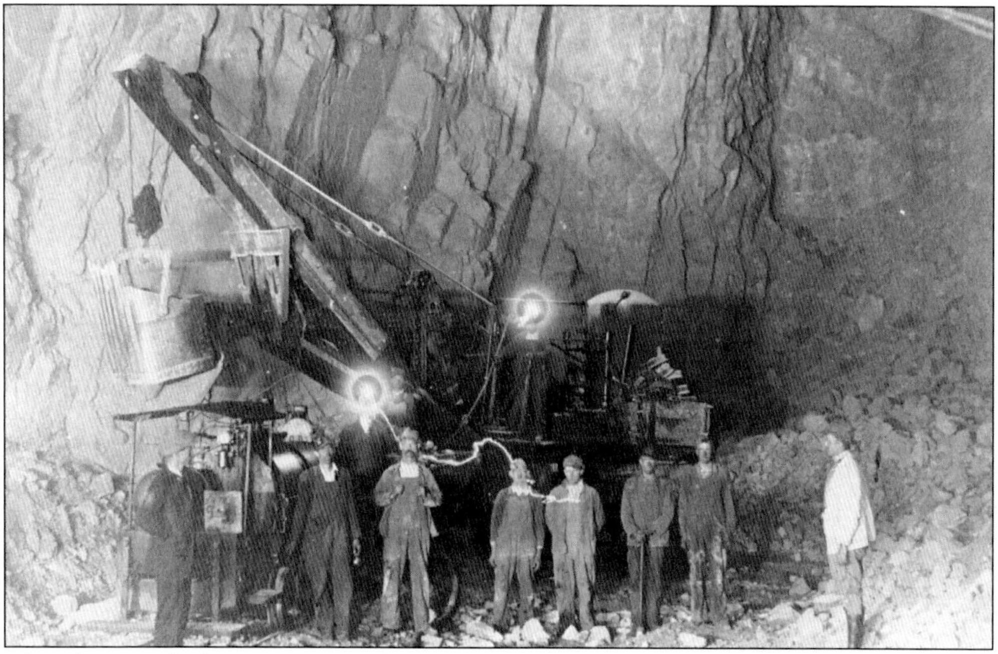

This photograph shows miners in the limestone quarry near the Low Moor Iron Company. Limestone was used in the purification processing of iron ore. During the smelting process, it helped create slag by combining with the impurities in the iron ore. The use of carbide lamps indicates that the photograph was taken after 1900. (COHS.)

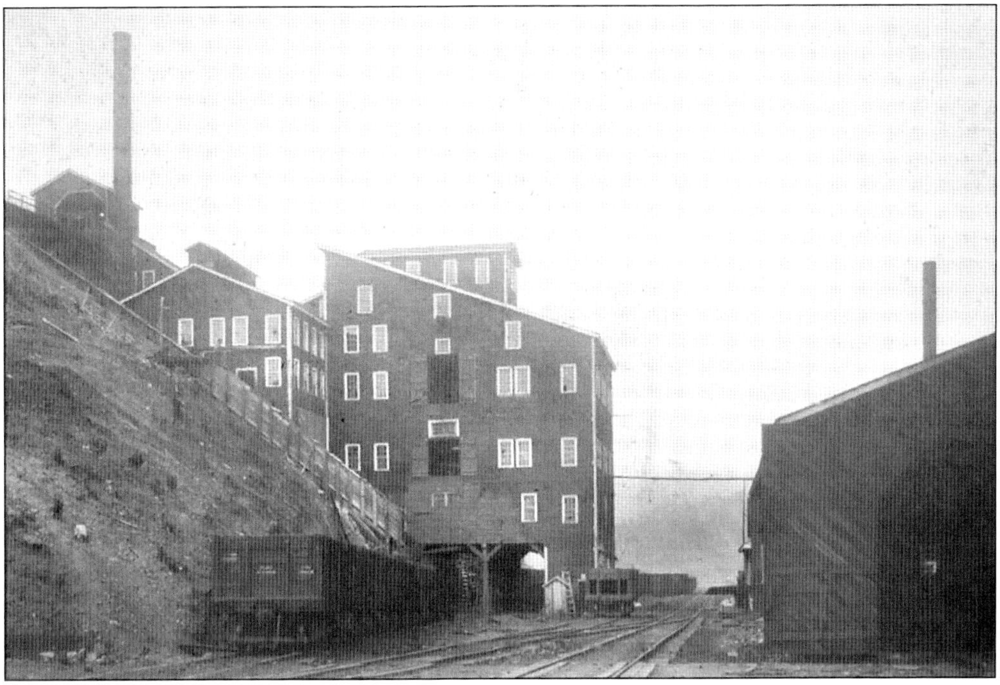

In 1907, the C&O Railway built the Potts Creek branch line from Covington to Jordan, extending it to Bess in 1908. It was built to allow the Low Moor Iron Company to access iron deposits in the Potts Creek valley. The mines around Jordan were deep shaft mines rather than the surface mining typically encountered in Alleghany County. The iron proved to not be the quality and quantity hoped for, and the track was retired in 1934, just five years after Low Moor Iron Company liquidated. These two pictures show the Jordan Mine tipple and ore washer. The above picture shows the locomotive house on the right. A portion of the branch line remained in use to service Industrial Rayon, Hercules, and Applied Extrusion Technologies operations. (Both, AHS.)

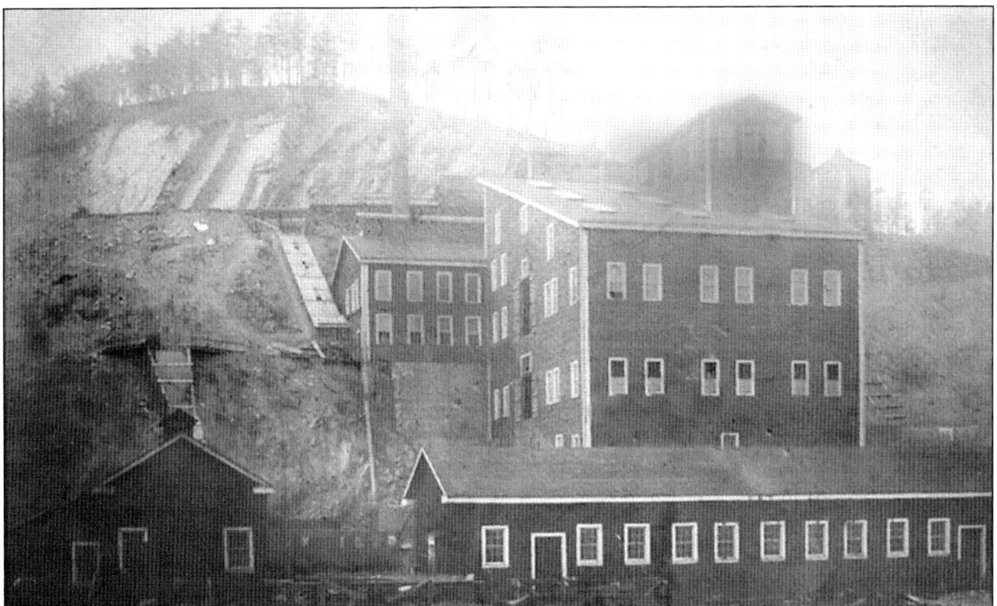

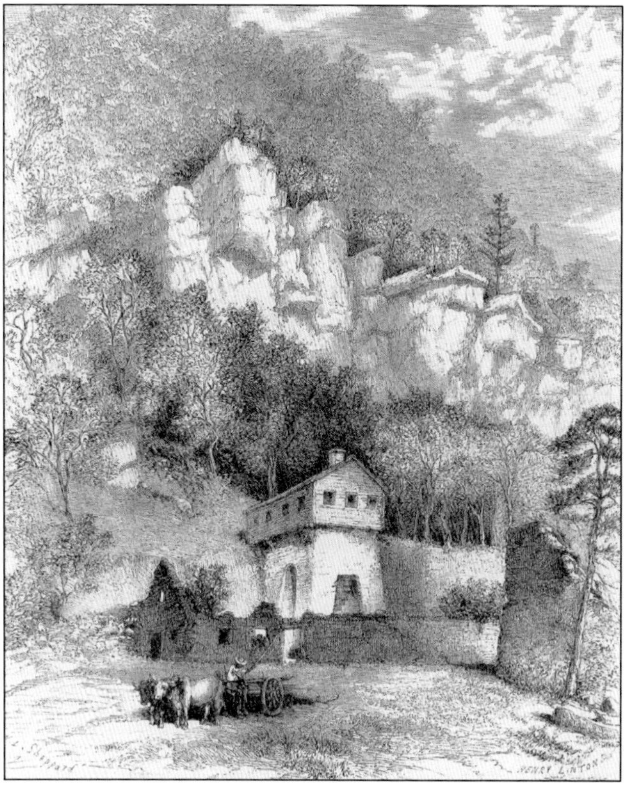

Clifton Forge was a cold-blast iron forge located southeast of the town of Clifton Forge. It is located across the river from Rainbow Rock. It was built in 1846, probably by John Jordan and John Irving, and was sold to William Alexander. Alexander continued operation until 1859. This illustration from the book *Picturesque America* shows Clifton Forge abandoned in 1872. (AHS.)

The limestone structure of old Clifton Forge still stands today beside Highway 220. The James River line of CSX runs beside the forge and can be seen from the highway. This photograph was taken by Charlie Hammond in 1980. The appearance of the forge has not changed in recent years. (HH.)

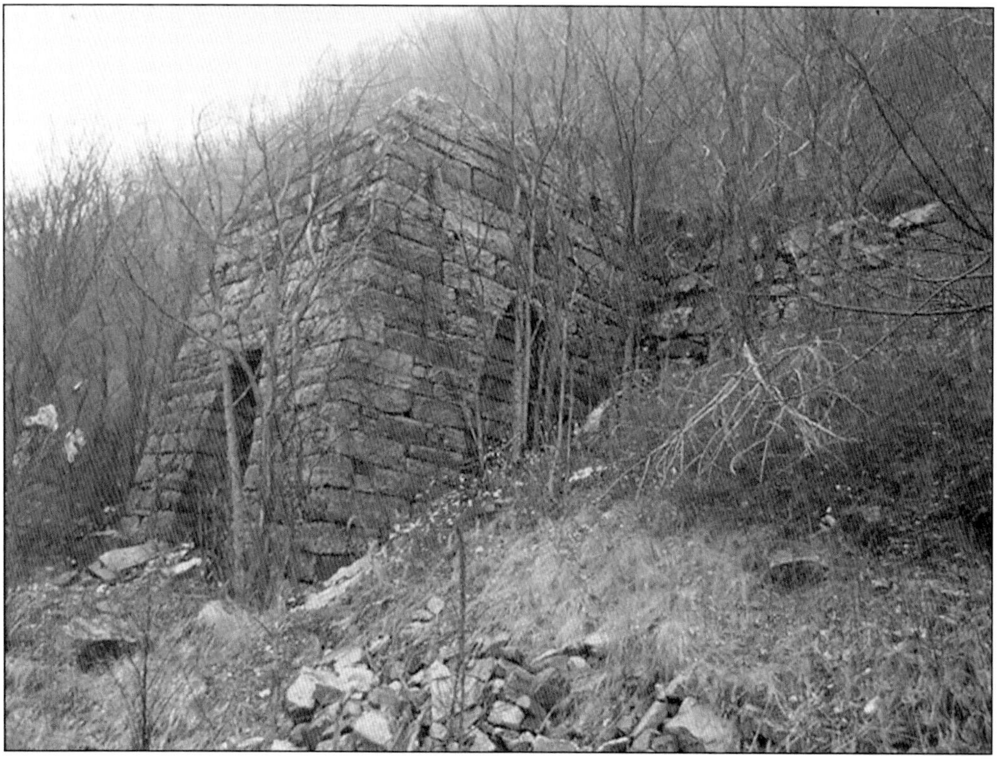

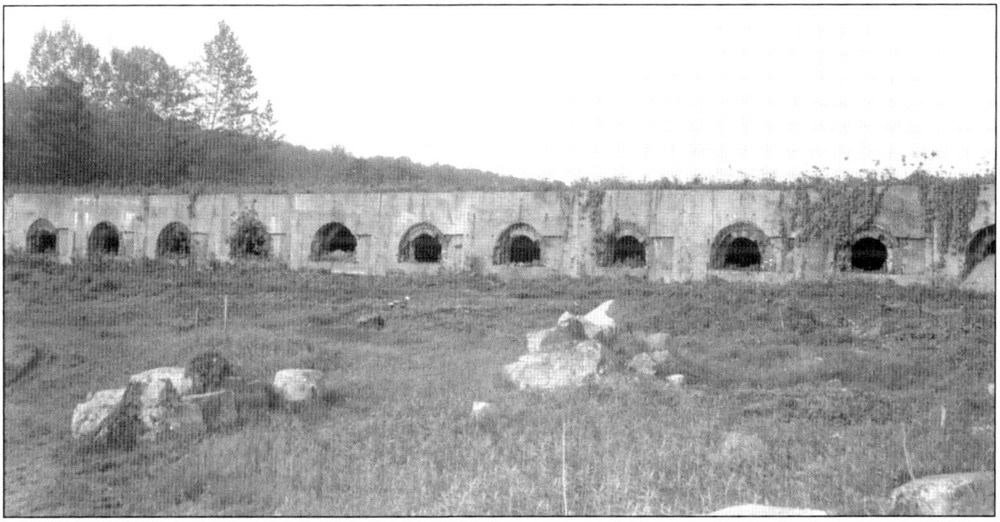

This is the row of "new" coke ovens that were used by the Low Moor Iron Company. They were located on property that today is adjacent to the Alleghany County Governmental Complex. They have since been removed, and the area is slated for commercial development. Coke is a fuel made by partially burning coal to refine it. It produces much hotter furnace temperatures than charcoal. (AHS-VR.)

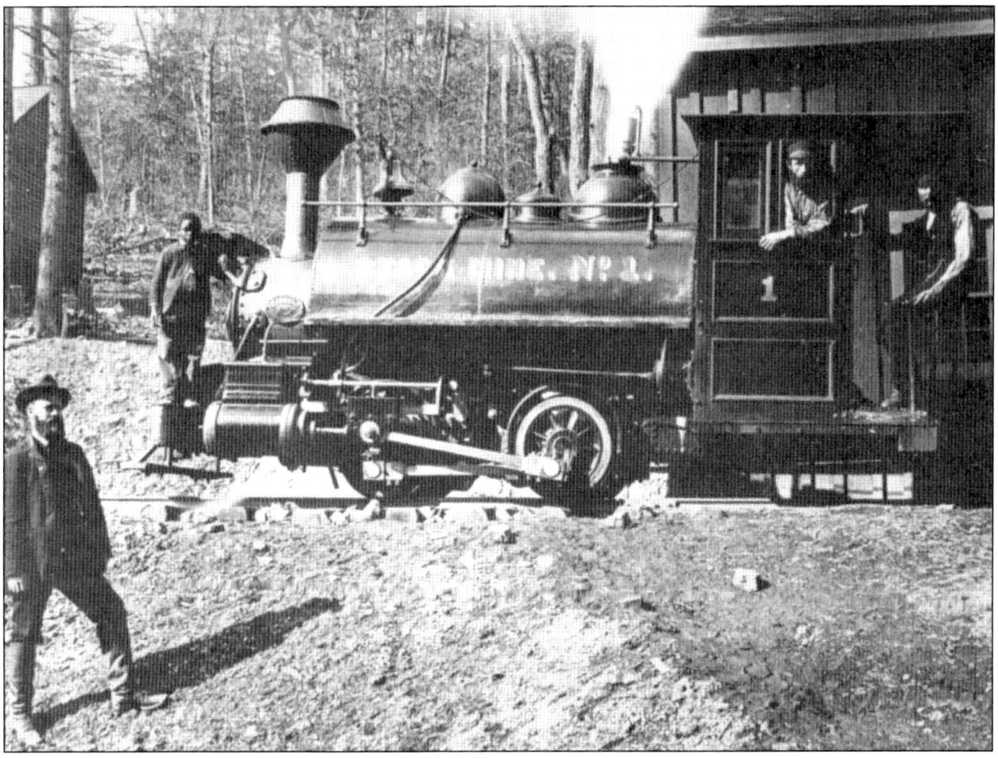

This is the Stack Mines dinky No. 1. The Stack Mines were surface mines active from 1893 to 1910 near Dunlap. The narrow-gauge railroad transported the ore to a tipple at Backbone, where it was transferred to C&O Railway cars. A fire in the iron ore washer in 1910 resulted in the closure of the operation. (COHS.)

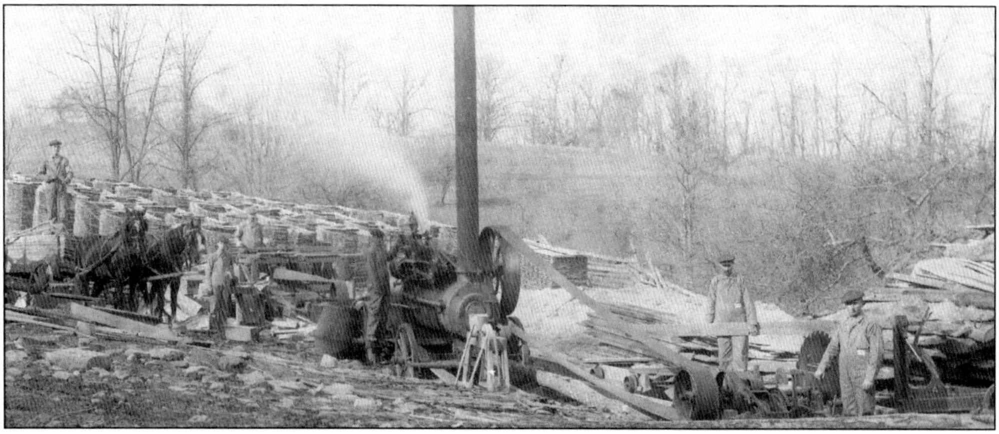

Wood was an important commodity for building as well as for making paper and rayon. This is a photograph of a small steam-powered sawmill operated by Allen Byrd Humphries in Rich Patch around 1910. The earliest sawmills were "up and down" mills run by water power, but circular saw blades saw widespread use beginning around 1820. (AHS.)

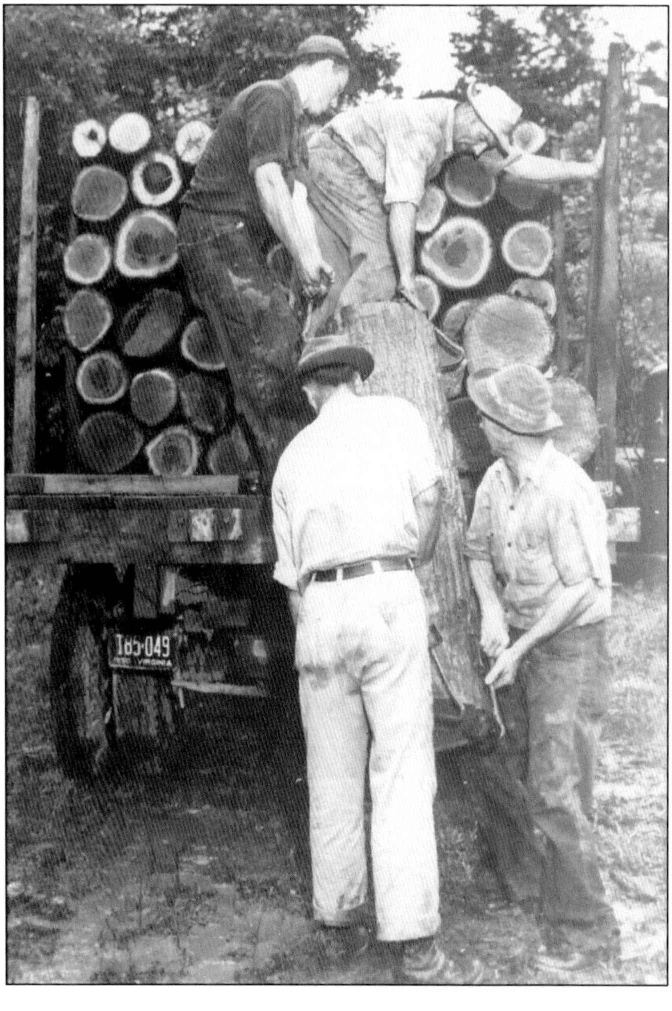

This photograph from 1950 shows unidentified loggers loading pulpwood onto a logging truck destined for Westvaco. The company originally had specific standards for lengths and types of wood used for making the pulp in the paper manufacturing process. Today, the mill's wood processing operations can handle both random logs and wood chips shipped to the mill. (AHS-VR.)

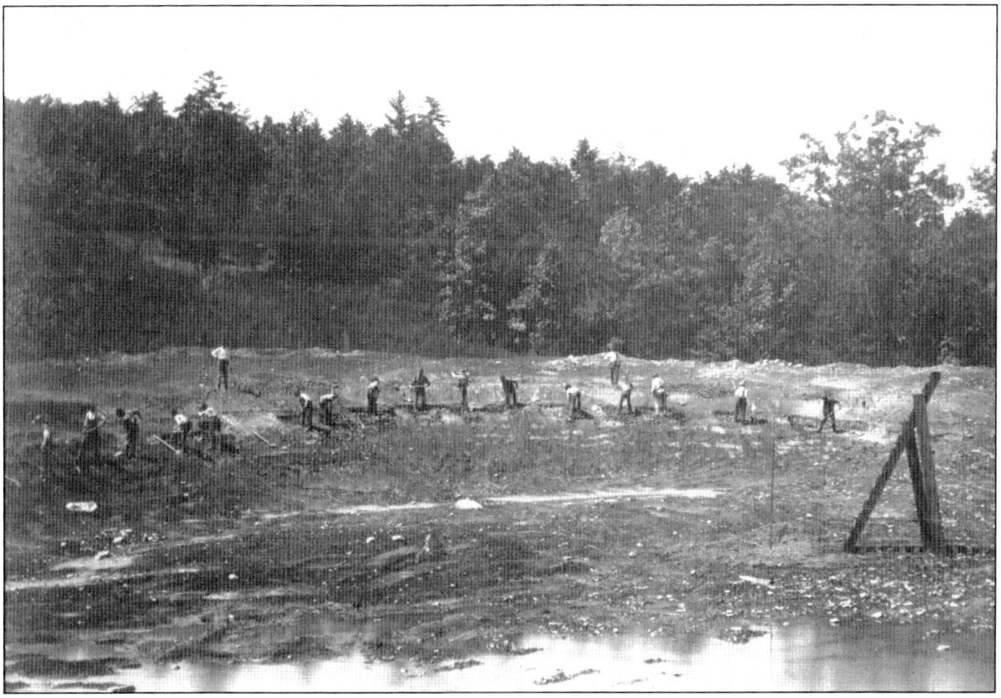

The West Virginia Pulp and Paper Company initially wanted to locate on the Greenbrier River in West Virginia. However, the people along the river did not want an industrial operation in the area. The company chose to locate in Covington in 1899. The location of Covington on the main line of the C&O Railway and its natural resources made it a desirable location. The area had a long history of industrial operations and welcomed the addition of the new paper mill. This 1899 photograph shows workers digging the foundation by hand. (AHS-VR.)

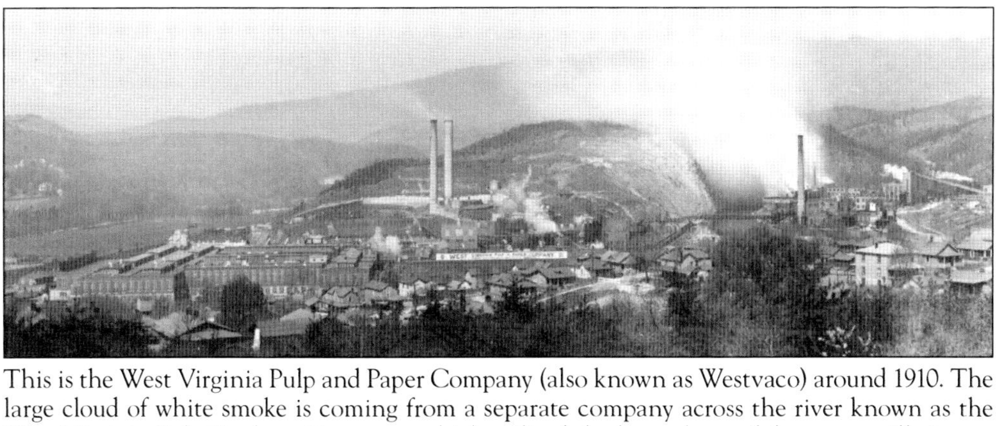

This is the West Virginia Pulp and Paper Company (also known as Westvaco) around 1910. The large cloud of white smoke is coming from a separate company across the river known as the West Virginia Pulp Products Company, which utilized the byproducts of the paper mill. Across the river, notice the small early wood yard. Rows of company houses stand in the foreground. (AHS-VR.)

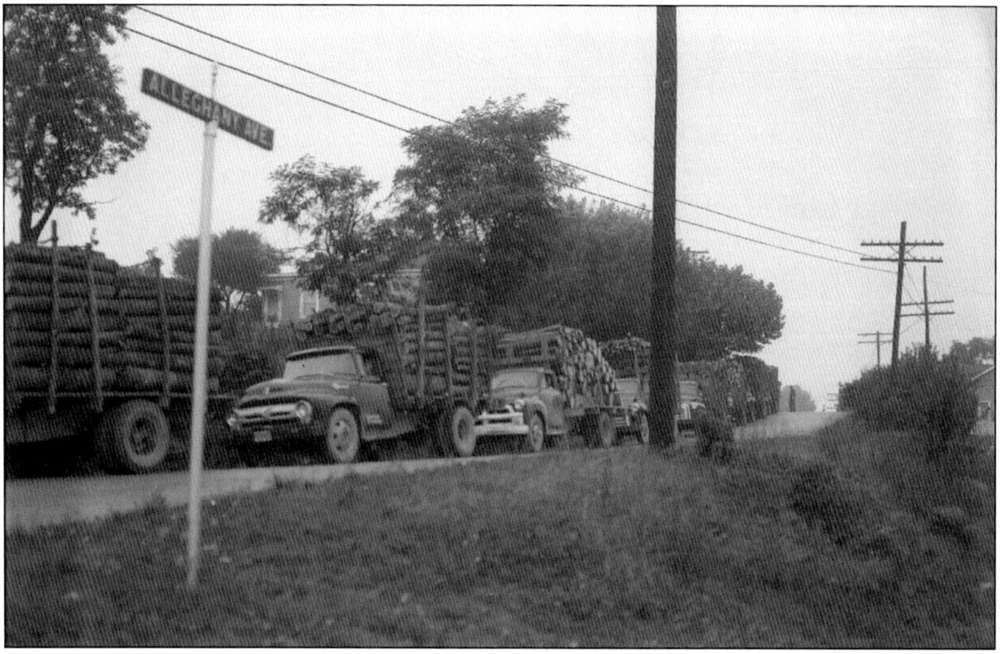

This late 1950s photograph shows a row of loaded pulpwood logging trucks backed up on Alleghany Avenue waiting for their turn to unload at the wood yard. The demand for pulpwood is significant and is supplied by local loggers and large-scale operators who can deliver both wood and chips by truck and rail. (AHS-VR.)

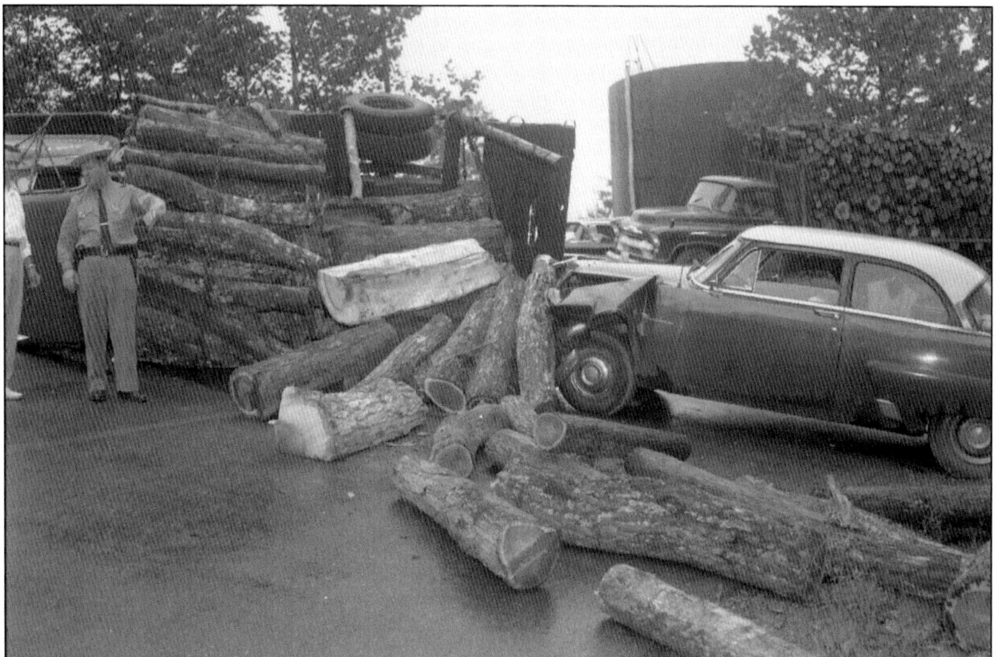

This pulpwood truck accident involving a passenger car happened on July 30, 1959. The driver of the truck was Roscoe Moyer, and the car was driven by Edward C. Crow of Baltimore. No injuries were reported as a result of the mishap. (AHS-VR.)

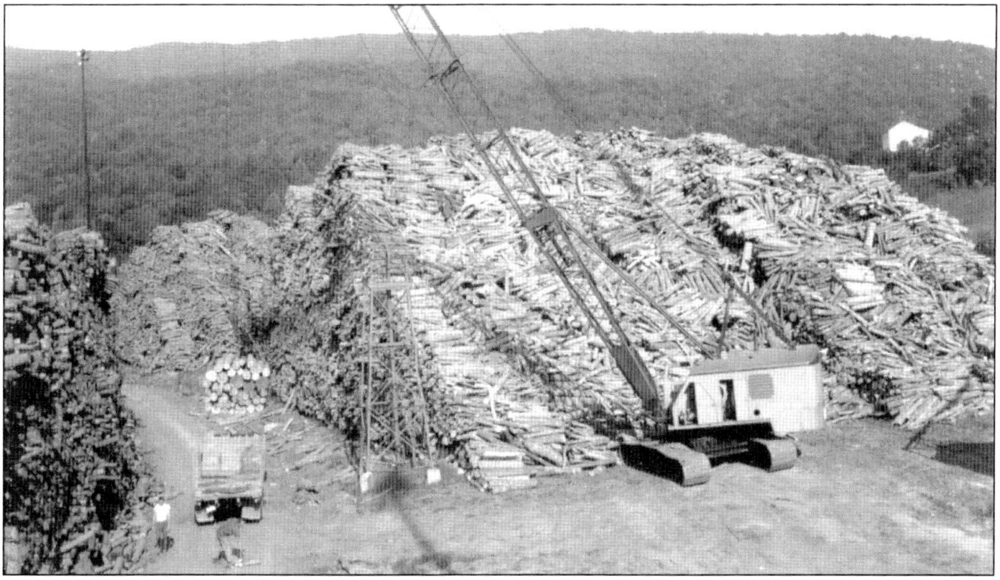

The wood yard is the location for processing the wood coming into the paper plant. This late 1940s photograph shows wood being taken off a truck by crane. The pulpwood is stacked in one section of the yard and then debarked and ground up for pulp. Wood chips delivered to the mill are stacked elsewhere and are ready for processing. (AHS-VR.)

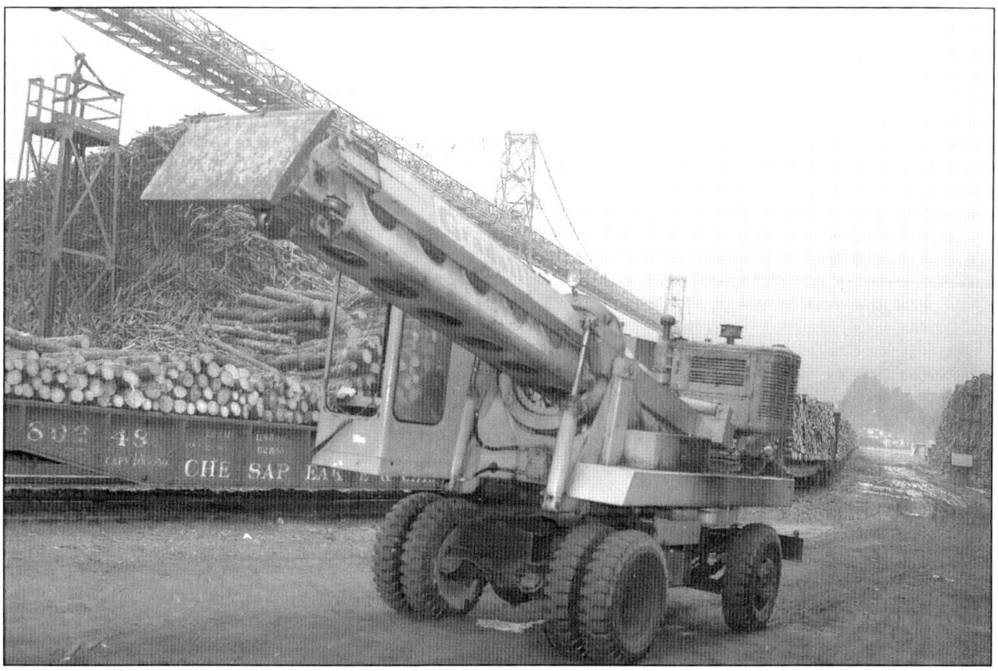

This 1956 photograph shows a trainload of logs delivered to the paper mill. The railroad delivered logs to the mill by the train in the background. While cranes usually unloaded trucks, this unloader simply pushed the logs off the train. Notice a firefighting tower on the left that could be used to extinguish any fires in the yard. (AHS-VR.)

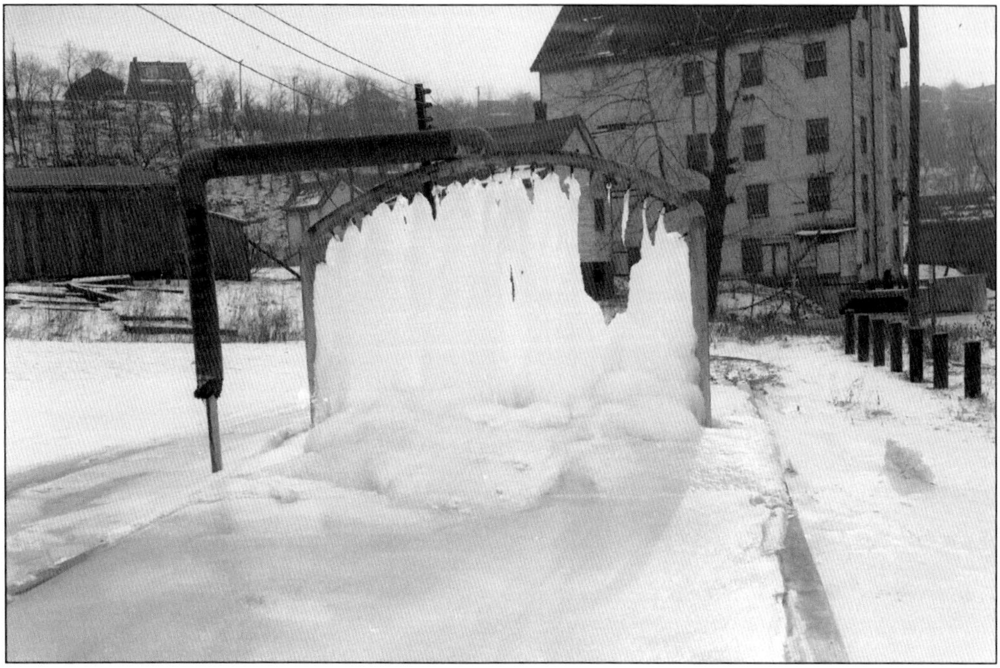

A carwash was provided by the plant to help residents keep their cars clean due to some fallout from the operations. This carwash, located near McAllister and Bell Mill (background), was left on in 1956 to try to keep the pipes from freezing. It was apparently not a good idea. (AHS-VR.)

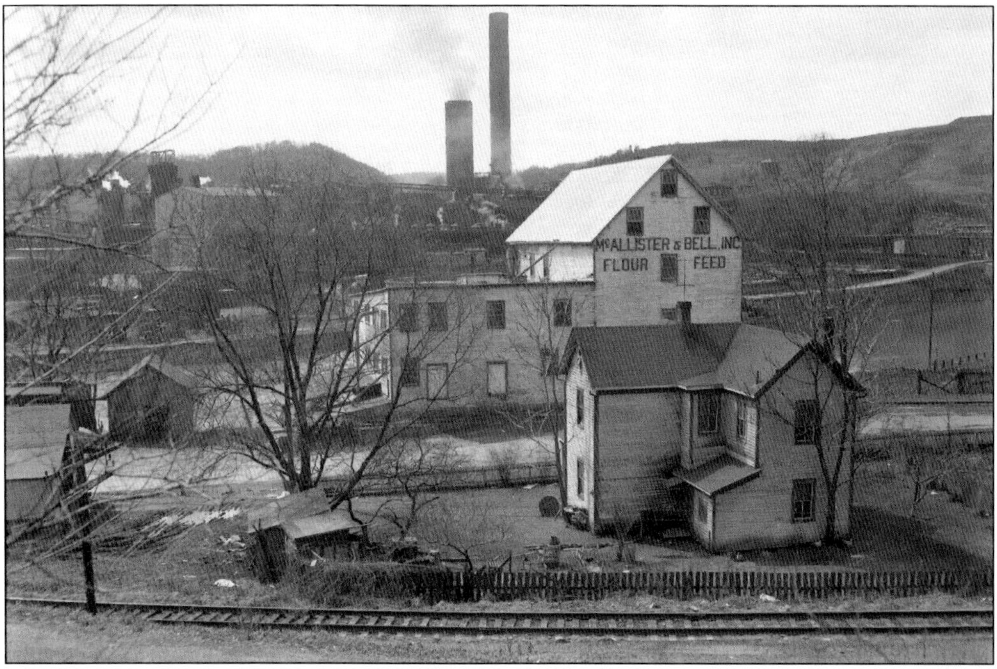

The McAllister and Bell Flour and Feed Mill was located near the wood yard across the river from the Westvaco paper machines. McAllister and Bell had been in operation for over 100 years by the time the mill was torn down and replaced by Allied Chemical in 1962. The dam was left in place. (AHS-VR.)

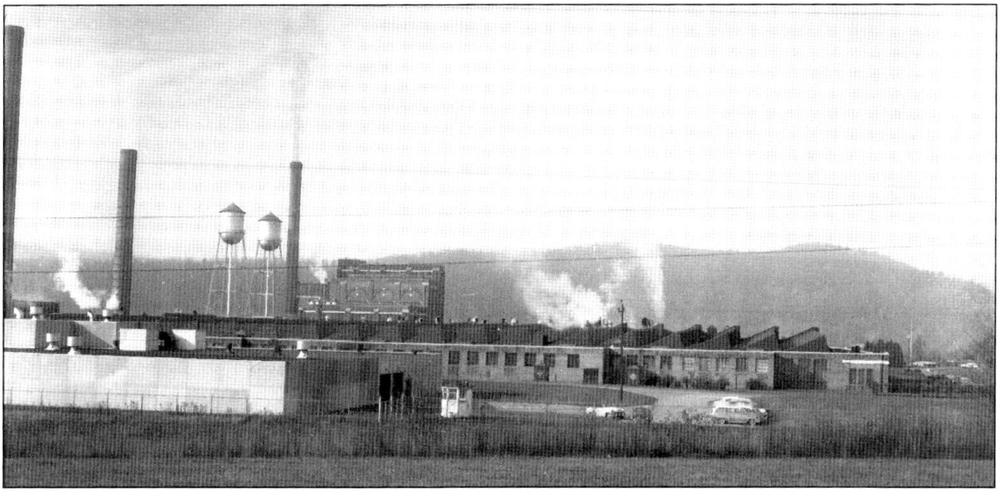

The Industrial Rayon Corporation came to Covington in 1928 and utilized fibers of the red spruce tree to spin synthetic yarn. Westvaco provided the rayon plant with the raw materials from its operations in Cass, West Virginia. This photograph was taken in 1959 just prior to the plant being bought by Hercules Inc. Hercules produced synthetic fibers and later expanded to produce a clear plastic packaging material. A fire in 1980 shut down the fiber production. The clear packaging material continued being produced, and the plant was later sold to Applied Extrusion Technologies. It ceased operations in 2008. (AHS-VR.)

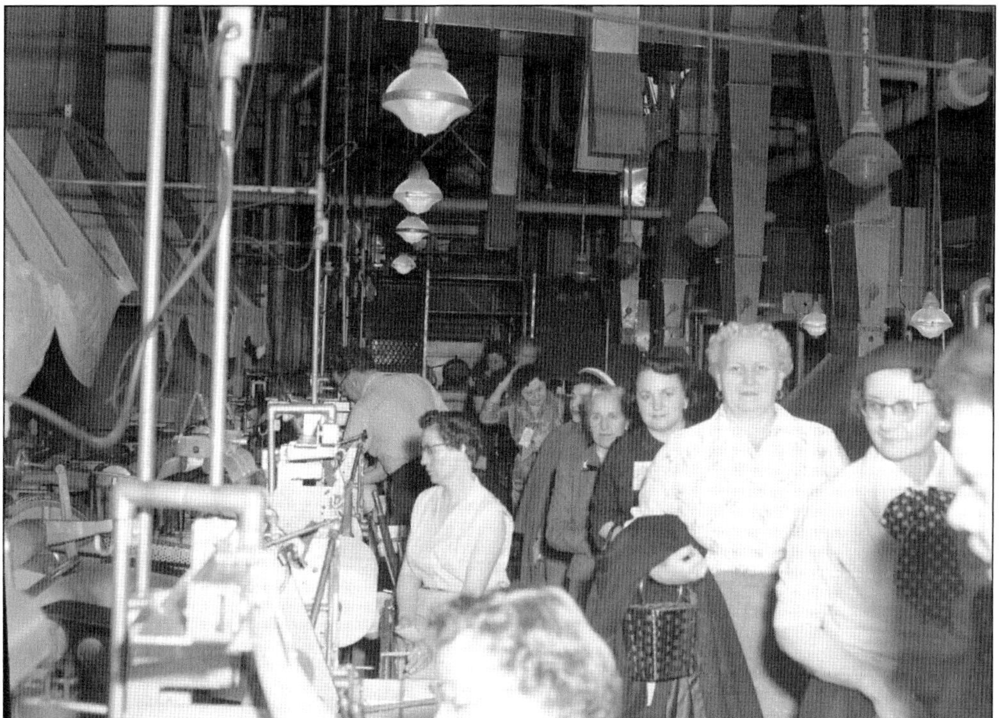

In 1958, the Business and Professional Women's Club took a tour of Industrial Rayon. Women were among the skilled workers needed to monitor the machinery in the production process. Notice the 1920s-style lighting. (AHS-VR.)

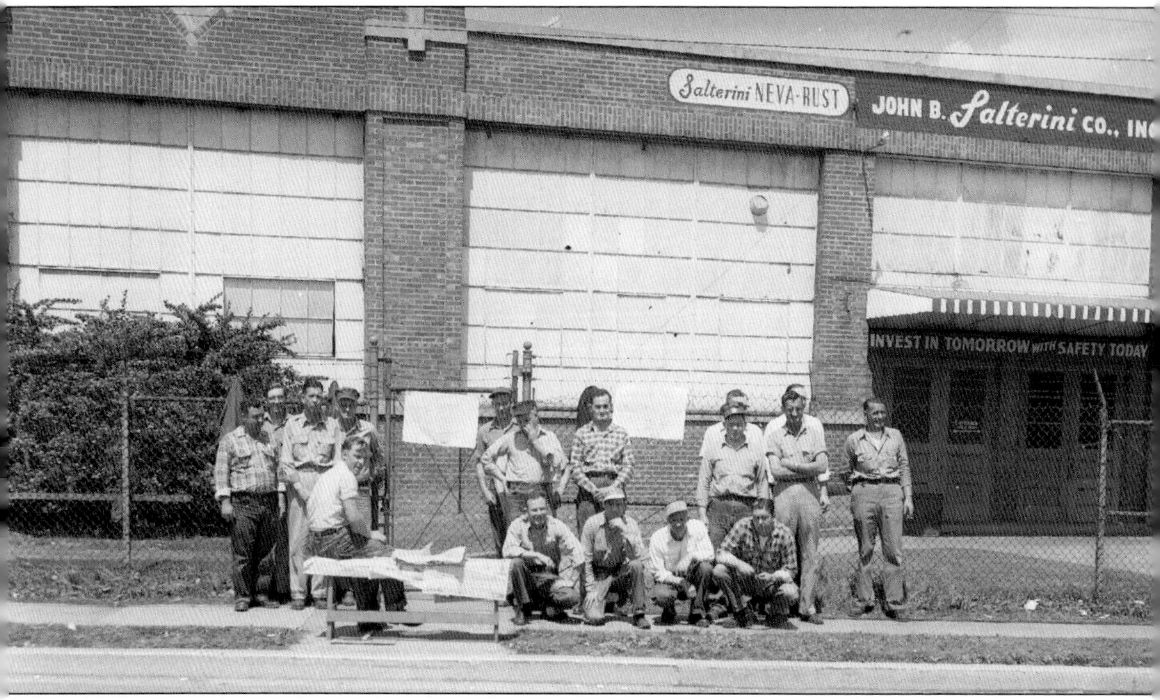

A silk mill was operated by the Schwarzenbach Huber Company in 1918 on Hawthorne Street in Covington. It later became the Covington Weaving Mill, operated by William Klopman and Son. After the weaving mill closed, the John B. Salterini Company began producing custom-made wrought iron furniture. This 1962 photograph shows workers from the plant on strike for living wages. Because the patio furniture had a protective outer coating, it was marketed under the brand name of Neva-Rust. (AHS-VR.)

Salterini furniture was made out of hollow iron tubing. This photograph shows a blacksmith working at his forge to shape the tubing. Different shapes were then assembled into the final product. (AHS-VR.)

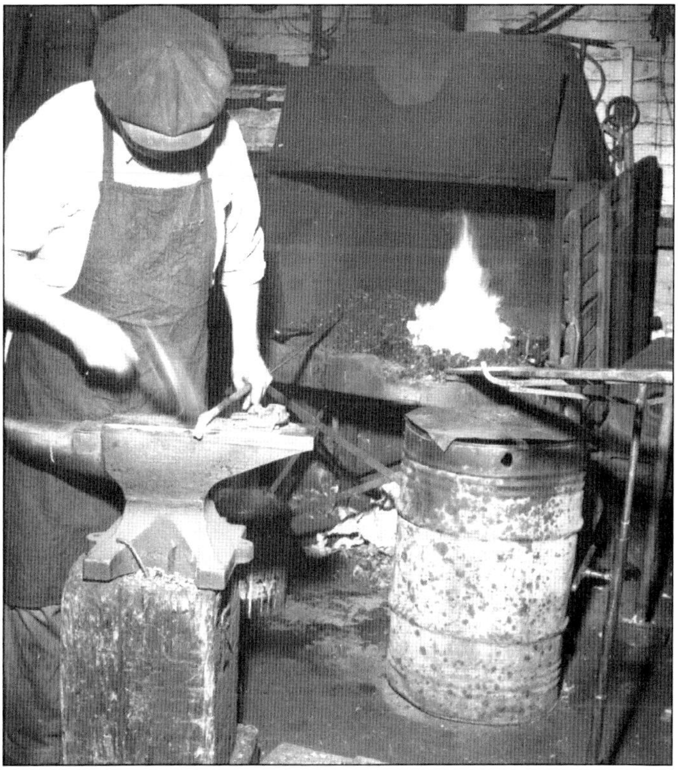

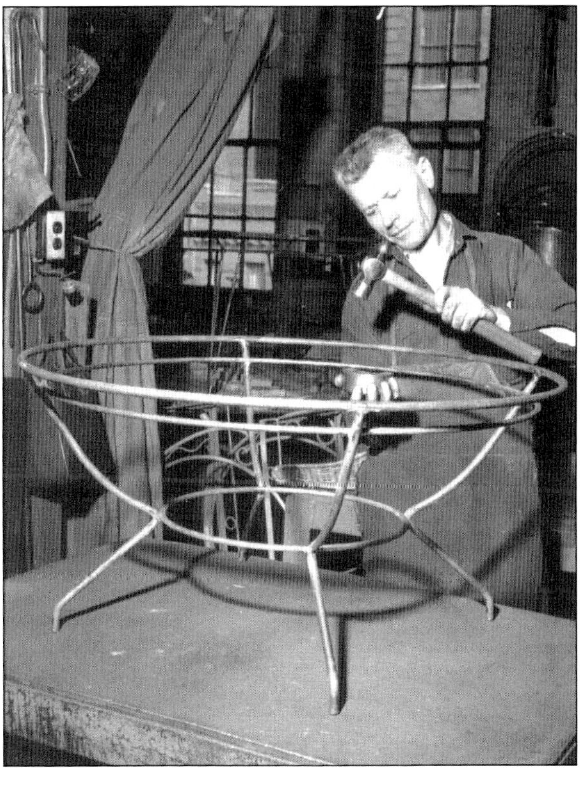

This table has final shaping done by a machinist to make sure that the top surfaces are smooth and level. He carefully hammers on the metal while holding a lead weight below, which softens the blow. The furniture came in a wide variety of styles and is still popular today because of its durability. (AHS-VR.)

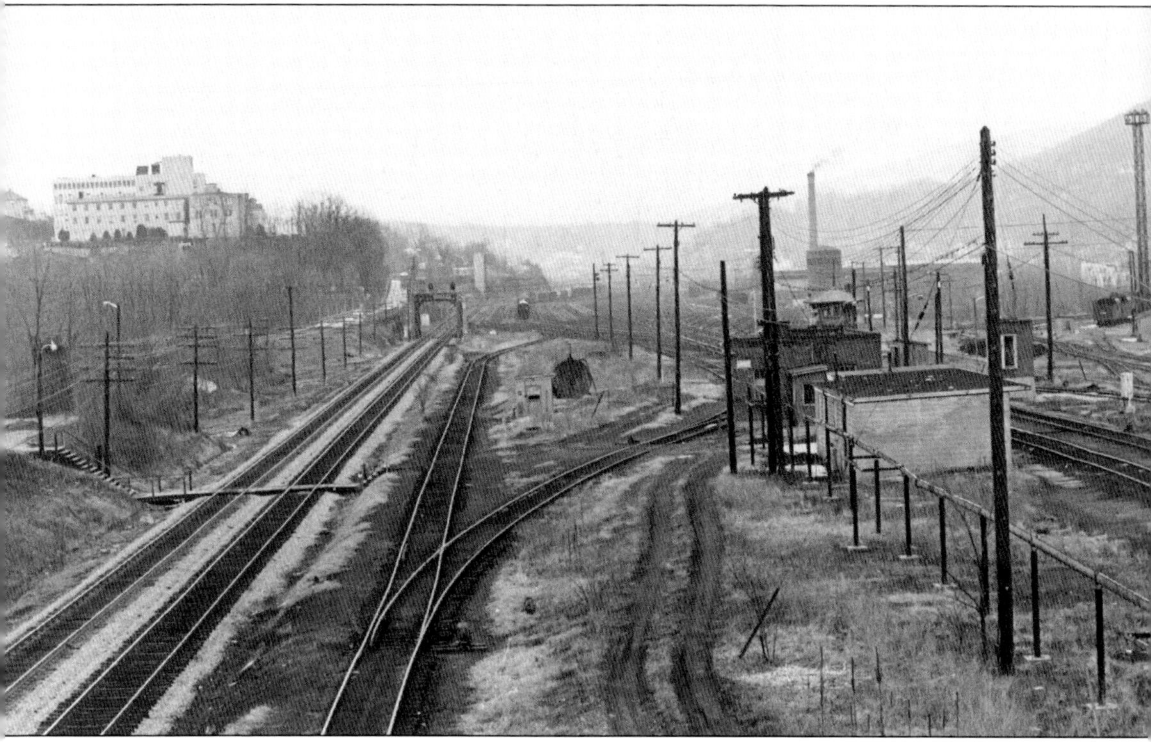

This undated photograph of the west end of the C&O Clifton Forge yard shows the C&O Hospital atop the hill on the left. The two main lines of the railroad are on the left. The tall smokestack from the C&O Shops is visible in the center background. A signal tower can be seen in the foreground in front of the stack. (AHS-VR.)

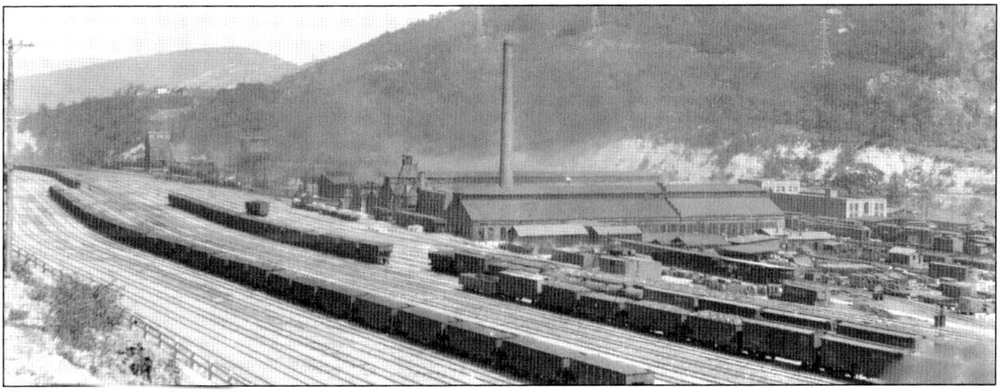

The building of the Clifton Forge C&O Shops began in 1890, and they were in operation by 1896. Clifton Forge was chosen because it provided the most land for the shops between the Blue Ridge and Alleghany Mountains. The photographs on this page show the shops in the 1930s or 1940s. (AHS-VR.)

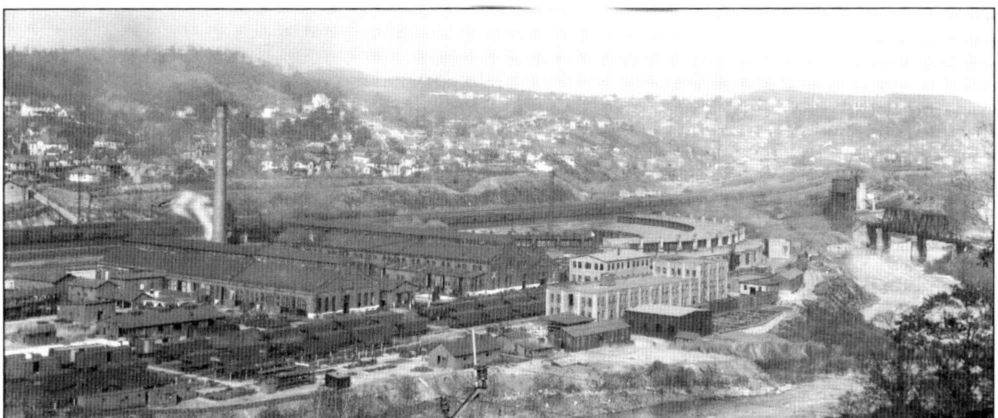

The shops housed a comprehensive engine repair operation and first serviced the steam locomotives operated by the C&O. The shops were then repurposed in the 1950s when the railroad shifted to diesel engines. (AHS-VR.)

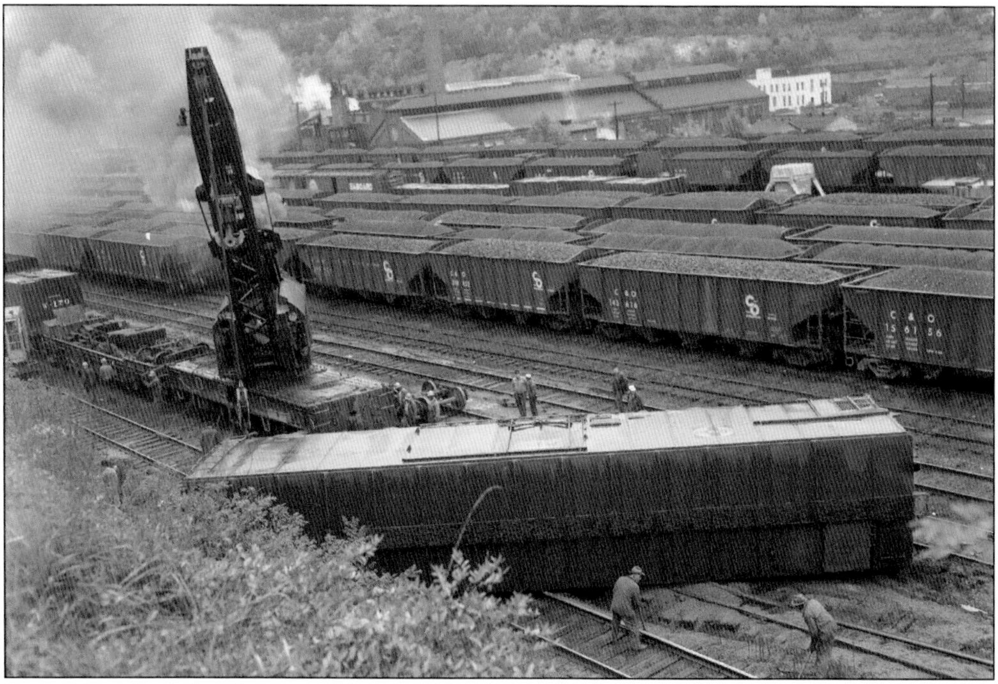

Long after the railroads stopped using steam locomotives, they continued to use steam power for other purposes. These two pictures show the steam crane from the Clifton Forge wreck train being used to pick up the trucks from a derailed boxcar in the early 1960s. A tender left over from the steam era provides the water needed for the steam crane. While the crane clears the wreckage, notice the track section gandy dancers already making repairs to the damaged track. (Both, AHS-VR.)

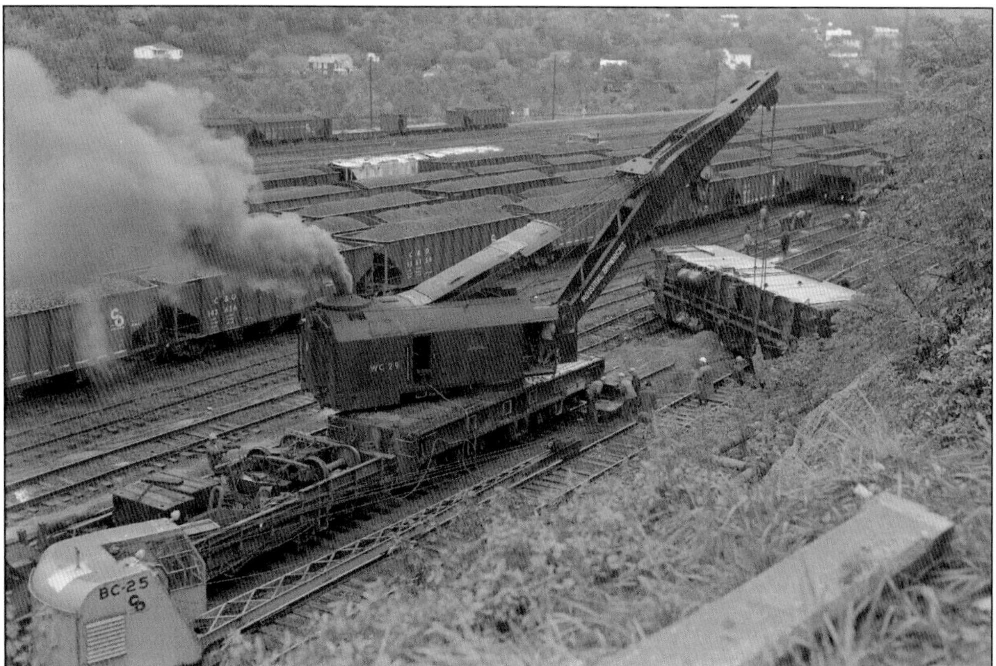

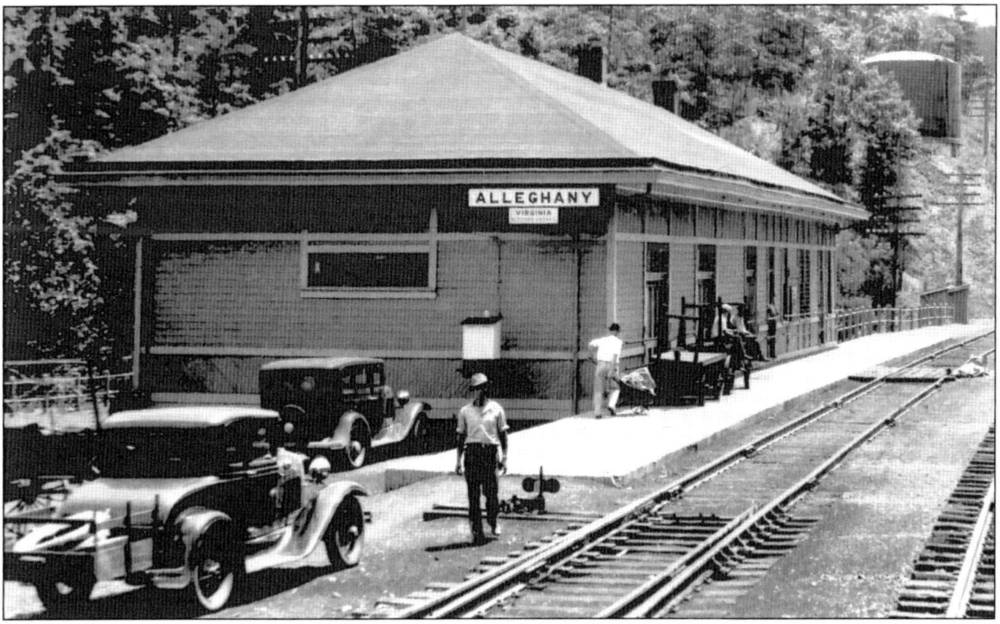

Prior to the Interstate Highway System, railroads were the primary mode of passenger transportation, particularly over long distances. Many small communities had a train station or flag stop. Alleghany Station was located on the C&O Railway near the West Virginia state line on Highway 311. Despite being in a rural section of the county, this 1930s photograph shows a busy station with people waiting for the next train. (COHS.)

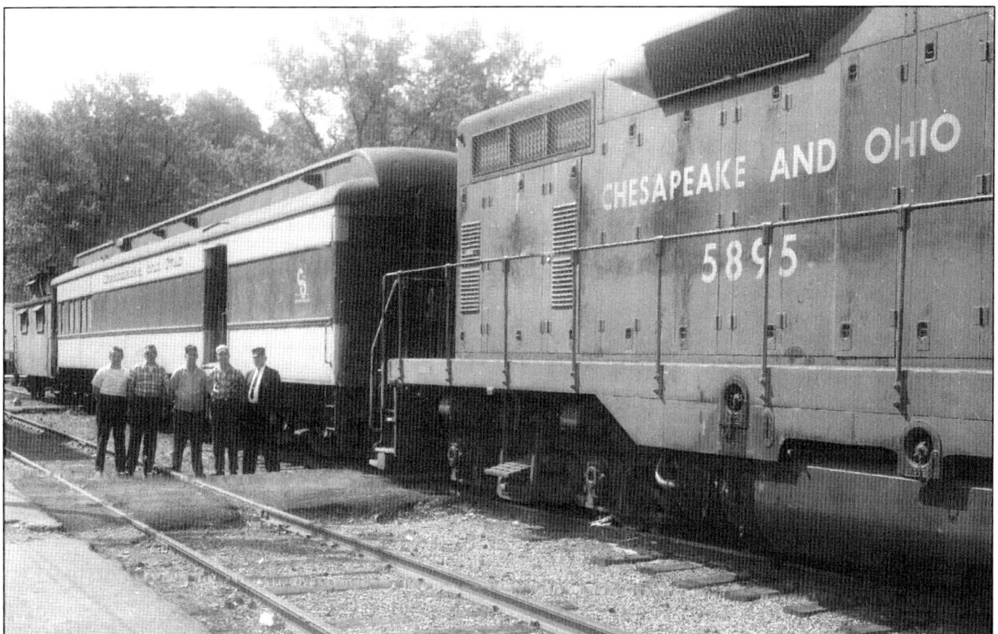

The C&O Railway's Hot Springs branch opened service for passengers in 1891. The 24-mile line was finished in only six months. It continued to carry passengers to the Hot Springs resort until early 1970. This photograph shows the last passenger train on the Hot Springs branch in February 1970. (AHS-VR.)

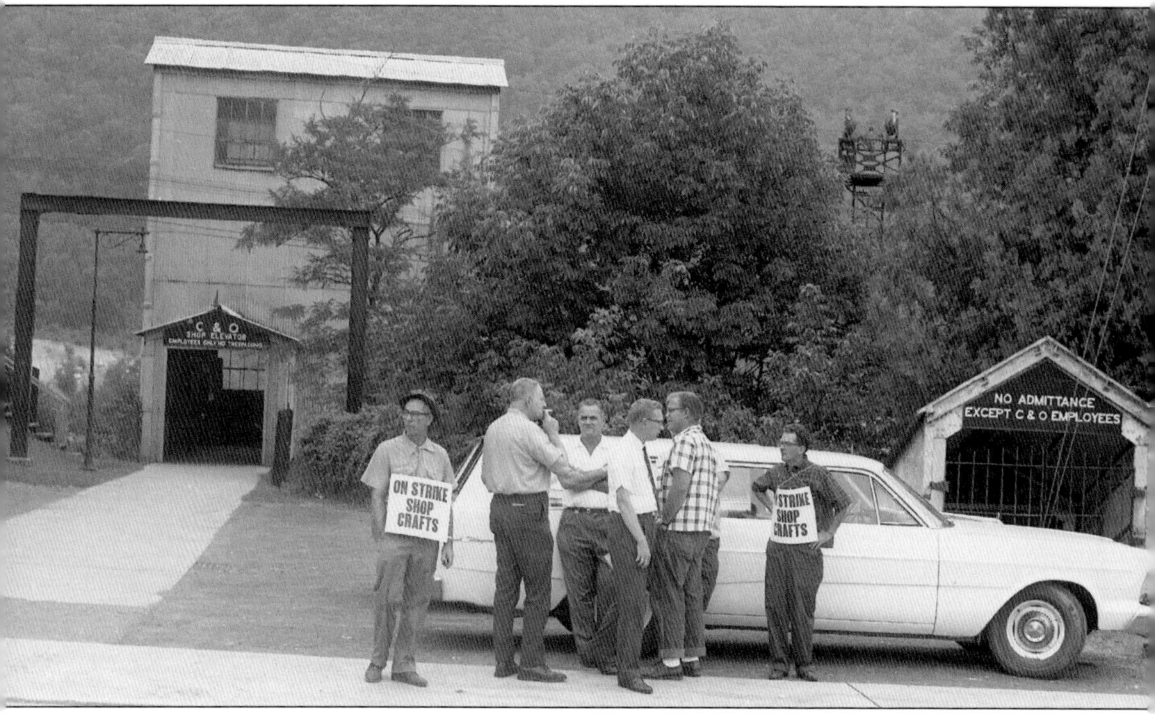

The Shop Crafts Union went on strike in July 1967 for better wages and working conditions in the Clifton Forge Shops. This photograph was taken near the entrance of the elevator and walking tunnel leading to the shops. The signs at these entrances were restored in 2015 based on their appearance in this photograph. (AHS-VR.)

Four

Recreational Opportunities

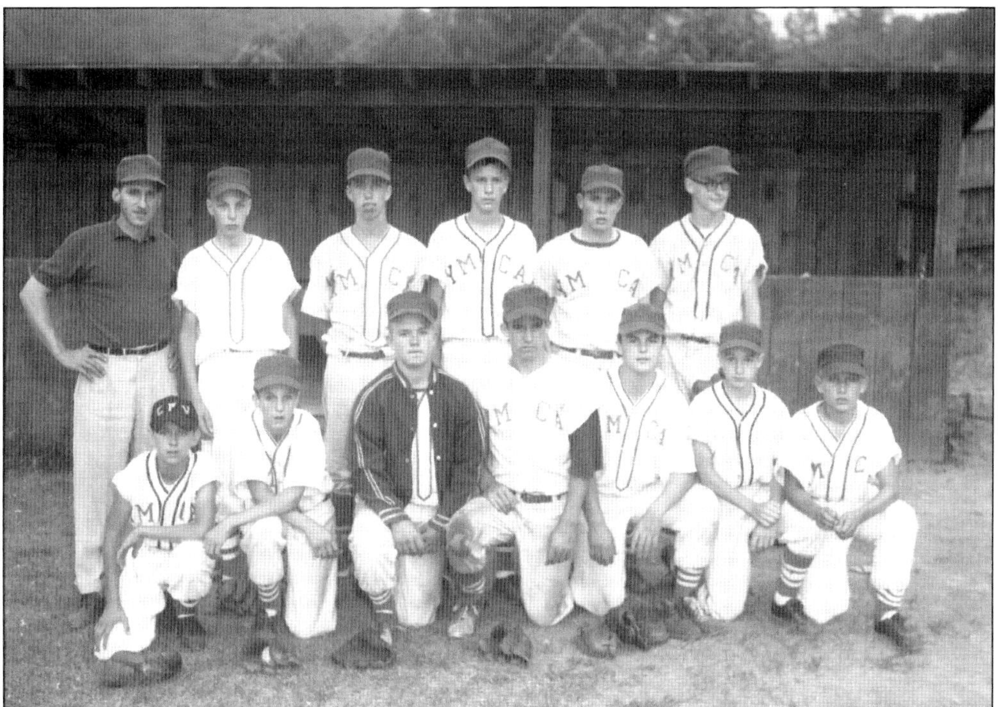

This 1960s photograph shows the Clifton Forge YMCA little league team coached by Mike Fuhrman. Also pictured are Benny Wilkerson, Donnie Kyle, Bud Hall, Dale Hall, Richie Fuhrman, Danny Watts, Steve Craft, David Skelding, and Jerry Nicely. (AHS-VR.)

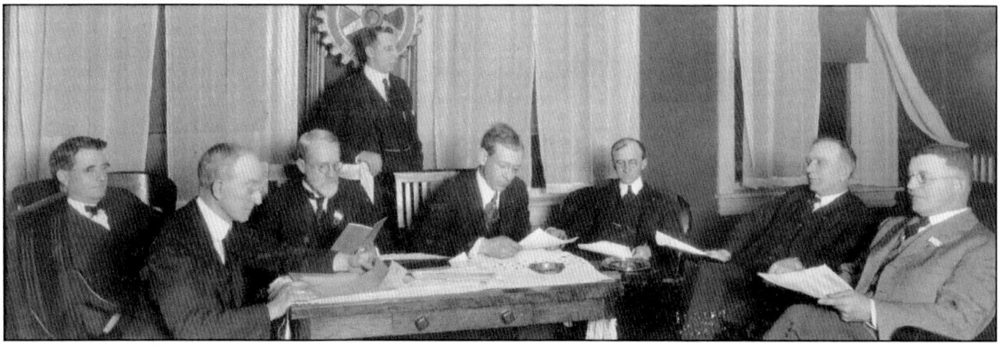

These are the first directors of the Covington–Hot Springs Rotary Club. The photograph was taken on November 12, 1920. From left to right are Joe McAllister, Joe Carpenter, "Uncle Lew" Cowardin, Frank Humbert (standing), Lanier Pole, George Miller, Will McAllister, and Tom Gathright. President Col. Richard Stokes is not pictured. (AHS.)

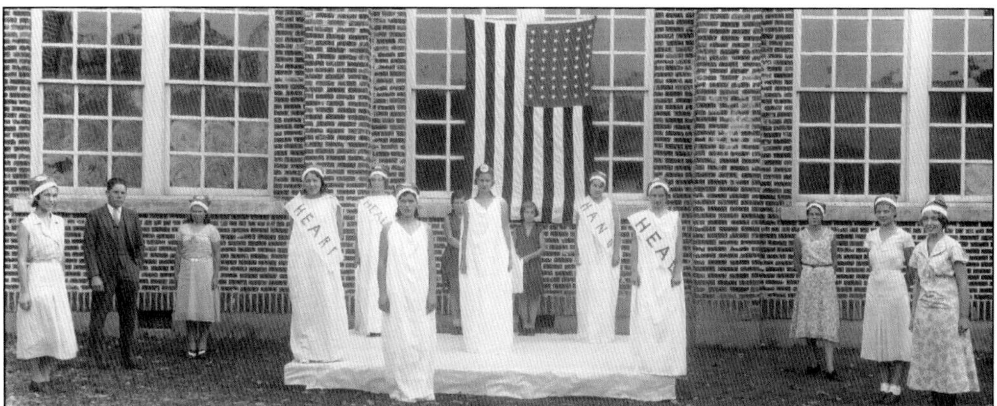

The national 4-H organization was created in 1914 as a youth program under the Cooperative Extension Service. It became known as 4-H in 1924 when the clover leaf insignia was adopted. This photograph was included in the board of supervisors paperwork from a report of the county extension worker. It shows the Falling Spring 4-H Club pageant on Achievement Day, October 29, 1932. (AHS.)

This photograph from December 6, 1956, shows Brownies giving a check for the Community Chest to Lt. Ronald Greene of the Salvation Army. Others pictured are, from left to right, (first row) Pamela Hodges; (second row) Donna Rice, Mildred McCabe (cookie sale chairwoman), and Shirley Umbles. Donna Rice in Troop 2 sold 70 boxes, and Pamela Hodges in Troop 11 and Shirley Umbles in Troop 9 sold 60 boxes each. (AHS-VR.)

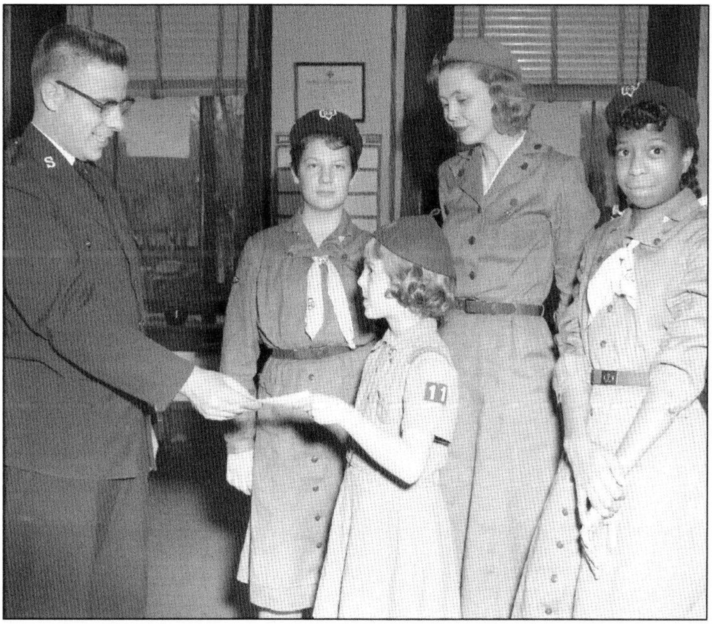

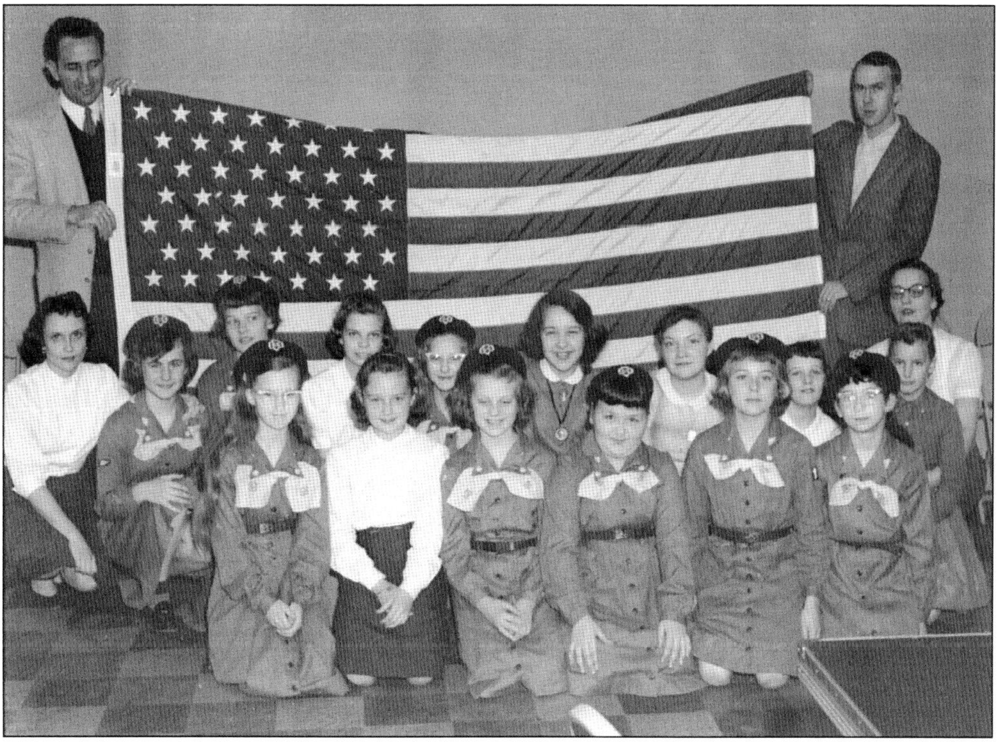

This is Selma Troop 13 with its new 49-star US flag on March 11, 1959. From left to right are (first row) Carletta Nelson, Linda Kirts, Carnell Wrenn, Brenda Kraft, Emily Mays, and Dawn Hall; (second row) co-leader Mrs. James A. Collins, Betty Jo Stockdale, Fay Tyler, Sandra Maydian, Loretta Creamer, Sylvia Broughman, Patricia Harlow, Genie Van-Buren, Wanda Jean Carter, and co-leader Mrs. L.M. Carter Jr. Holding the flag are C.B. Weikel (left), president of the fire department, and D.L. Carter, treasurer. (AHS-VR.)

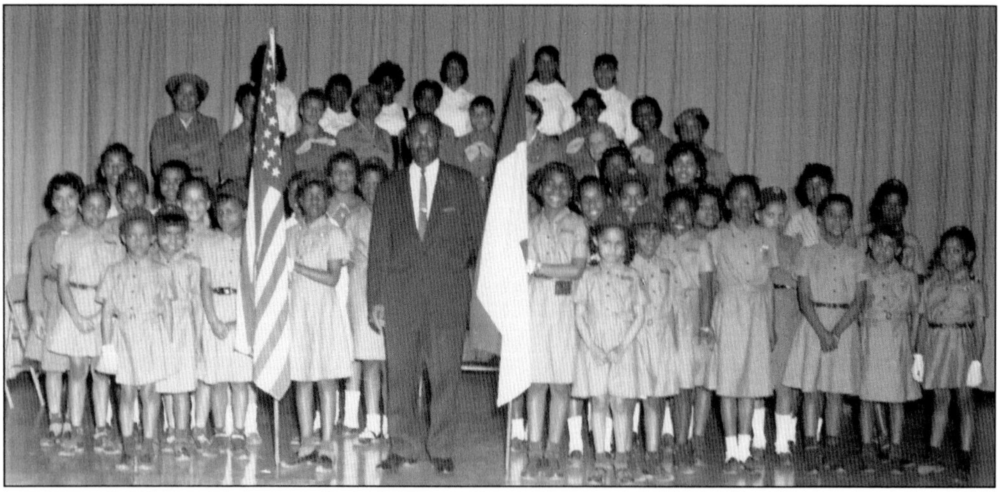

County schools were segregated until 1964, as were civic organizations. Girl Scout Troop 9 from Covington is pictured at Watson High School in March 1962. Notice that the group is still using a 48-star US flag three years after Alaska and Hawaii joined the Union. (AHS-VR.)

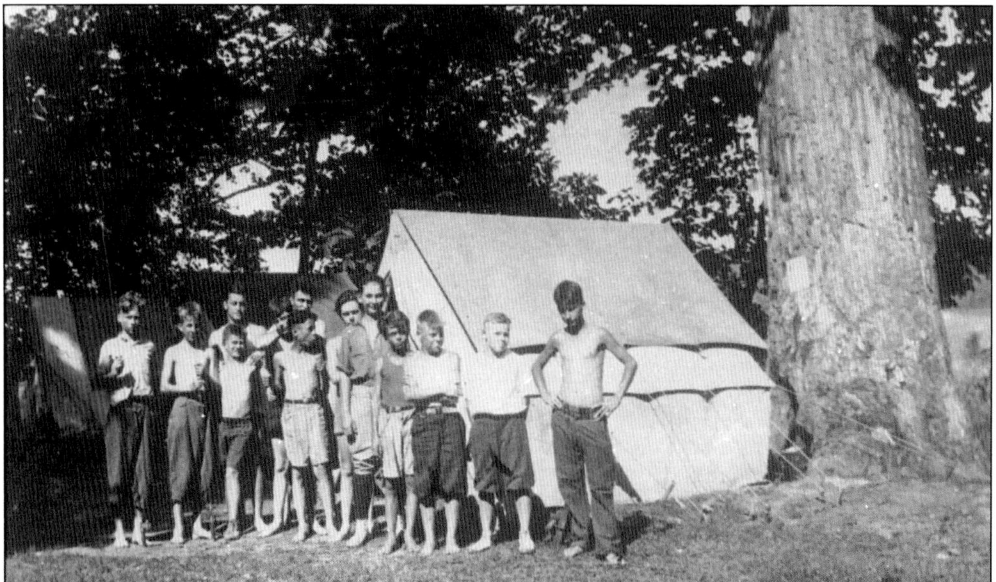

Boy Scout Troop 2 was organized in 1919 and is the oldest continually sponsored troop in the United States. Here is a picture of Scouts in their camp in 1925. This campsite was photographed well before Douthat State Park was built, and the site is thought to have been in Longdale. (AHS-VR.)

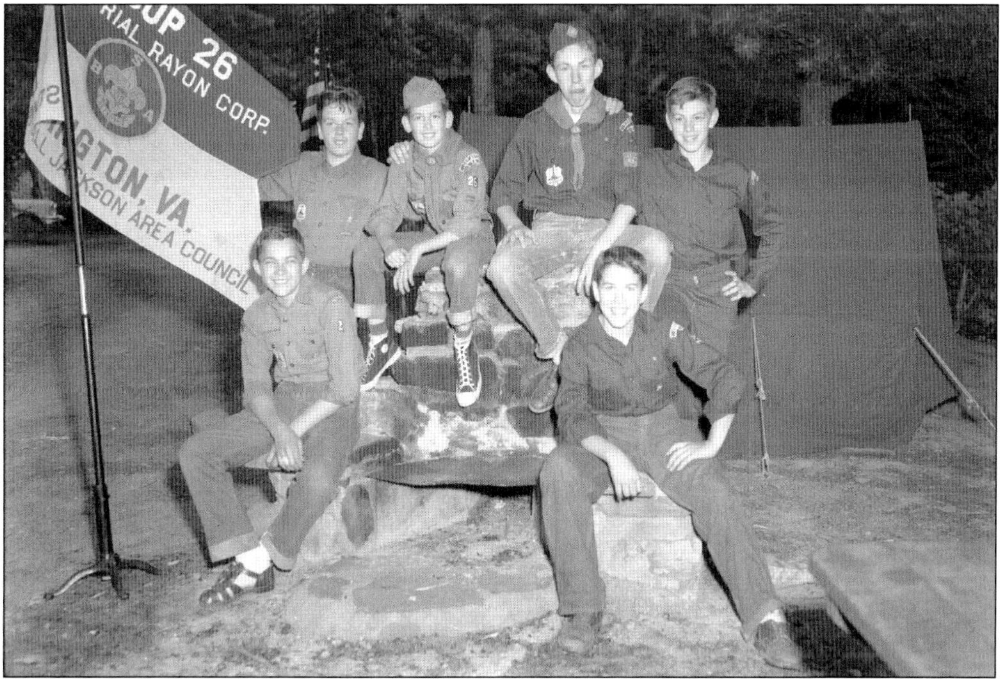

Many local businesses sponsored different teams and civic organizations. This May 18, 1958, picture shows Boy Scout Troop 26 of Covington, which was sponsored by the Industrial Rayon Corporation. From left to right are (first row) David "Sardie" Linkenhoker and unidentified; (second row) Jerry Carpenter, Rick Griffith, Sammie Persinger, and unidentified. (AHS-VR.)

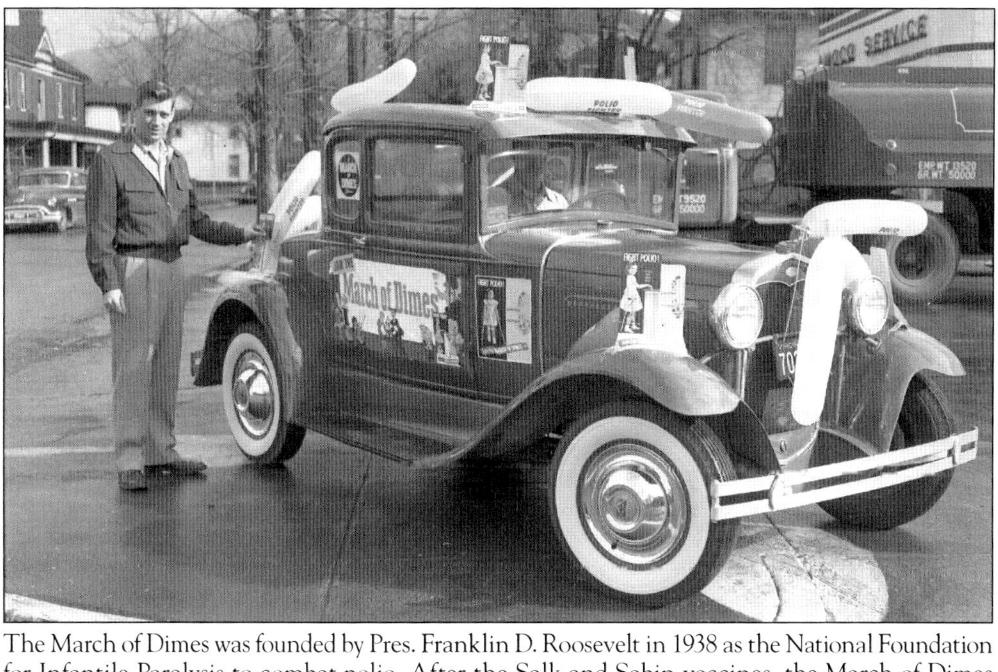

The March of Dimes was founded by Pres. Franklin D. Roosevelt in 1938 as the National Foundation for Infantile Paralysis to combat polio. After the Salk and Sabin vaccines, the March of Dimes changed its focus towards general heath for pregnant women and babies. This 1950s photograph shows an anti-polio March of Dimes fundraising car. (AHS-VR.)

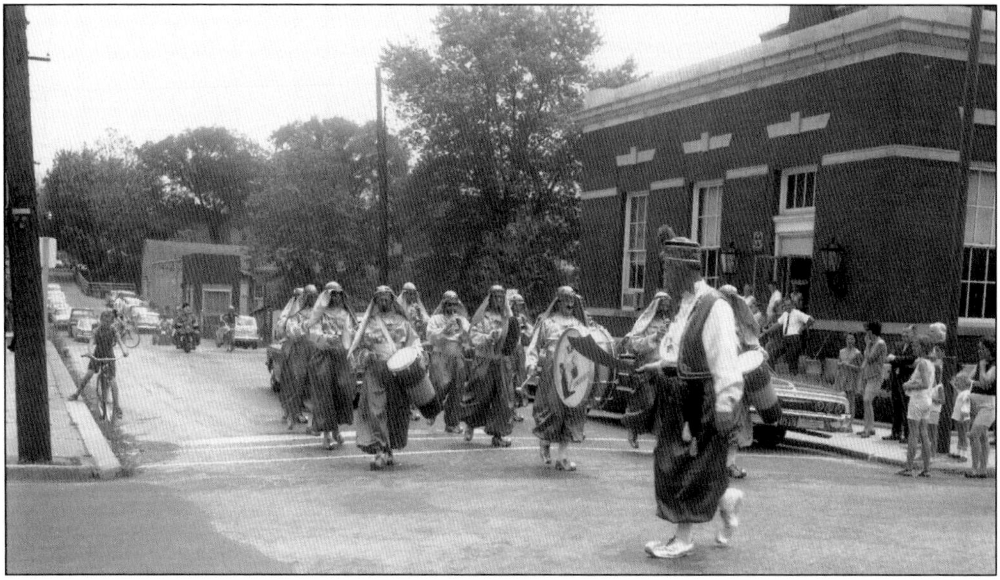

The Shriners have been an important organization in this community for many years supporting Shriners' children's hospitals. This June 1966 photograph shows a parade in Clifton Forge going down Church Street, with the Shriners in their ceremonial outfits walking in front of the post office. (AHS-VR.)

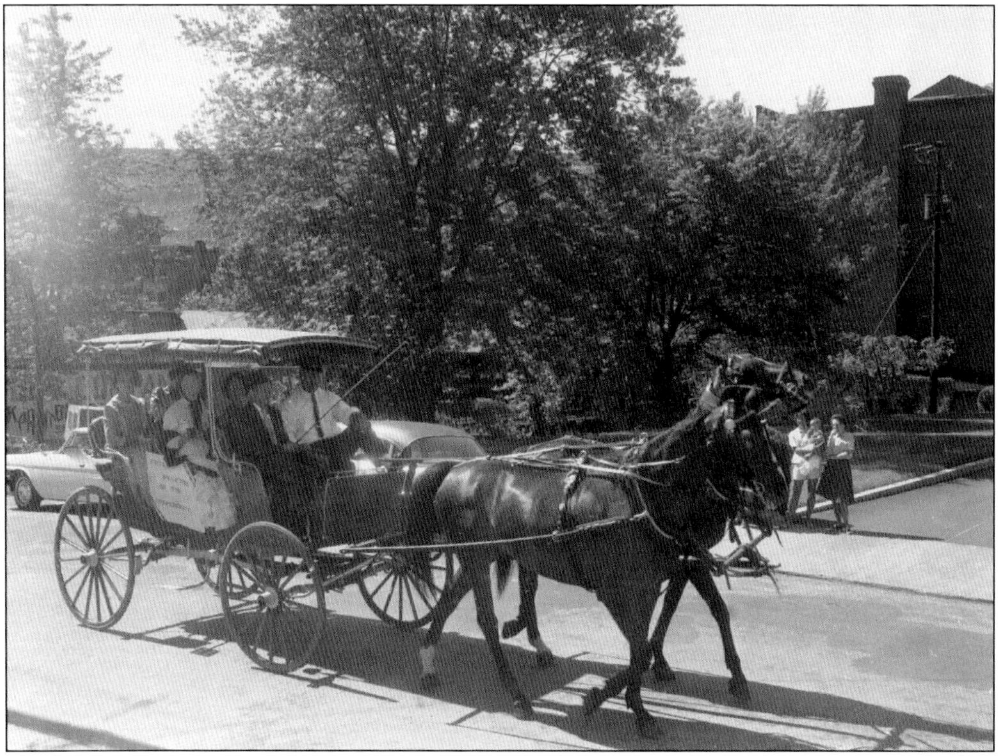

This photograph, taken during the same parade, shows the United Daughters of the Confederacy. This section of Church Street between Jefferson and Commercial Avenues provides a view of the post office parking lot and the back of the Masonic Theatre. (AHS-VR.)

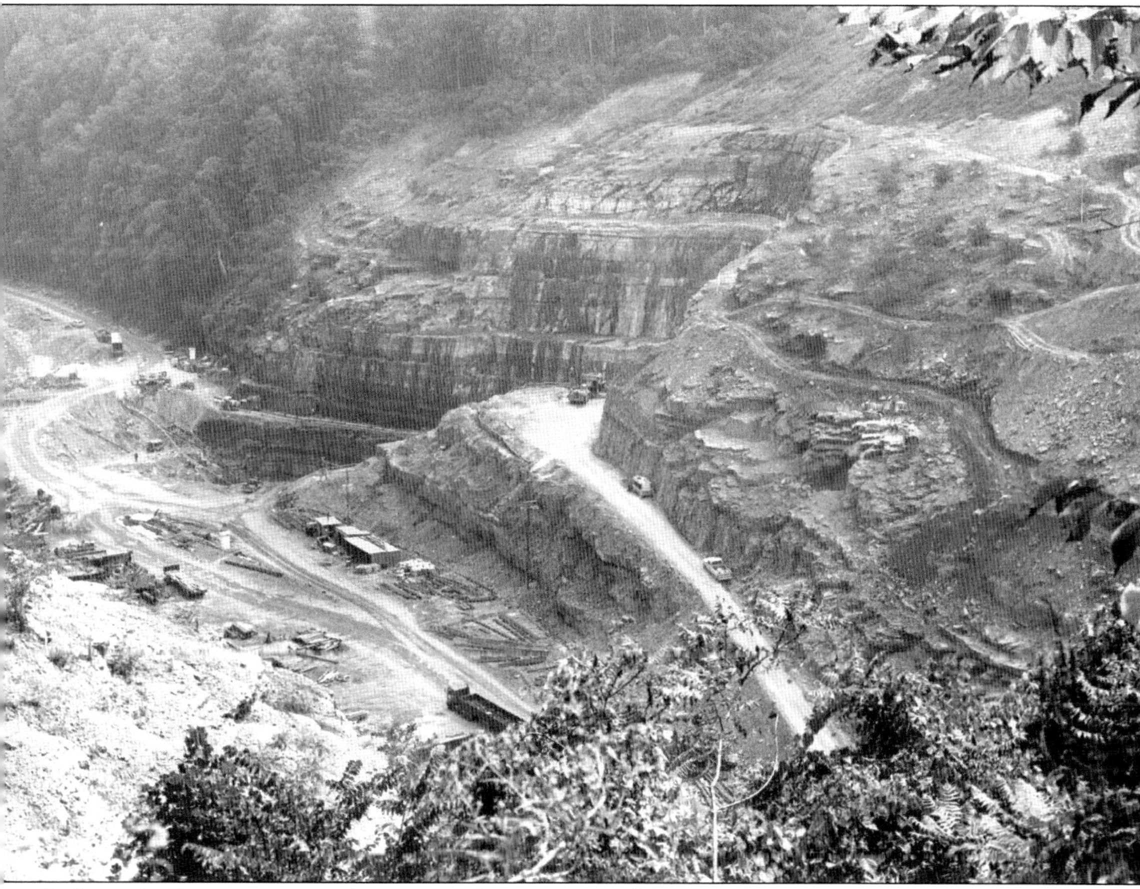

Perhaps the biggest project of recreational interest in Alleghany County in modern times was the building of the Gathright Dam to create Lake Moomaw. Work began on the project in the summer of 1968. This photograph shows work in 1974 creating the underground spillway to carry the lake water back to the bed of the Jackson River. (AHS-VR.)

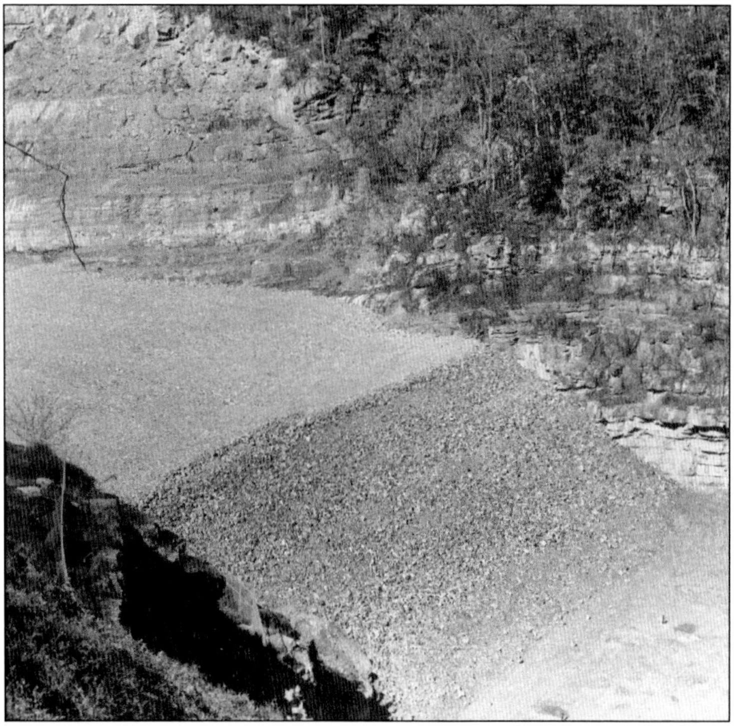

This photograph shows the construction of the earthen dam, which was built with crushed rock and a clay core. The dam was completed in 1979 and was built primarily for flood control and recreational activities. The lake was opened to the public in 1982 and provides bathing beaches, a number of picnic areas, and several boat landings. (AHS-VR.)

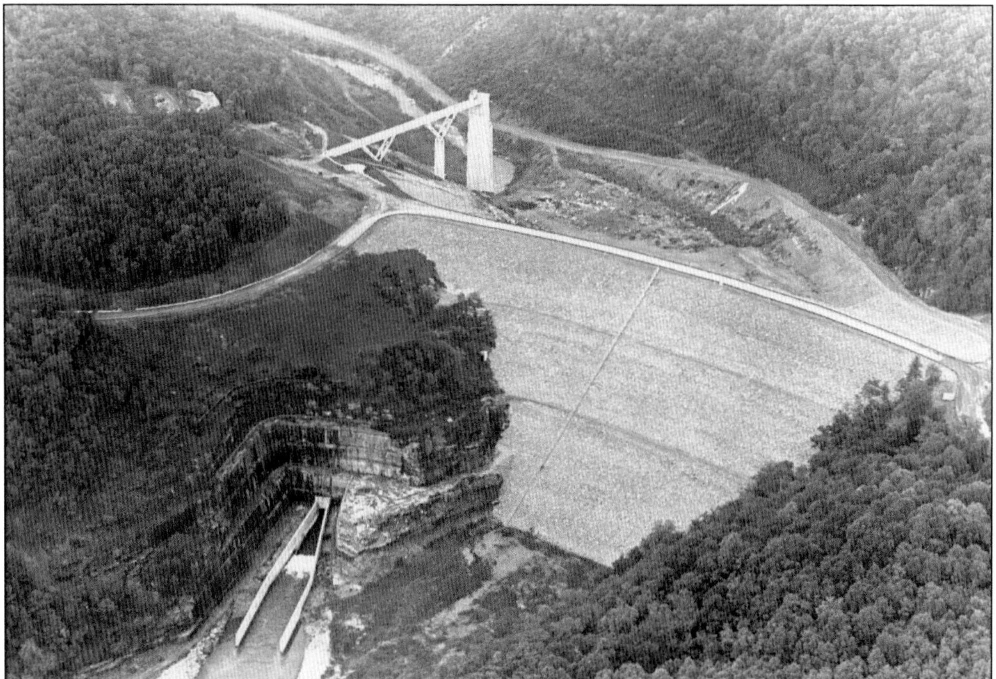

This 1979 photograph shows the completed dam. The large tower at the top provides the intake for the spillway. It is capable of releasing water from several levels of the lake. At the time this picture was taken, the tower was not yet in operation, as evidenced by the fact that the lake has not begun to fill. The river is flowing unchecked through the spillway. (AHS-VR.)

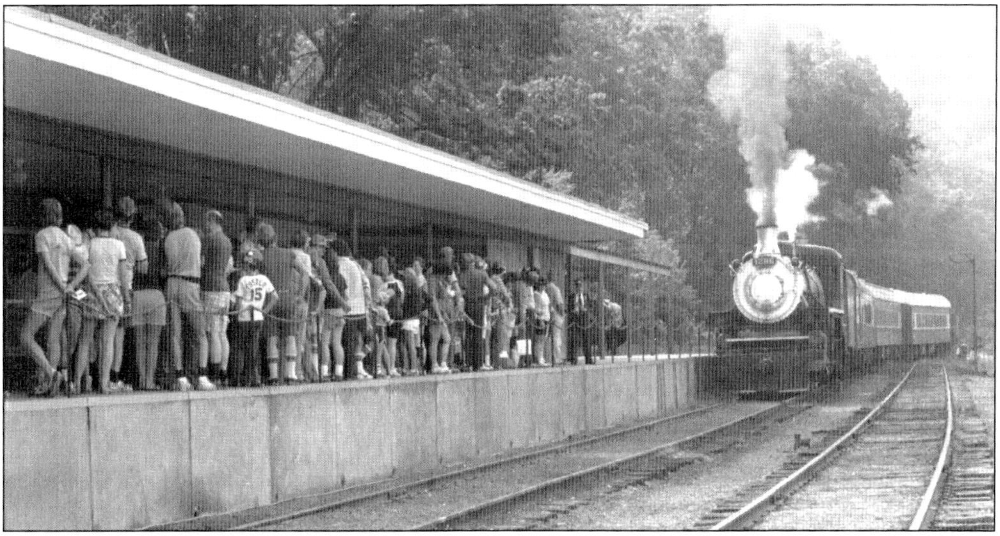

When the C&O Railway ended passenger service on the Hot Springs branch in early 1970, the rails remained in place. The branch was used by the scenic excursion Alleghany Central Railroad in the 1970s until its closing in 1983. This picture shows steam engine No. 1286 coming into the Intervale Station with passengers in line waiting for their ride. (AHS-VR.)

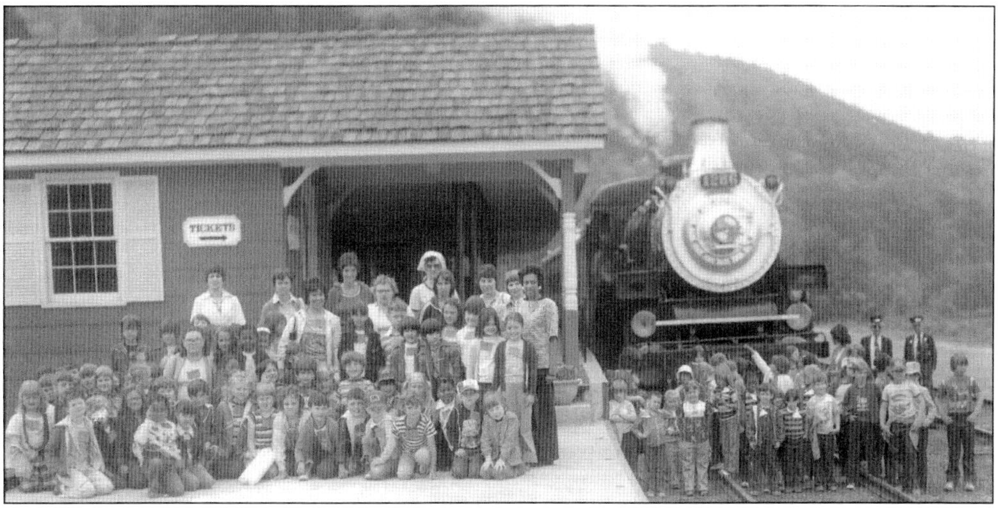

The Alleghany Central was run by Jack Showalter, who built a passenger station at Intervale. This picture shows a school group in front of the station and engine after the conclusion of their trip. The rails of the Hot Springs branch have since been removed, and the abandoned rail bed is now used as a walking and biking trail. The trail is owned and was developed by Alleghany County and is called the Jackson River Scenic Trail. (AHS-VR.)

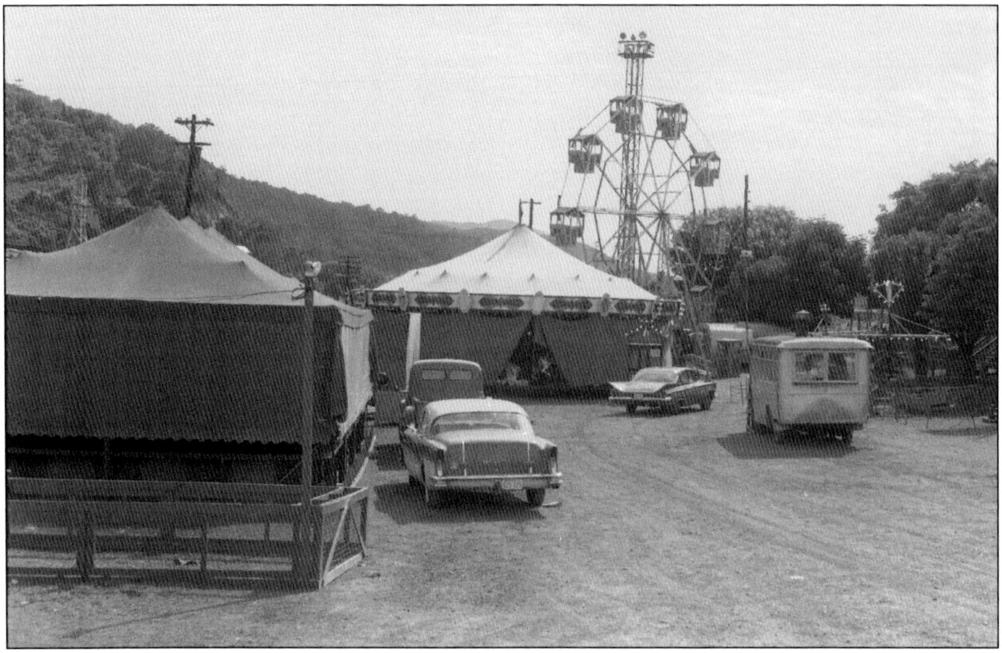

The county fairgrounds were located in Mallow where the Mallow Mall now stands. The first county fair was held in 1915. The fairgrounds were used for a variety of community recreational functions besides the county fair. This photograph shows a carnival that came to the fairgrounds in June 1959. (AHS-VR.)

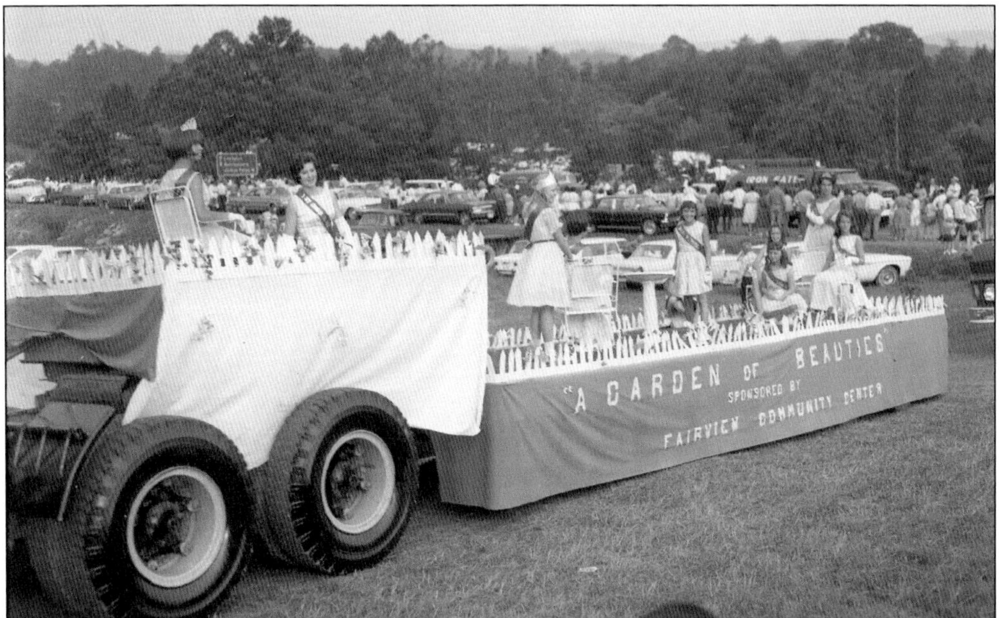

The fair provided a number of activities besides the carnival. A large exhibit tent provided opportunities for the display of local agriculture, homemade delicacies, and handmade quilts, needlework, and other crafts. This photograph shows a parade as part of the fair activities in the late 1960s including beauty pageant contestants and various fire engine companies. (AHS-VR.)

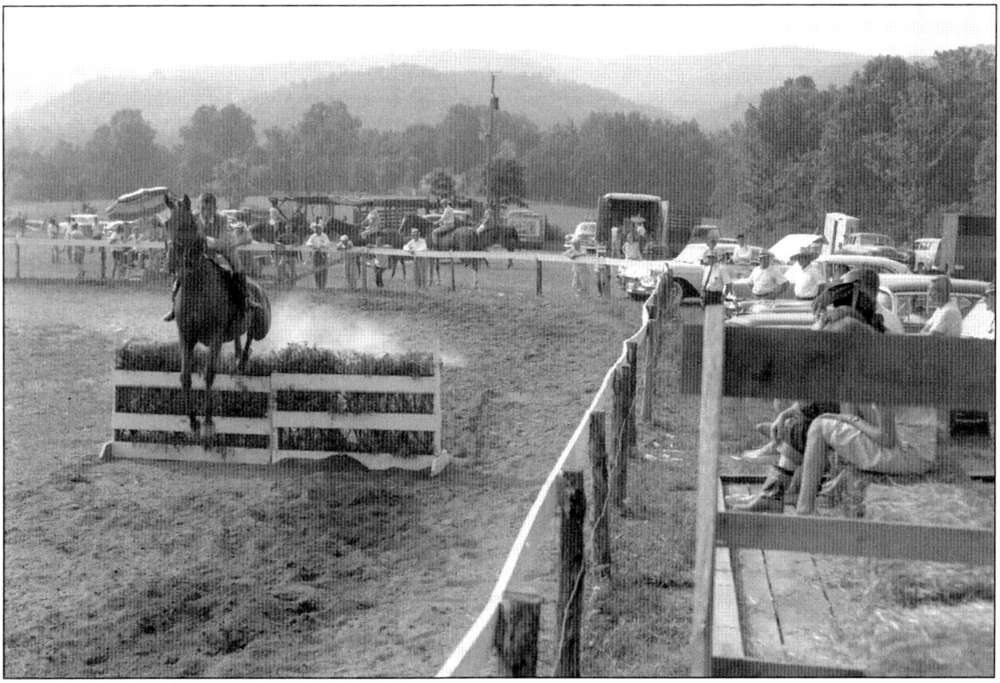

The fairgrounds also featured stables and a race track. Competitions included both race horses and show horses, as seen in this 1950s jumping event. Other events included trick riders and roping contests. (AHS-VR.)

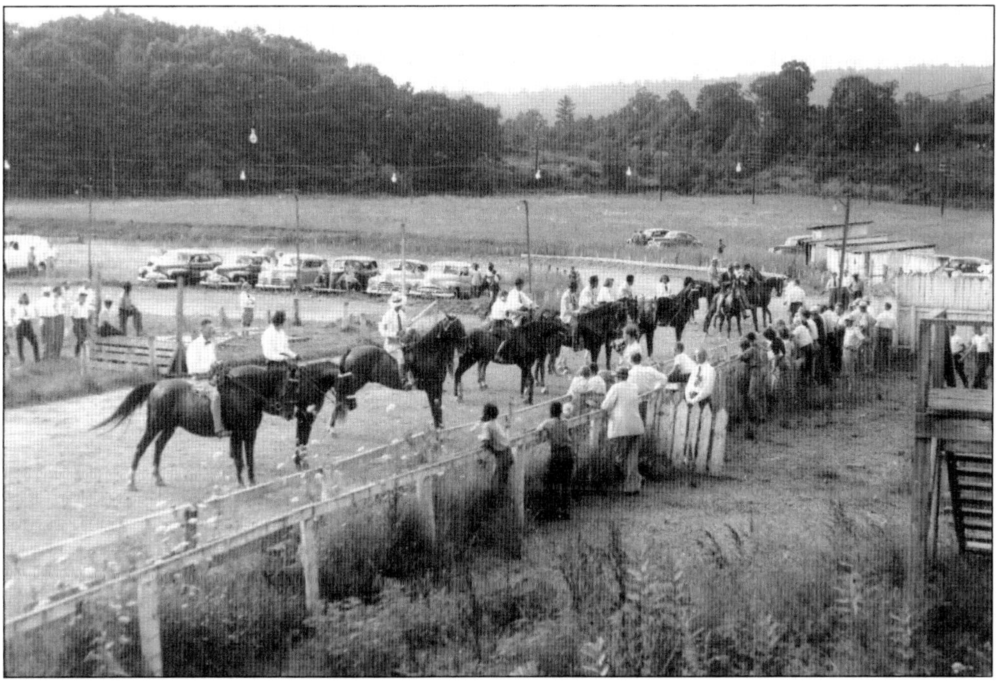

This is a horse judging competition on July 21, 1948. Notice the interesting early arrangement for outside lighting at the fairgrounds, featuring open lightbulbs strung 15 feet above the ground. (AHS-VR.)

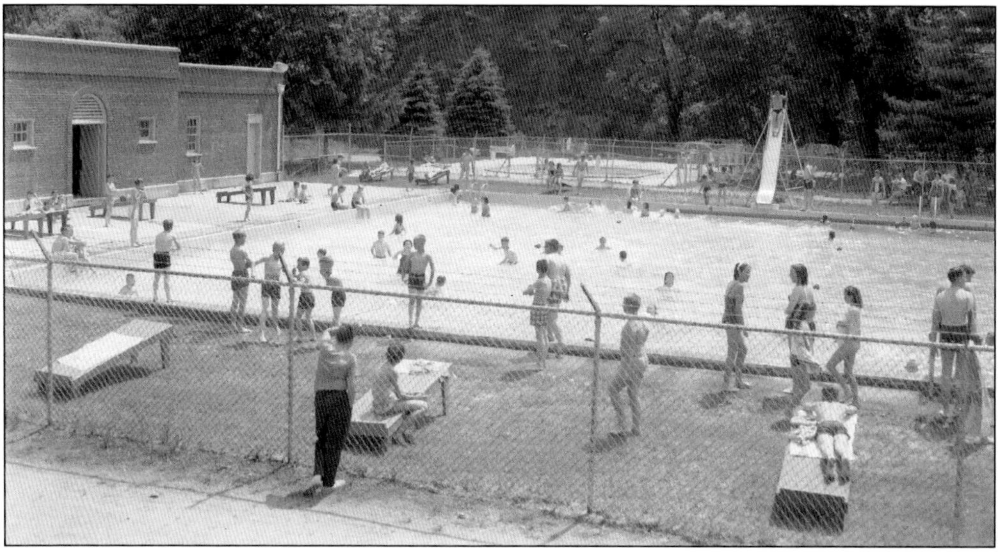

A favorite recreation spot in Covington was the City Playground, which featured a pool, bathhouse, playground, and ballfield. This June 1961 photograph of the old Covington pool is evidence of its popularity. The large section was for swimmers, and the wading pool in the background was for smaller children. The children's wading pool had fish painted on the bottom. There is now a new pool at this location. (AHS-VR.)

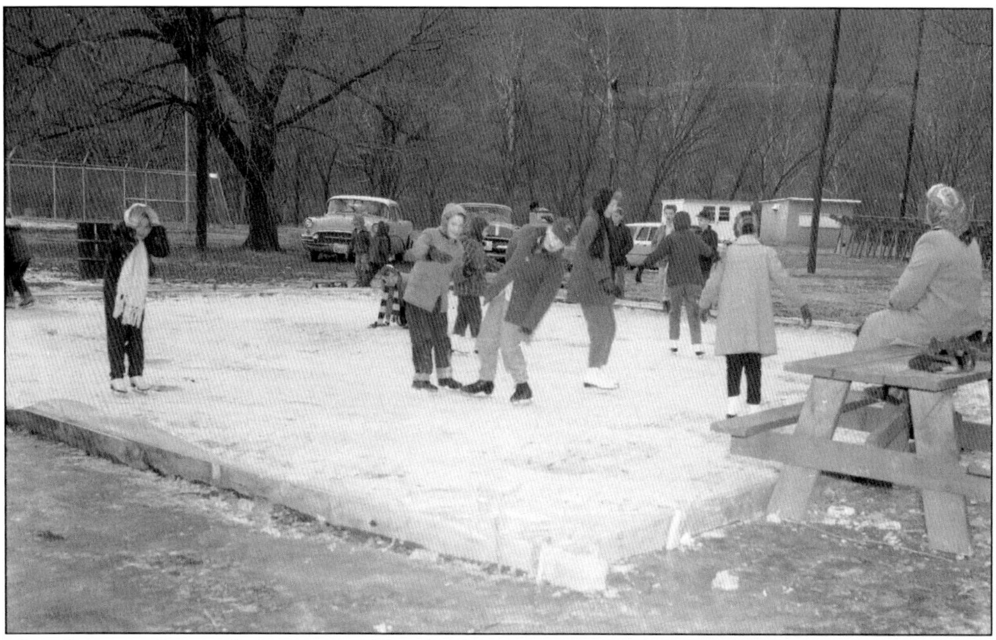

The playground provided year-round fun for the community. This photograph from January 1960 shows skaters on a makeshift ice rink. The pool and baseball field can be seen in the background. (AHS-VR.)

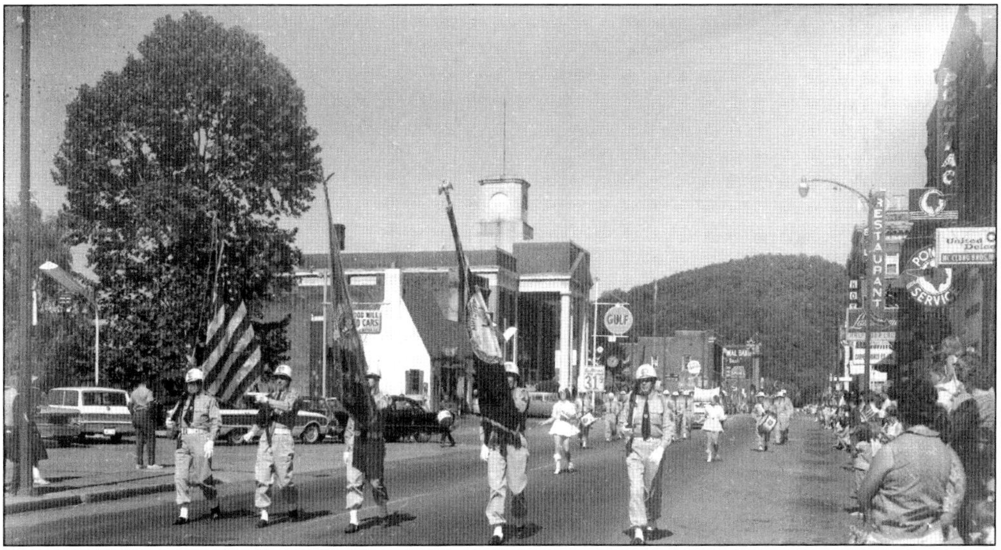

Everyone loves a parade, and Alleghany County was the site of many. This is an Independence Day parade proceeding down Main Street in Clifton Forge on July 4, 1963. The Drum and Bugle Corps of the Veterans of Foreign Wars Post 1033 leads the parade, followed by the C&O School of Nursing. The gasoline price at the Gulf station in the background was 31.9¢ per gallon. (AHS-VR.)

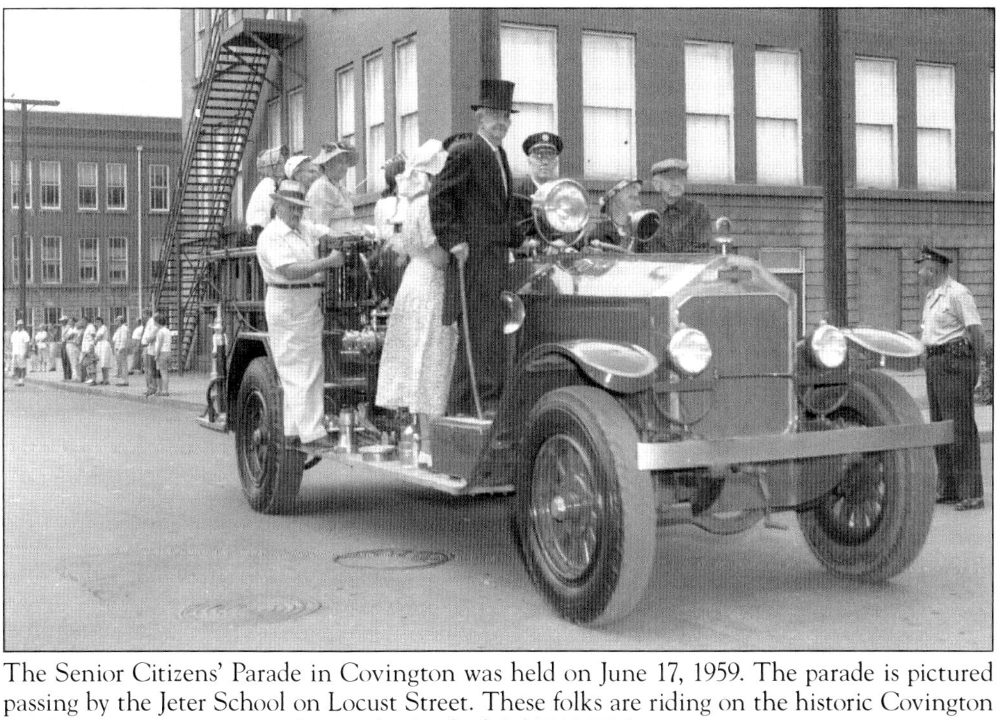

The Senior Citizens' Parade in Covington was held on June 17, 1959. The parade is pictured passing by the Jeter School on Locust Street. These folks are riding on the historic Covington Fire Department engine, nicknamed "Hezekiah." (AHS-VR.)

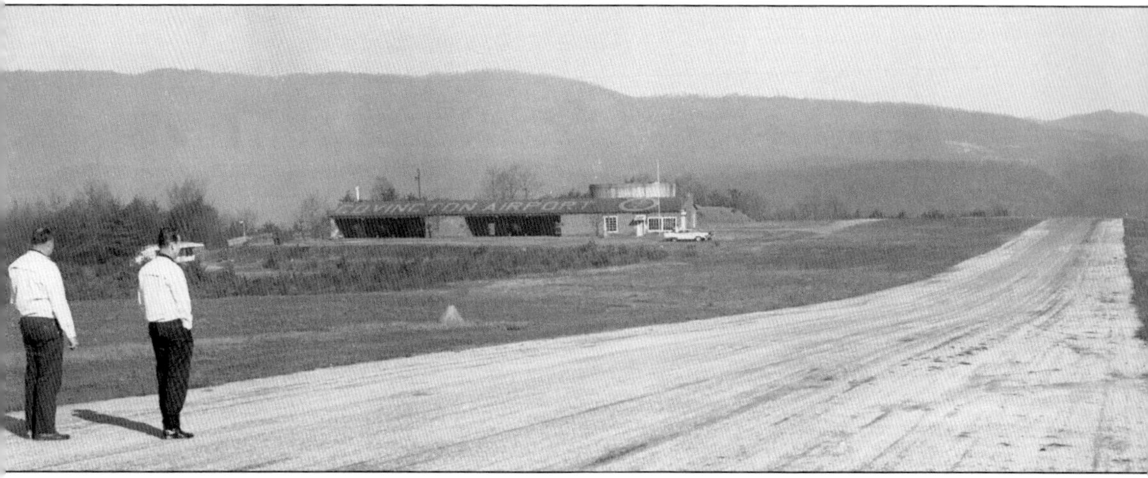

Covington Airport was built at the top of McAllister Hill in the early 1950s and was used by several of the prominent businesspeople in the area for charter flights and recreation. The airport was also used as a drag racing strip. Pictured here are two members of the Hidden Valley Dragsters looking over the runway. (AHS-VR.)

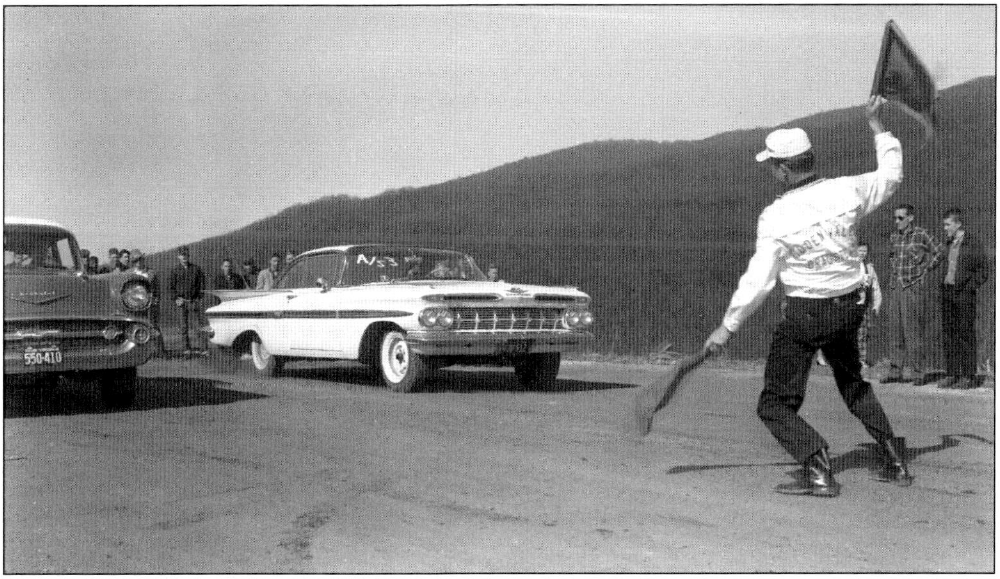

The Hidden Valley Dragsters used the airport as their drag strip until they could build their own track. This photograph shows Ernest Wickline of the Dragsters waving the flag to start one of the races between a pair of Chevrolets. (AHS-VR.)

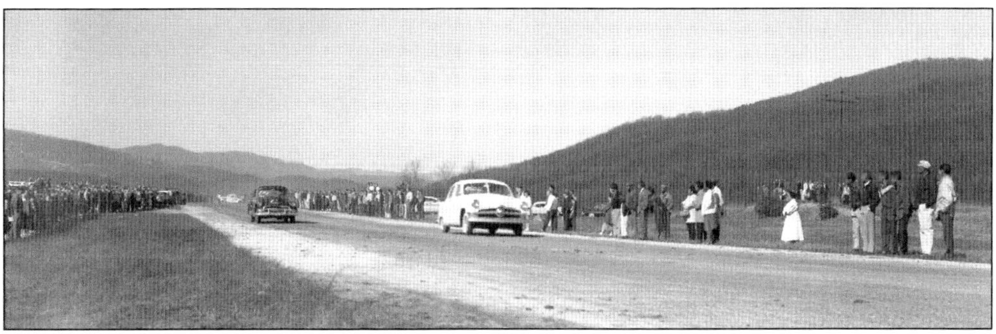

Here, a race is in progress with the audience lining the track. These photographs are from drag races in February 1959. Airport usage started to decline in the 1960s, and the Hidden Valley Dragsters started using their own track when the airport was shut down. High Acres Mobile Home Village now uses the runway for its main road. (AHS-VR.)

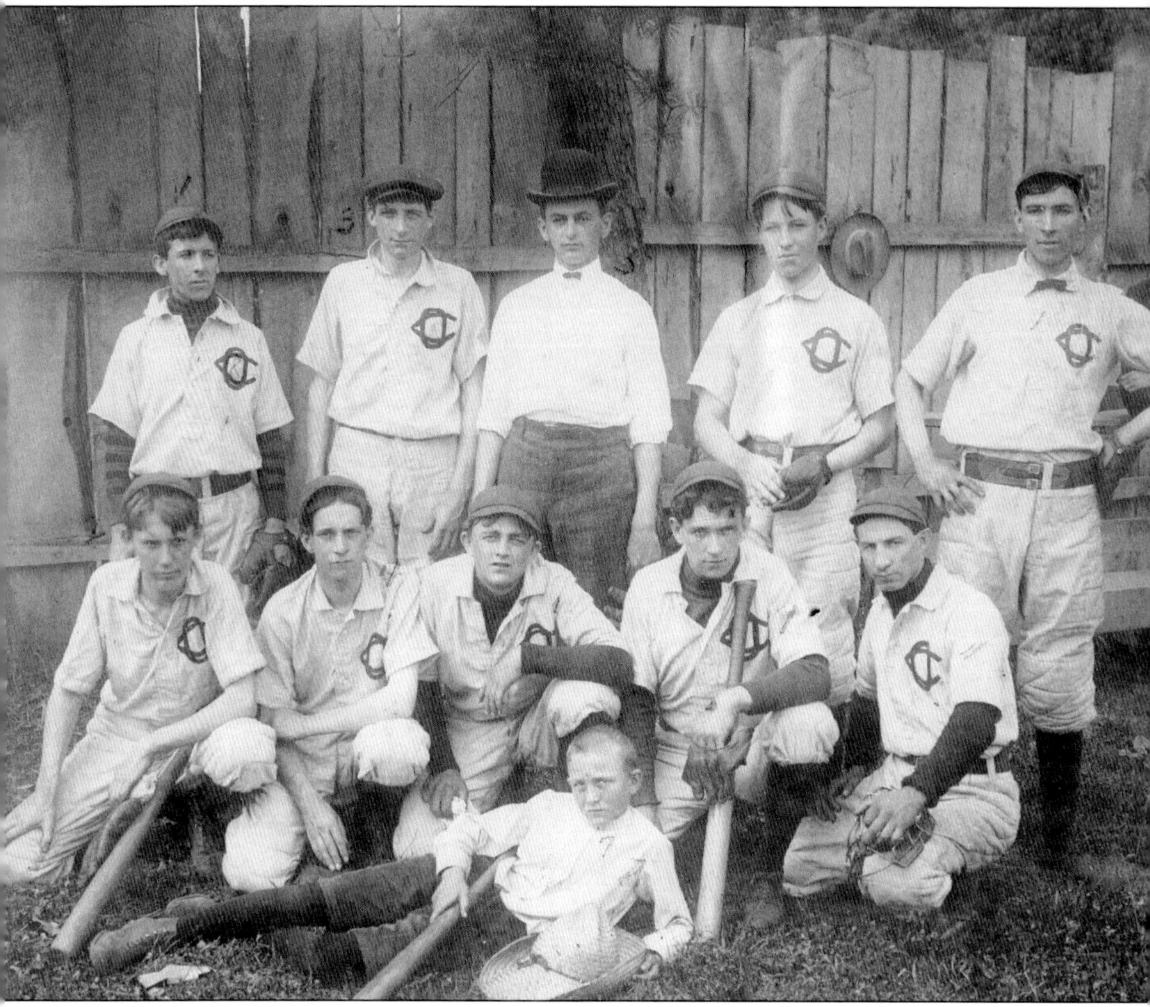

A variety of sports teams, both professional and amateur, have been sponsored by local communities and businesses. This is the semiprofessional C&O Railway baseball team from 1905. From left to right are (first row) Halton, mascot; (second row) Hope, third base; Simpson, manager; Halton, shortstop; Brown, right field; and D. ?, catcher; (third row) Mills, center field; Ham, first base; Shiplett; Haislett, pitcher; and Deacon, left field. They had nine victories and one defeat. (AHS-VR.)

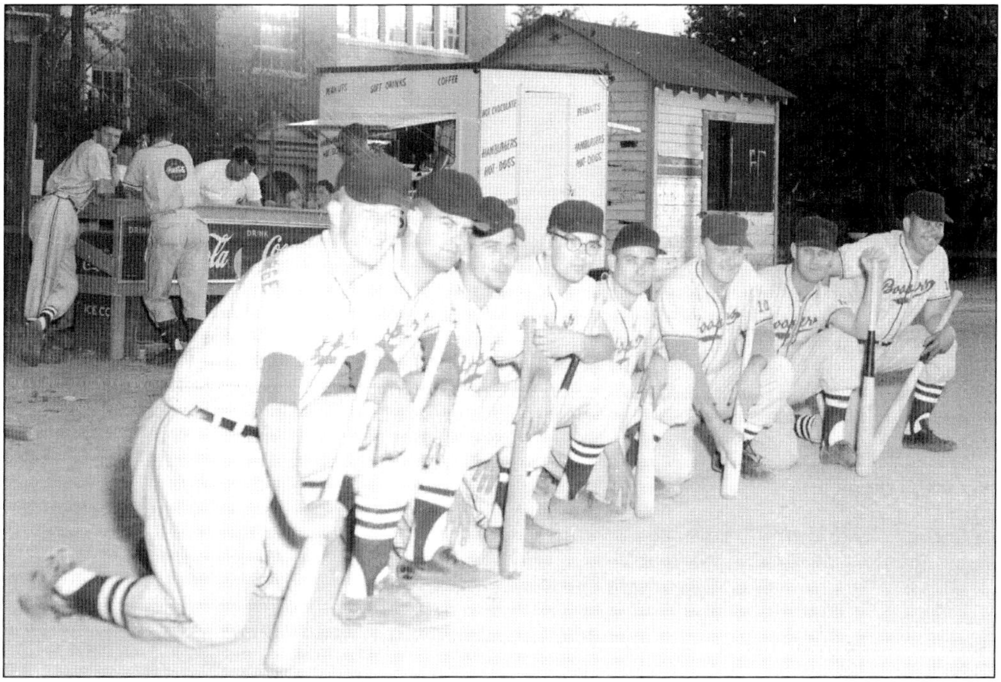

The original Clifton Forge Boosters were a semiprofessional team in the Valley League starting in 1921, but they disbanded in the 1930s. The team was reborn in the late 1940s as part of the Virginia Mountain League and remained in the league until it ceased play in 1960. This late 1950s photograph shows the team at Memorial Park in Clifton Forge. (AHS-VR.)

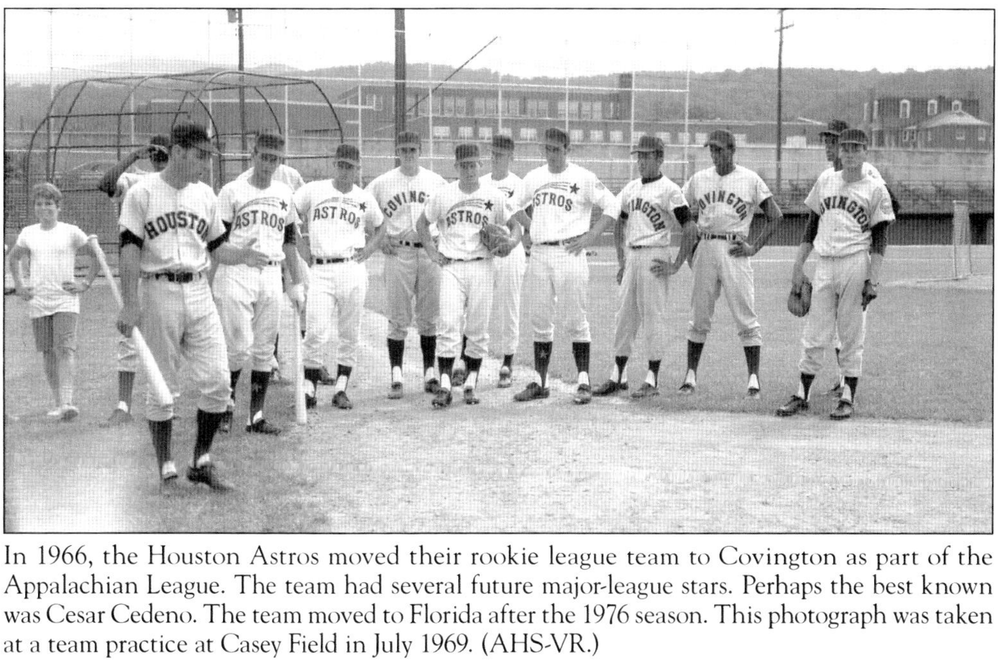

In 1966, the Houston Astros moved their rookie league team to Covington as part of the Appalachian League. The team had several future major-league stars. Perhaps the best known was Cesar Cedeno. The team moved to Florida after the 1976 season. This photograph was taken at a team practice at Casey Field in July 1969. (AHS-VR.)

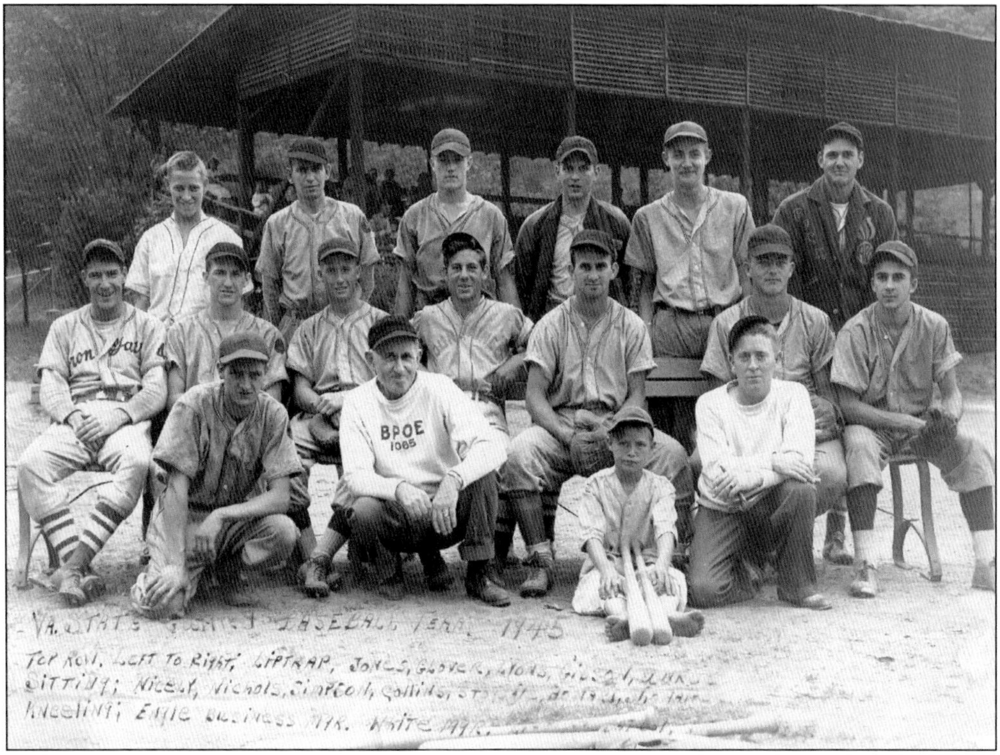

Some of the amateur teams in the area brought players from rival teams together. This is the 1945 Virginia State Guard baseball team in Clifton Forge. They are, from left to right, (first row) Engle (business manager), White (manager), Liptrap (batboy), and Rumball (assistant manager); (second row) Nicely, Nichols, Simpson, Collins, Stogdale, Howard, and Jack Showalter; (third row) Liptrap, Jones, Glover, Lyons, Gibson, and Unroe. Notice the Iron Gate and Clifton Forge uniforms. (AHS-VR.)

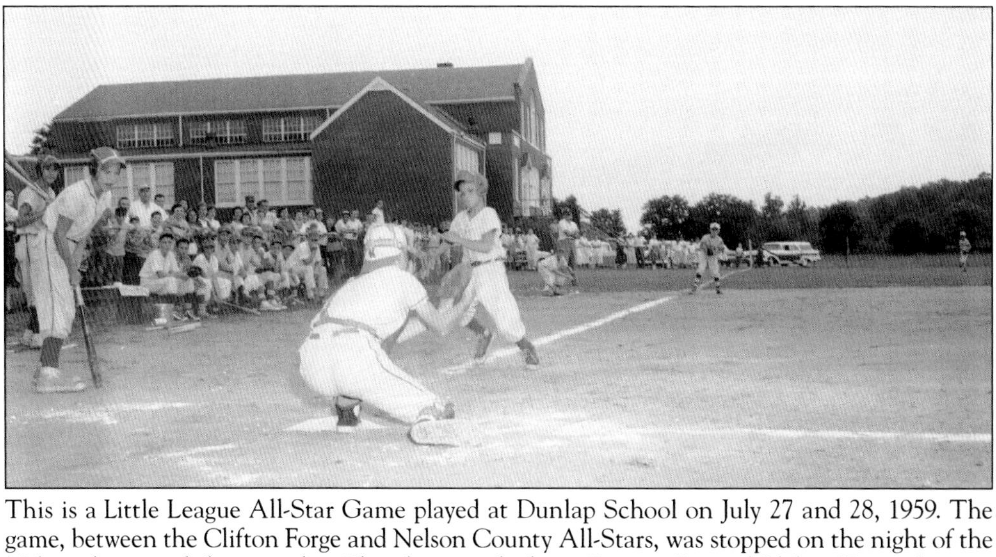

This is a Little League All-Star Game played at Dunlap School on July 27 and 28, 1959. The game, between the Clifton Forge and Nelson County All-Stars, was stopped on the night of the 27th and resumed the next day. The photograph shows Ronnie Fore of Clifton Forge about to slide safe at home. (AHS-VR.)

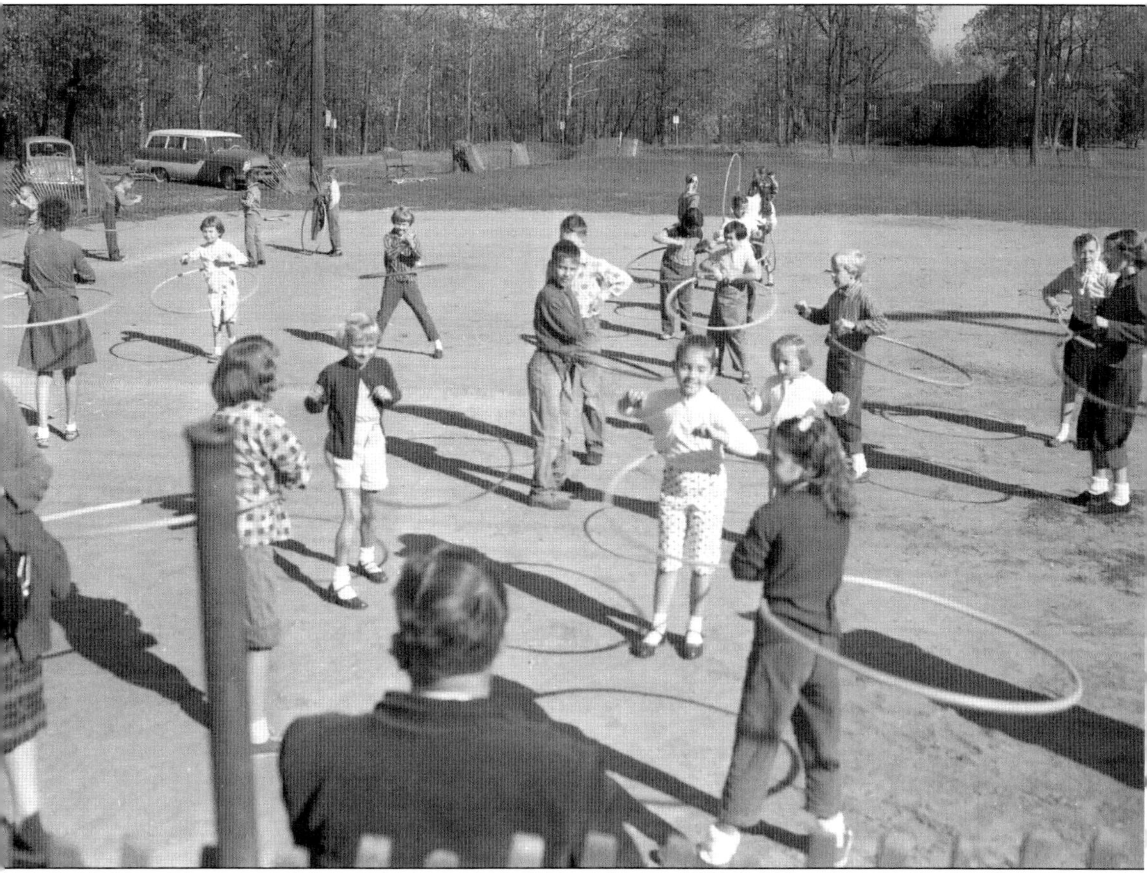

The modern plastic Hula Hoop was invented early in 1958 and was wildly popular at the time. Here is a Hula Hoop contest on the baseball field at the Covington City Playground on October 30, 1958, involving contestants from all over the county. (AHS-VR.)

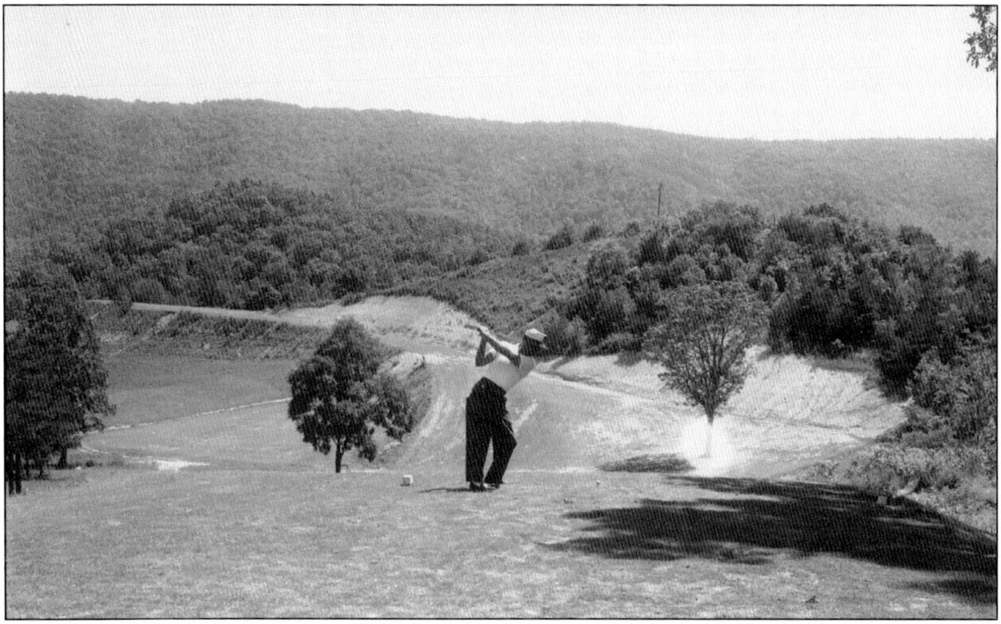

This undated photograph shows a golfer teeing off at the course of the Alleghany Country Club in Valley Ridge. It was a nine-hole course located adjacent to Alleghany High School and the Jackson River Technical Center. The course is no longer in use. (AHS-VR.)

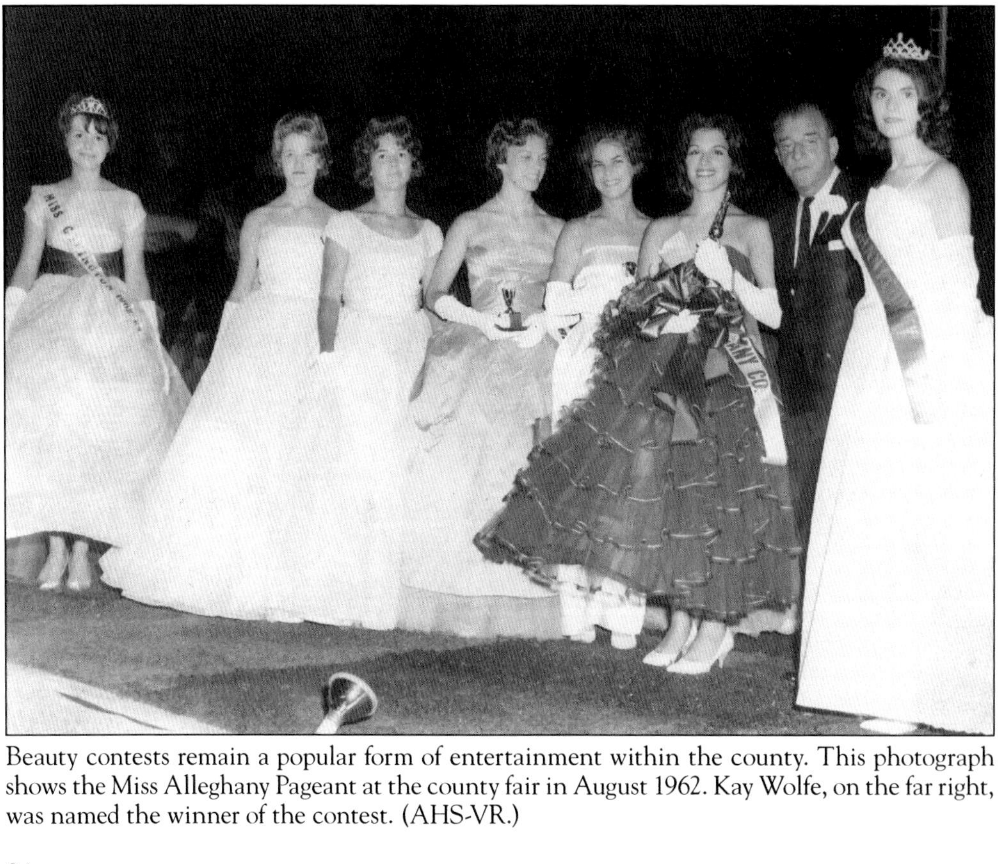

Beauty contests remain a popular form of entertainment within the county. This photograph shows the Miss Alleghany Pageant at the county fair in August 1962. Kay Wolfe, on the far right, was named the winner of the contest. (AHS-VR.)

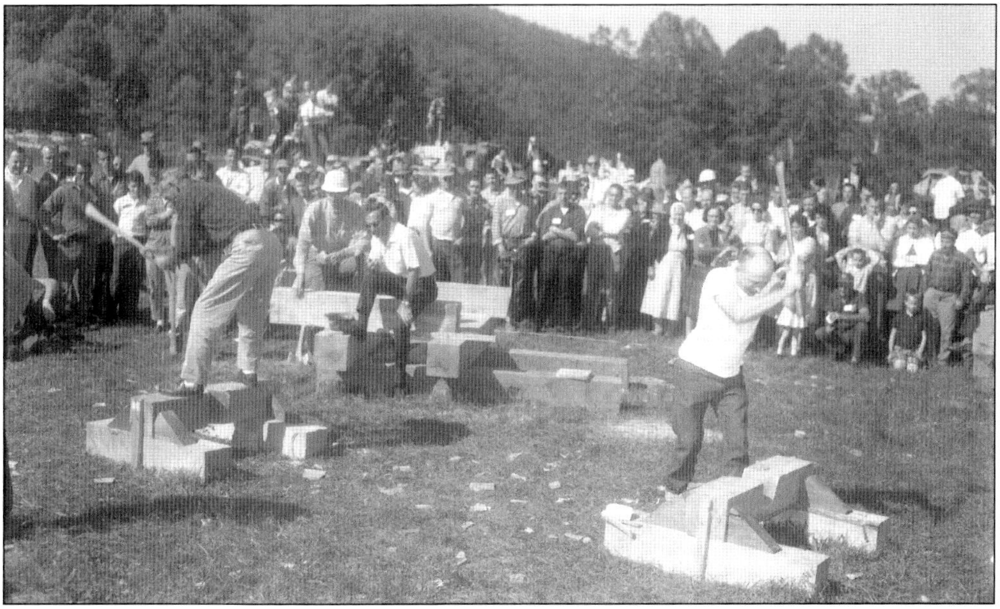

Labor Day is typically the largest celebration of the year in Covington. The events after the annual Labor Day Parade have varied through the years, featuring a number of different events, entertainment, and contests. This wood-chopping contest occurred during the 1963 celebration. The special events were sponsored annually by the labor unions in the area. Today, Covington Papermakers Union 675 sponsors the event. (AHS-VR.)

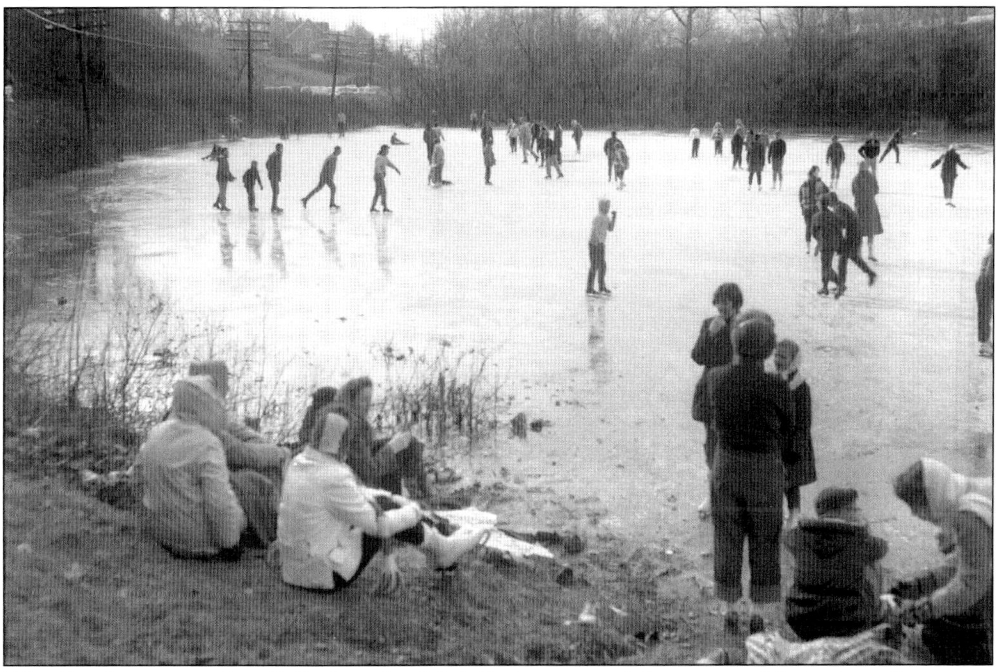

Pikes Pond was created in 1868 when the C&O Railway moved the course of the Jackson River near Low Moor. It has been a popular community attraction over the years. Here, intrepid ice skaters enjoy the thicker ice available during a cold day in January 1960. This activity is no longer permitted on the pond, as it poses a hazard due to the unknown thickness of the ice. (AHS-VR.)

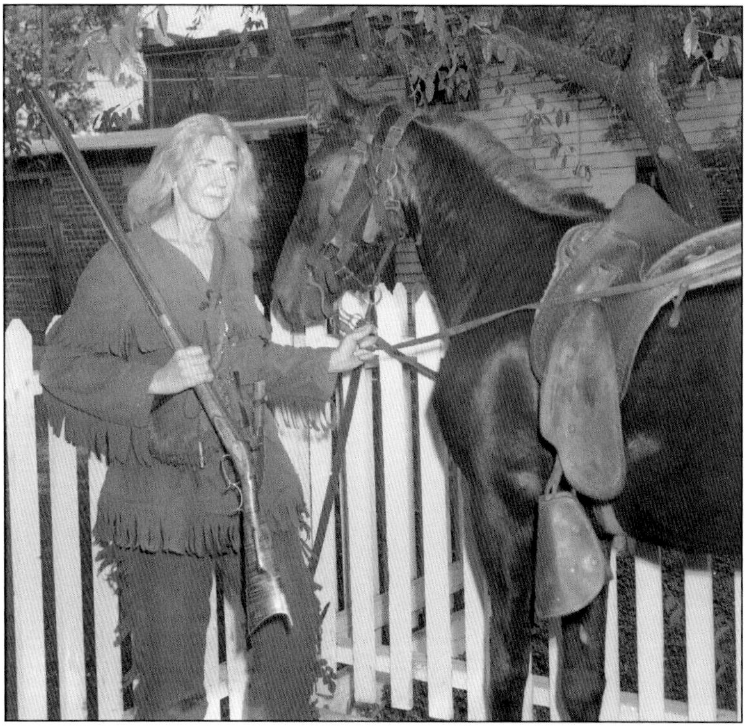

"Mad Ann" Bailey was a frontier woman well known for her exploits as an Indian fighter, message carrier, and army recruiter. Her husband was killed at the Battle of Point Pleasant, and she continued to live on her own until she remarried. She lived on Mad Ann Ridge in present day Alleghany County. Here, Mrs. Clarence "Cookie" Cook portrays Bailey in 1958. (AHS-VR.)

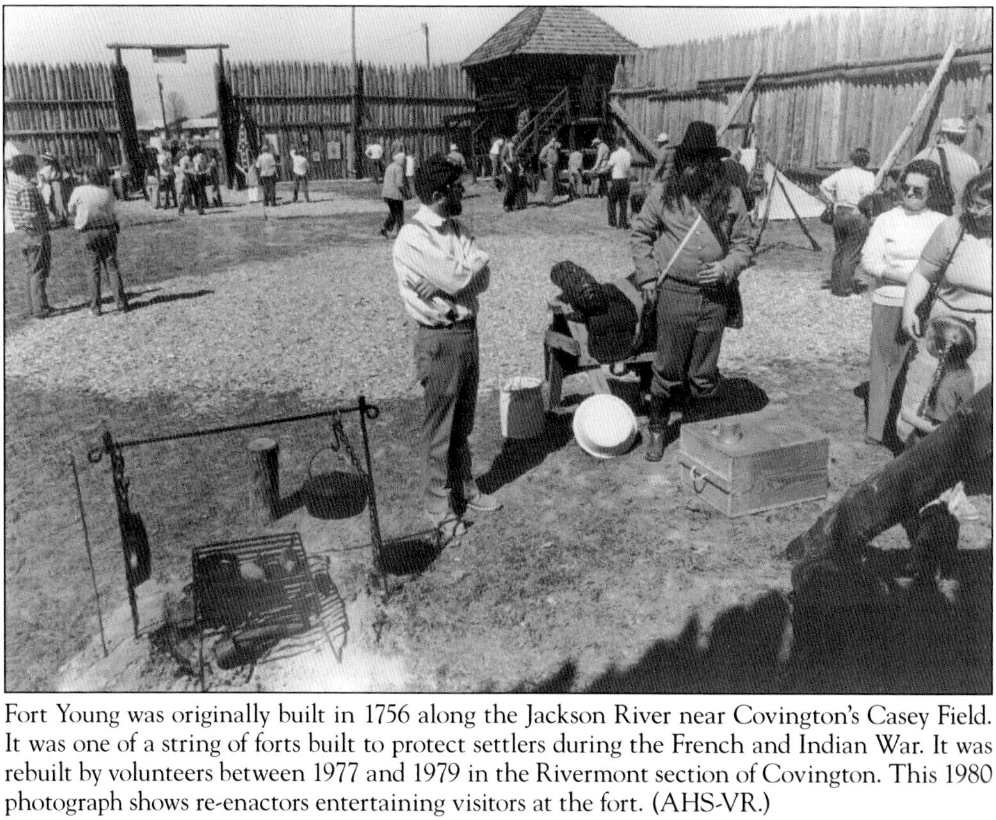

Fort Young was originally built in 1756 along the Jackson River near Covington's Casey Field. It was one of a string of forts built to protect settlers during the French and Indian War. It was rebuilt by volunteers between 1977 and 1979 in the Rivermont section of Covington. This 1980 photograph shows re-enactors entertaining visitors at the fort. (AHS-VR.)

Five

Fire and Rescue

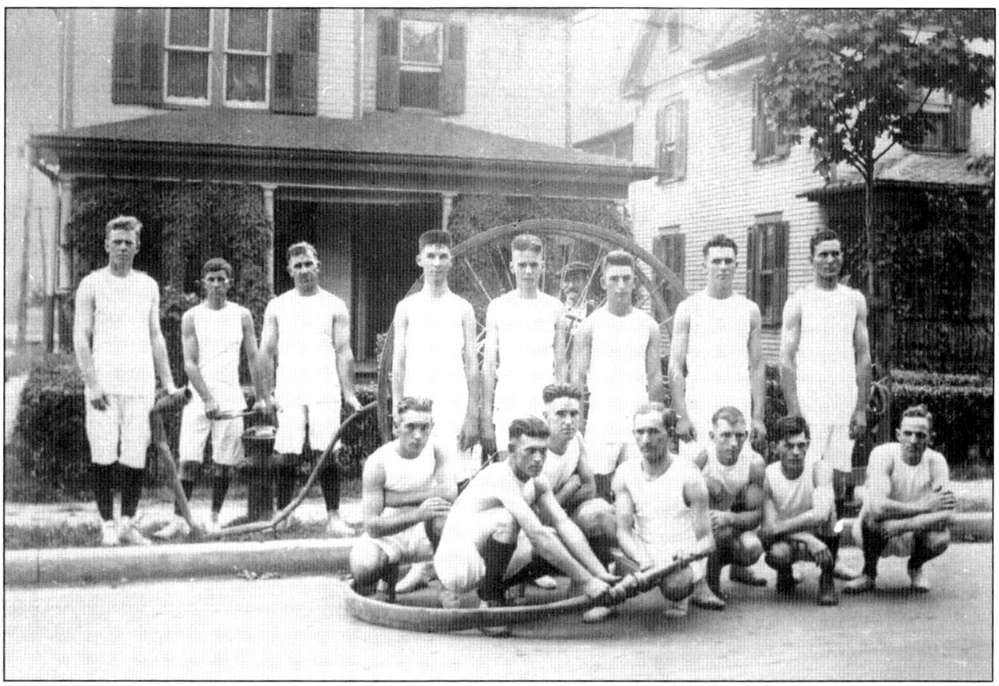

This 1906 photograph shows the Covington Fire Department race team with its new hose reel. The Virginia Fireman's Association holds an annual convention that includes a competition among the different departments for the speed at which they arrive on scene, hook up the hose, and start putting out the fire. (AHS-VR.)

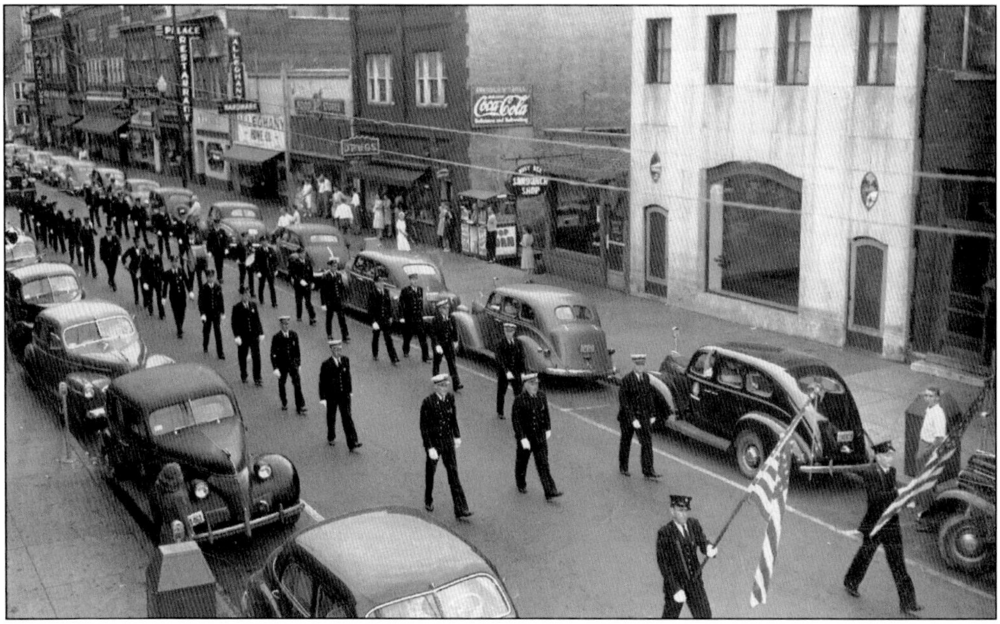

The Covington Fire Department is parading down West Main Street in Covington in preparation for the Firemen's Convention in 1948. The department's vintage pumper truck "Hezekiah" is visible in the background. Built in 1927 by American LaFrance, it was a workhorse for the fire department until its retirement in the 1960s. It has been restored and is still used in parades. (AHS-VR.)

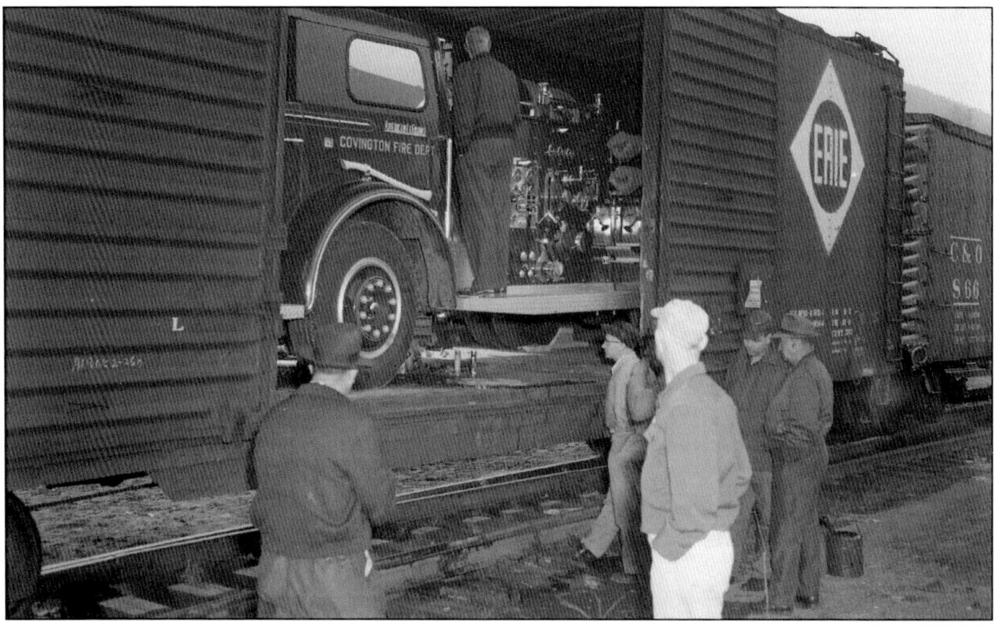

This unusual photograph, taken on March 3, 1959, shows the new Covington Fire Department hook and ladder fire engine being delivered by boxcar. It was made by American LaFrance and was used for many years for firefighting and demonstrations at Jeter School and public locations. The city used this fire engine to hang Christmas decorations, as bucket trucks were not yet in use. (AHS-VR.)

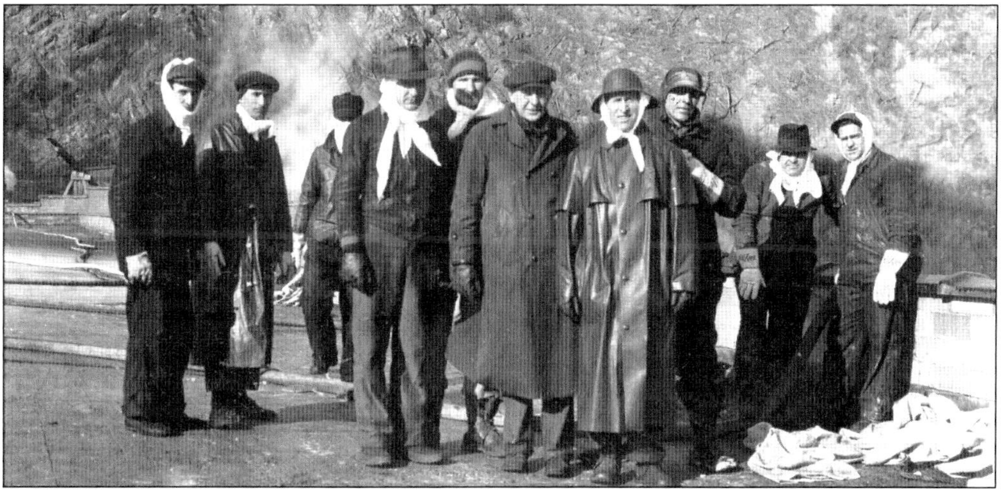

In early 1941, there was a fire in the Westvaco yard's paper roll storage. This photograph shows firemen in cold-weather gear on the roof at Westvaco after the fire had been contained. The size of the fire required the response of several fire companies. It is unknown which company these men represented. (AHS-VR.)

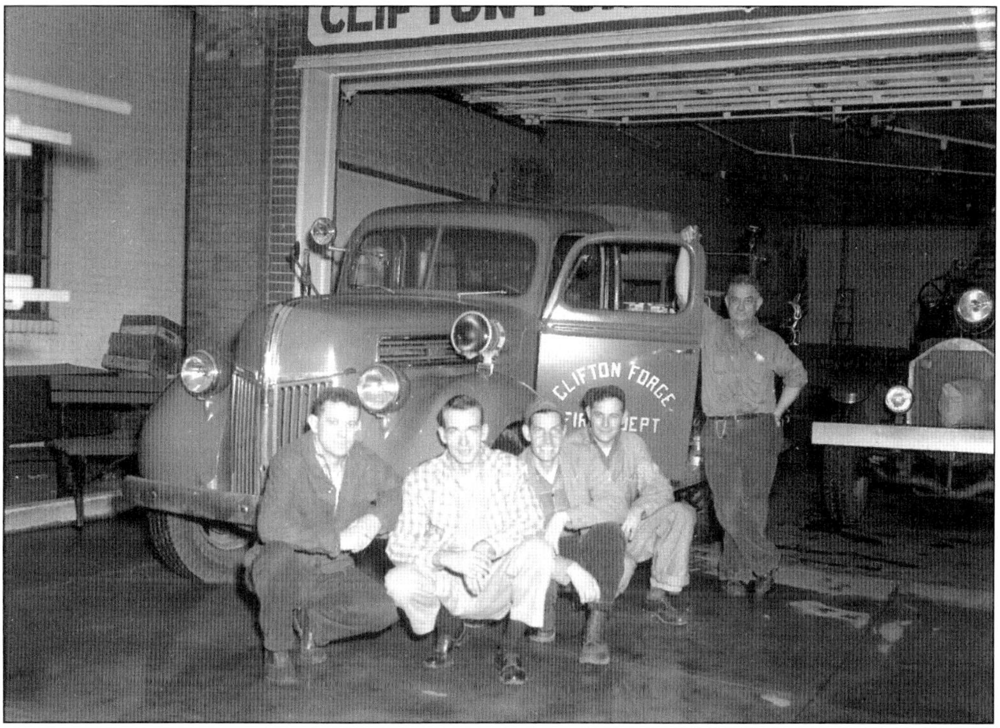

The Clifton Forge Fire Department stood beside the courthouse until December 1970, when a Pepsi truck ran into the building as it was coming down the Jefferson Street hill and lost its brakes. The building still stands and is currently being used as a laundromat, with a business incubator in the rear. This photograph was taken in February 1960. Clifton Forge had its own vintage fire truck, seen on the right. (AHS-VR.)

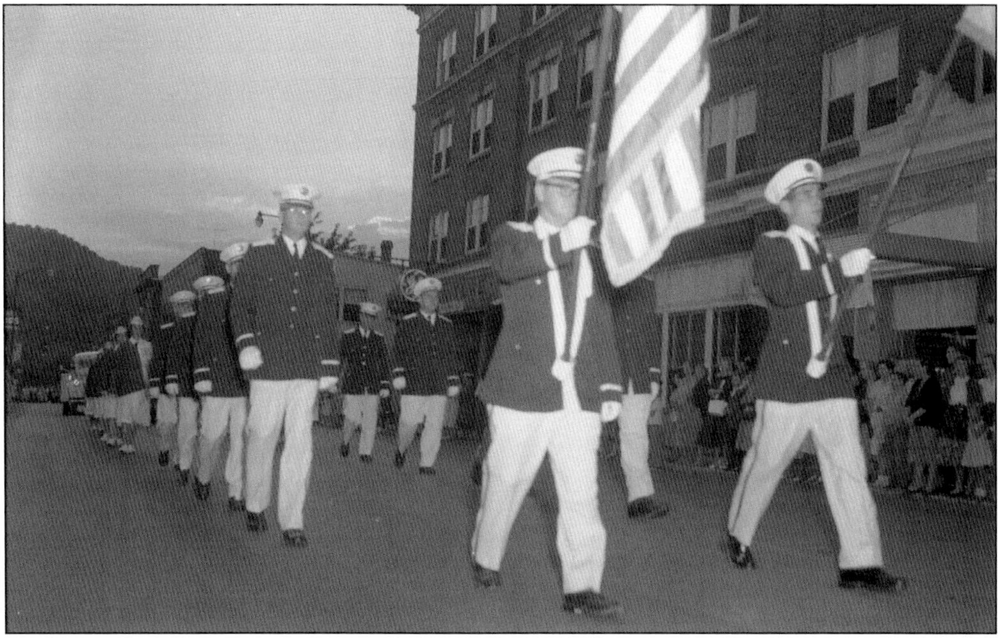

Clifton Forge hosted the Northern Virginia Fireman's Association Conference in June 1959. Fifty fire departments from all over Virginia and parts of West Virginia came to the conference to compete against their fellow firefighters. This photograph shows the Clifton Forge Rescue Squad in the firemen's parade on Main Street in Clifton Forge. The entrance to the Hotel Jefferson can be seen in the background. (AHS-VR.)

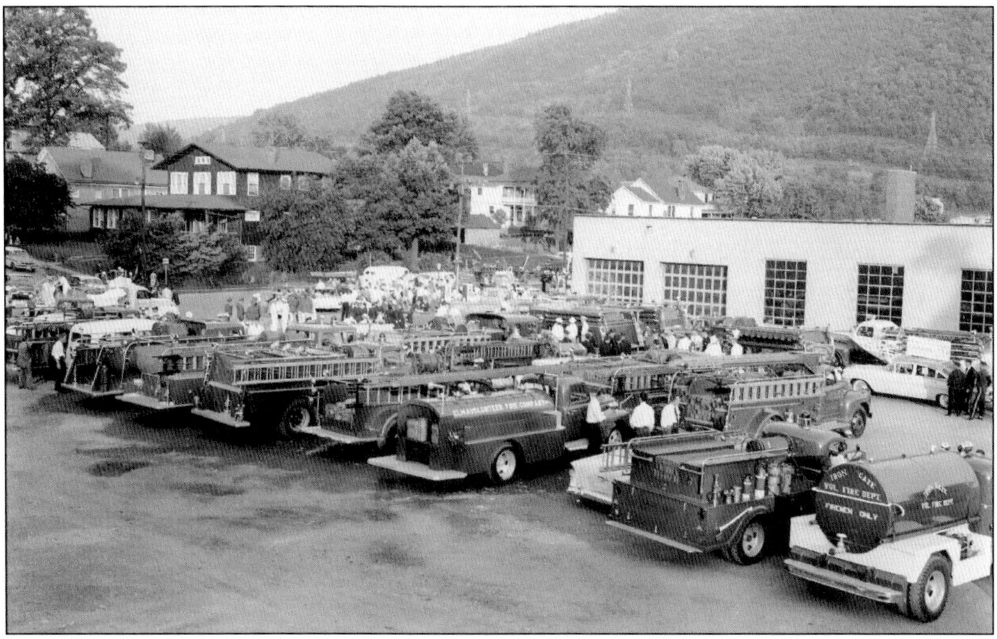

This photograph shows equipment from the different fire departments assembled behind Wood Chevrolet in Clifton Forge getting lined up for the parade. Iron Gate's water tanker is on the far right, and Selma's tanker is three vehicles down in the back row. Most of the vehicles from other locations are unidentifiable, but there are some from Fairfield and South Boston. (AHS-VR.)

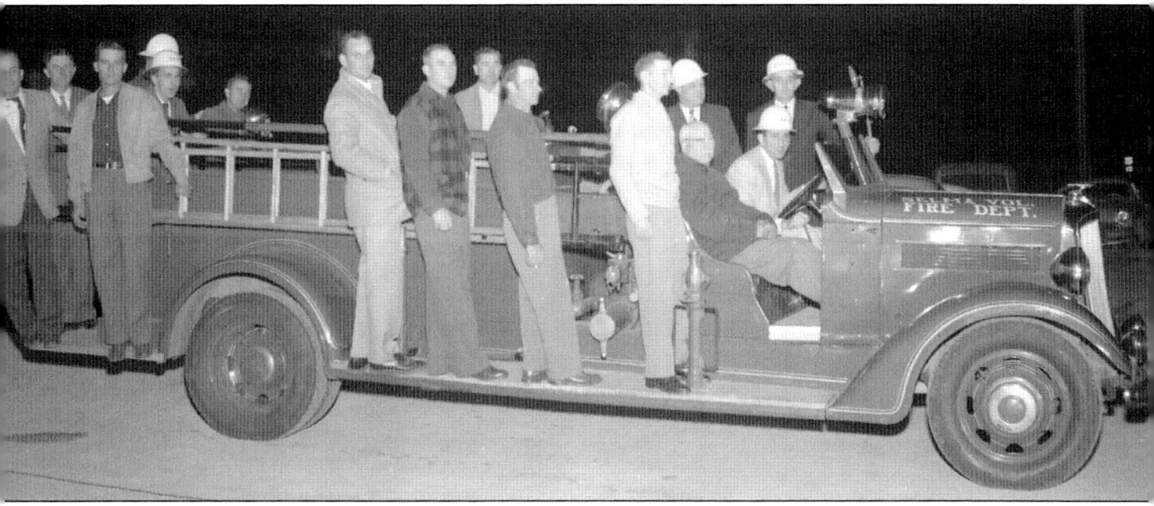

This 1950s photograph shows firemen of the Selma Fire Department on their ladder truck in front of the old Selma Fire Station next to Carter's general store. Open-air cabs were popular with early firetrucks. Try to find the smoker on the near-side running board. (AHS-VR.)

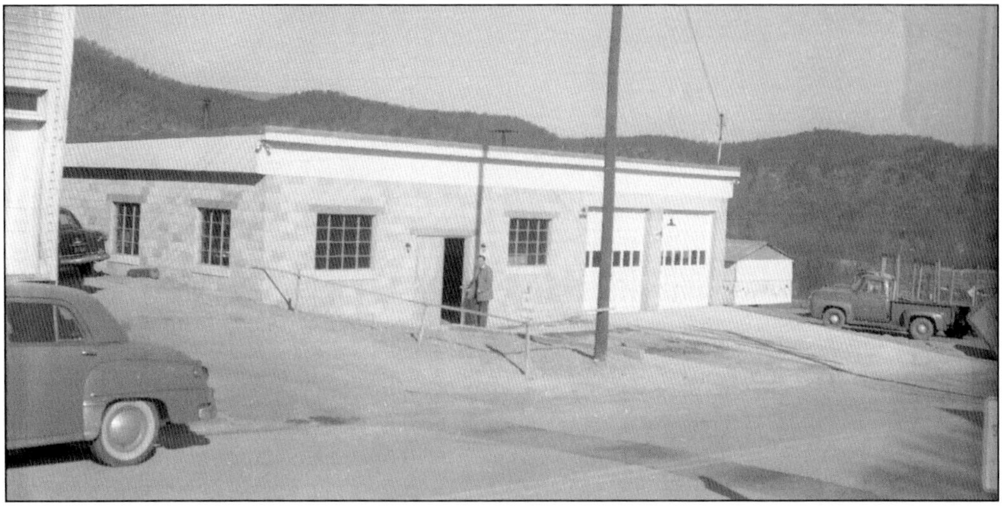

The above photograph shows the old Selma fire station. Visible on the left is the corner of Carter's store, which still stands today. This photograph is from the late 1950s. Notice the old bridge across the railroad beyond the pickup truck. The current Selma fire station was built in the late 1950s or early 1960s. The photograph below shows the ground-breaking for the building of the new station. The old station stood just to the west of the current building. (Both, AHS-VR.)

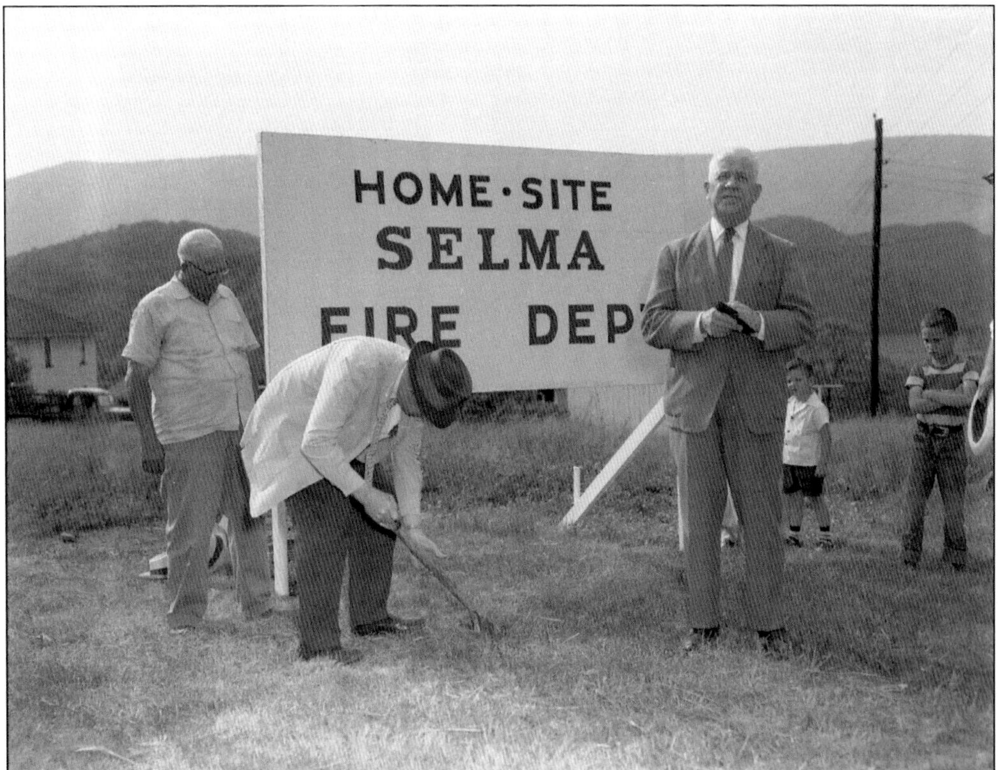

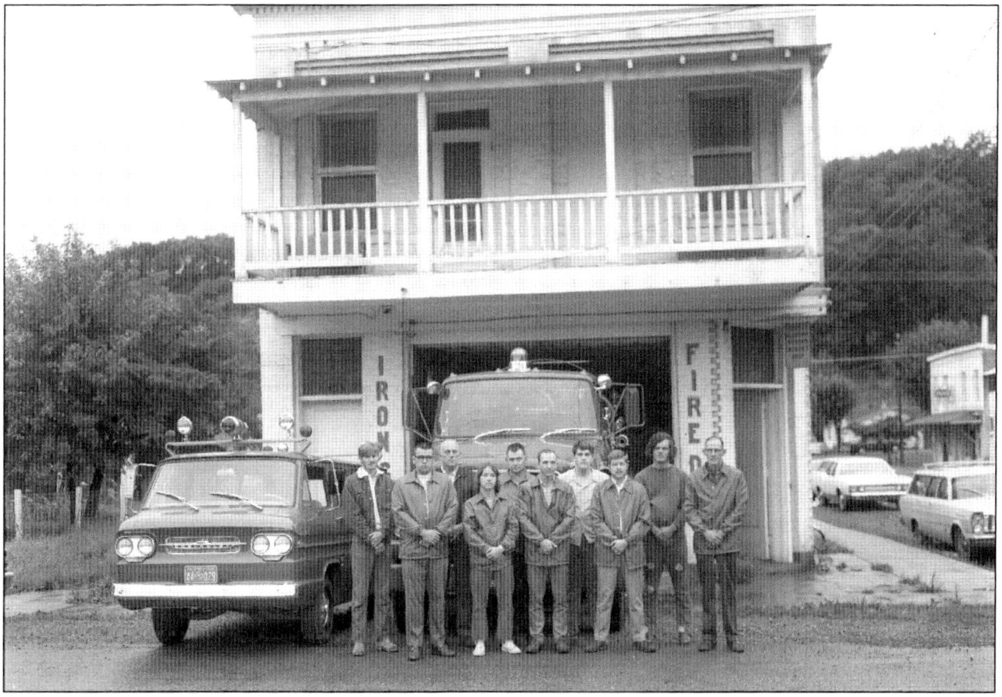

The firemen of the Iron Gate Fire Department were photographed in front of the old one-bay fire house in late 1973 with a pumper and utility van. Shortly after this was taken, a new building was constructed, and the old station was torn down. (AHS-VR.)

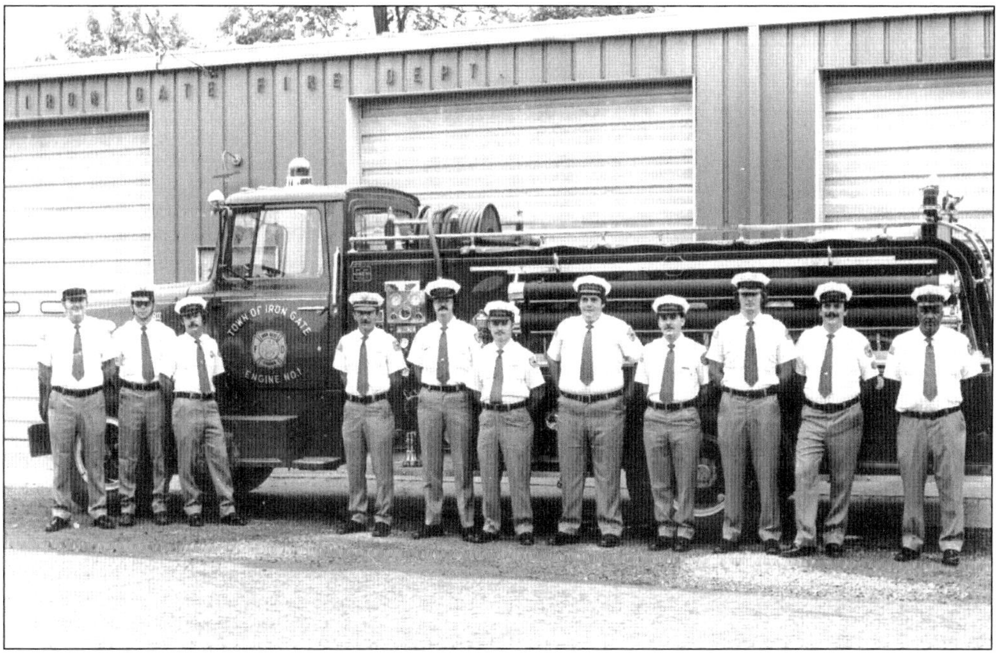

A few years later, the Iron Gate firemen gathered in front of their new, three-bay firehouse. It appears the department also received new summer uniforms with matching hats after the new station was built. However, the old pumper truck remained in use. (AHS-VR.)

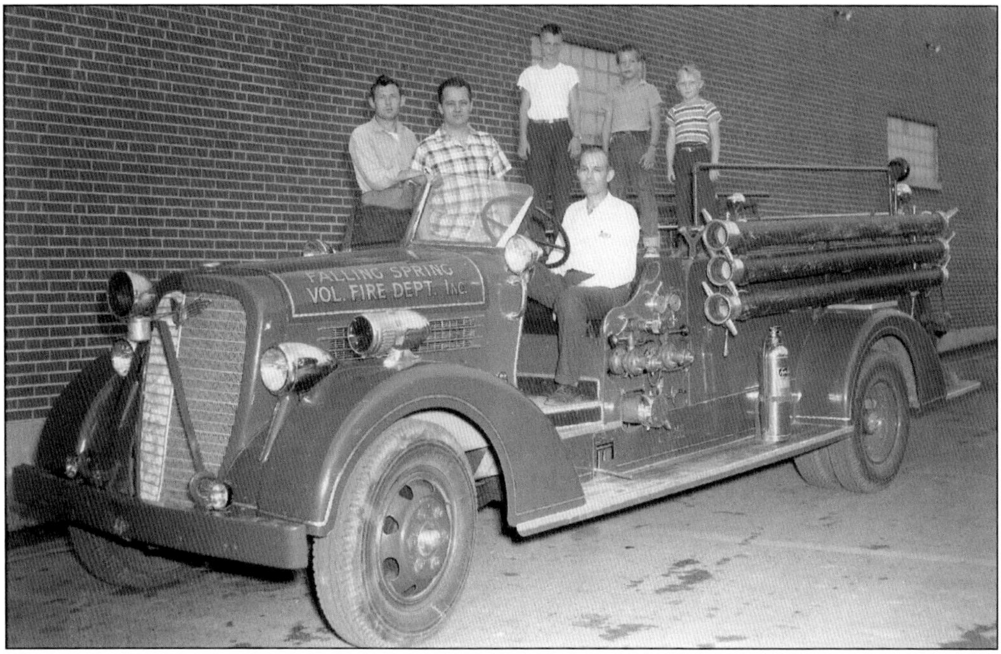

This May 1962 photograph of a Falling Spring Fire Department's open-cab fire engine was used as a promotion for a dinner social held by the department to celebrate the completion of a new building. Pictured are, from left to right, M.L. Jennings, J.J. Schoppmeyer, and T.A. Boggs of the fire department with "junior members" Gary Jennings, Larry Schoppmeyer, and Timmy Jennings standing on top of the engine. (AHS-VR.)

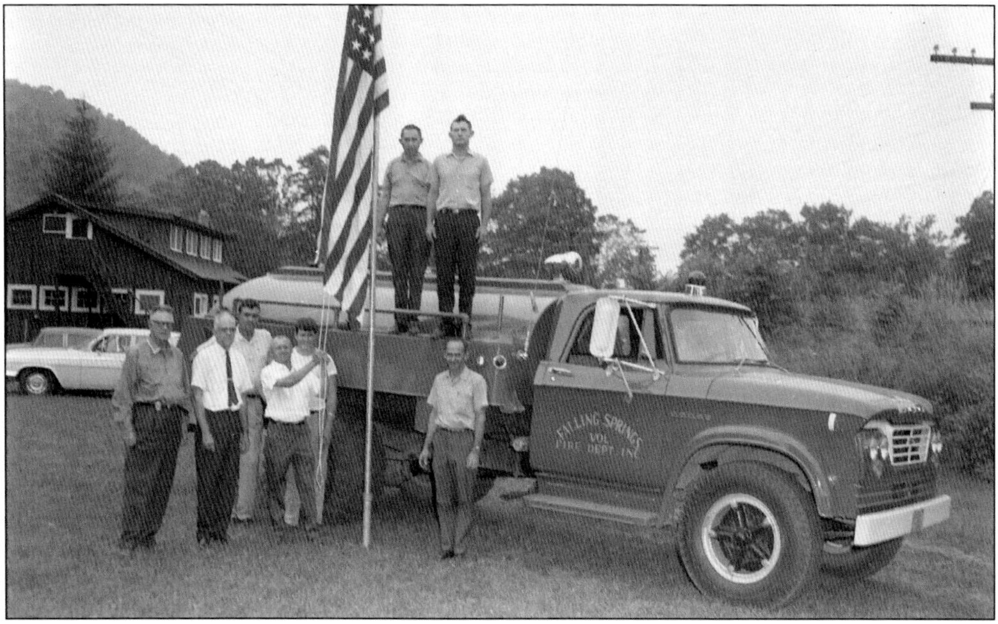

This March 1967 photograph shows a flag raising ceremony at Camp Appalachia along the Jackson River at the base of Morris Hill. Notice that the spelling on the vehicle in the previous picture was "Falling Spring," but the spelling on the tanker shown here is "Falling Springs." The debate over the "s" has gone back and forth, but there is only one spring above the falls. (AHS-VR.)

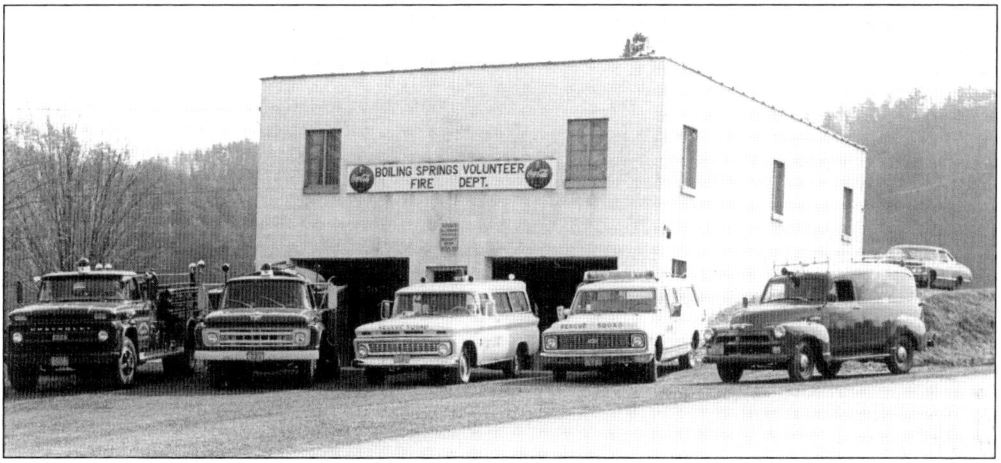

This early 1970s photograph shows the vehicles of Boiling Springs Fire Department and Boiling Springs Rescue Squad. This building and department remain active today, and there is also a debate in that community over the addition of an "s" on the word "spring." (AHS-VR.)

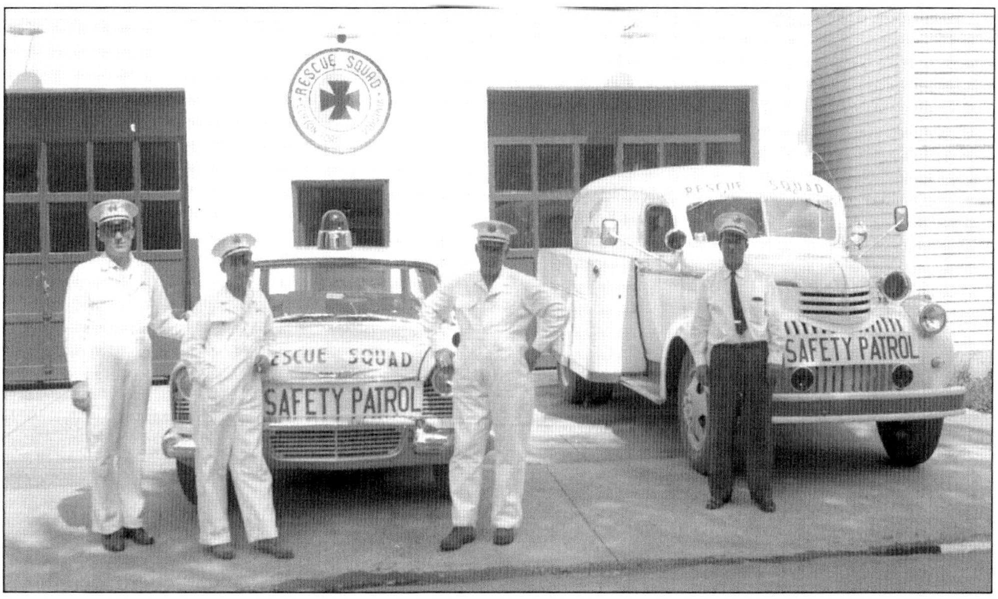

Each year around Memorial Day, the fire departments and rescue squads promote driver safety because of the high volume of traffic over the holiday weekend. This photograph shows the Clifton Forge Rescue Squad Memorial Day Safety Patrol on May 29, 1959. From left to right are Calvin Stayton, Buster Farrar, Ray Bowers, and Bob Warf Sr. (AHS-VR.)

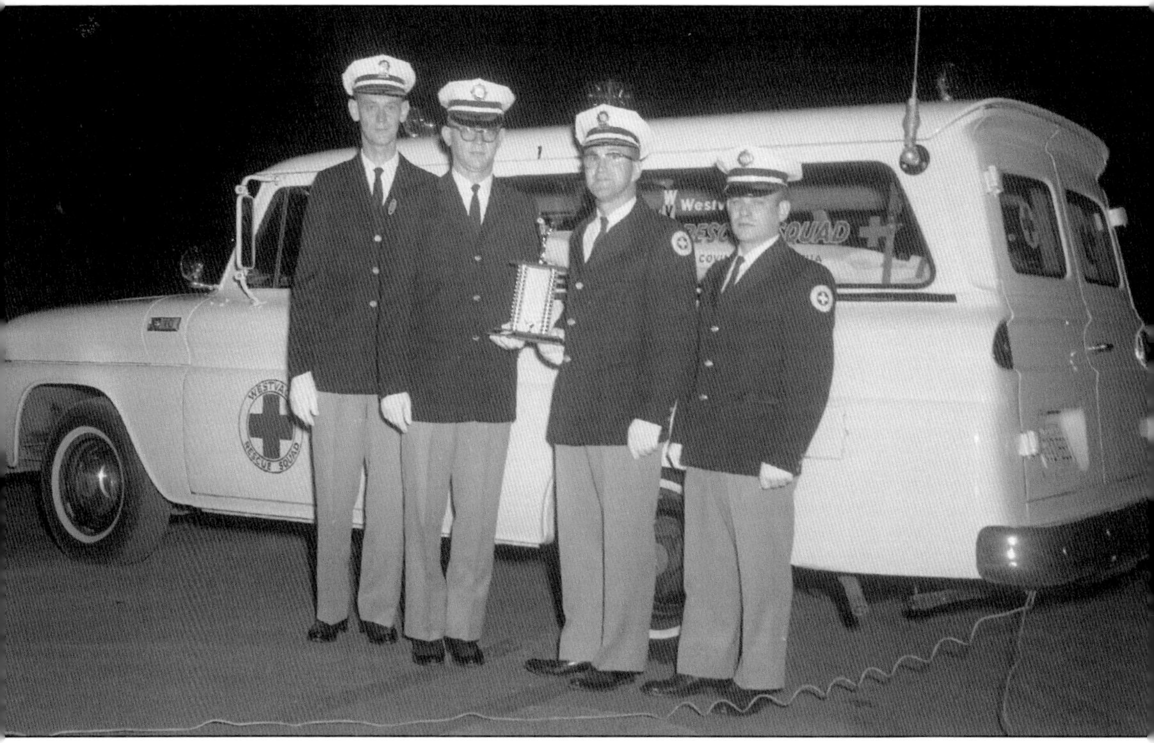

West Virginia Pulp and Paper Company, also known as Westvaco, was such a large mill in Covington that for the safety of its employees and the welfare of the community and company, it had its own fire department and rescue squad. These members pose with the trophy won by the Westvaco Rescue Squad during the state competition. From left to right are Buddy Ervin, Billy Ervin, John Clarke, and Jakie Kinsey. (AHS-VR.)

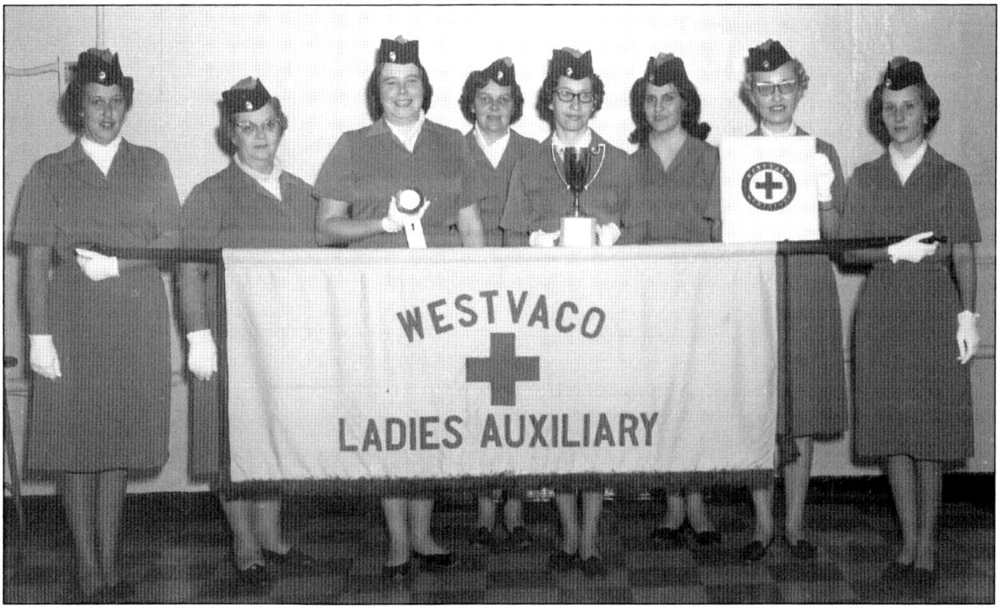

In 1956, several wives of the Westvaco Rescue Squad started the Westvaco Ladies Auxiliary. These ladies proudly display their first-place ribbon and trophy won in the 1966 state rescue squad competition. (AHS-VR.)

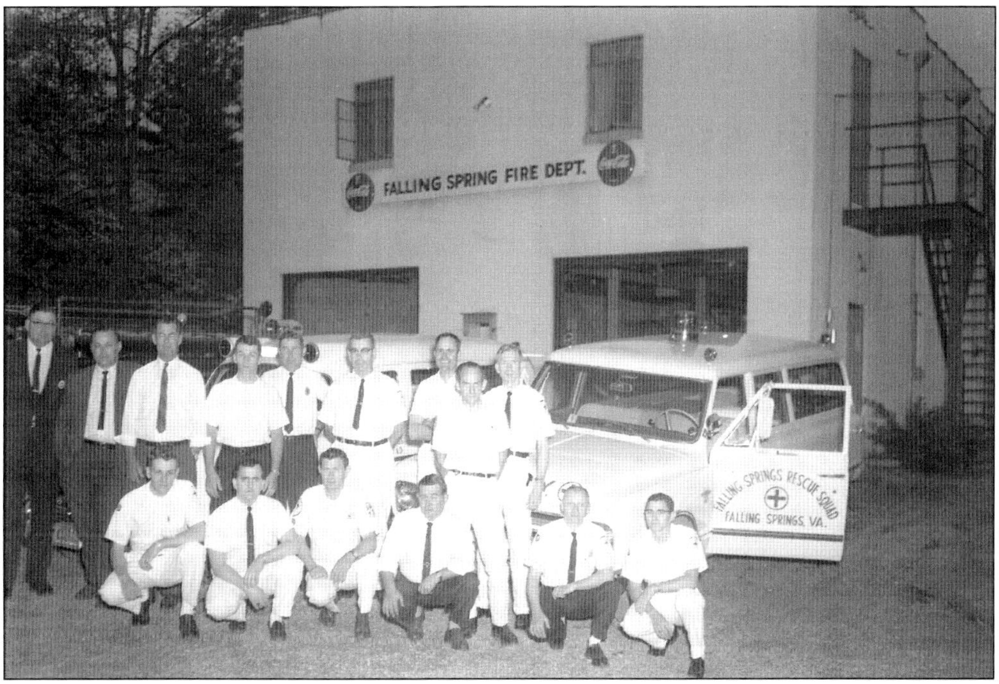

This late 1960s photograph shows the members of the Falling Springs Rescue Squad in front of the station shared with the Falling Spring Fire Department. There's still a difference over an "s" or no "s." As volunteer organizations, local fire departments and rescue squads sought support from local governments, individuals, and businesses. The sign was paid for by the Covington Coca-Cola Bottling Works. (AHS-VR.)

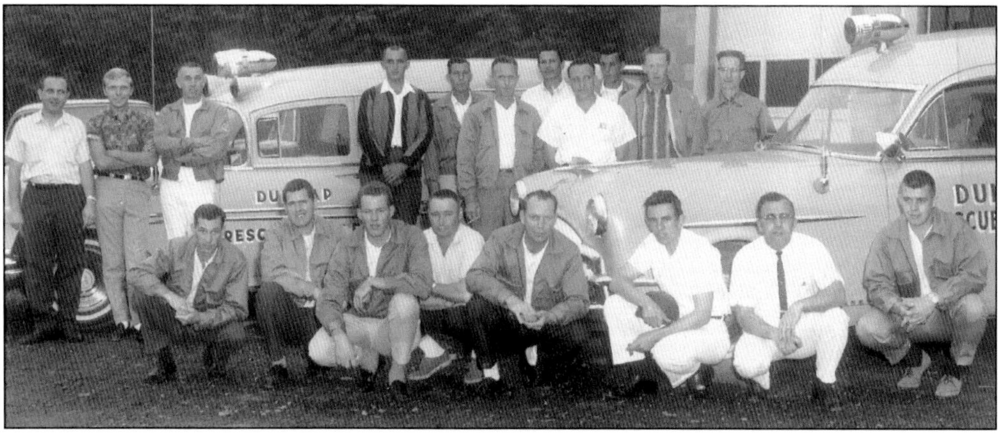

The Dunlap Rescue Squad is pictured in 1963 in front of the Dunlap station. Dunlap covered a large area and had a firehouse near Hematite to cover the Crows, Alleghany, and Sweet Chalybeate end of Alleghany County. Another station was located in Callaghan for that community and for citizens living on Ogles Creek, Johnson Creek, and Indian Draft. (AHS-VR.)

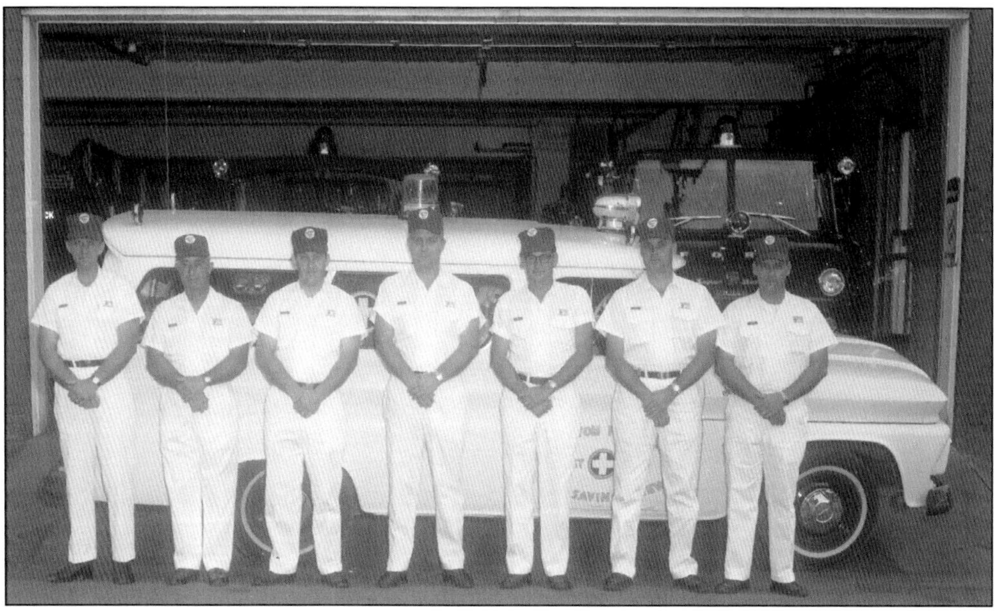

The Covington Rescue Squad members are in front of their ambulance at the fire station on Hawthorne Street around 1960. From left to right are O.L. "Slick" Williams, Howard Morris, Sylvia Entsminger, Roscoe Humphries, Jimmy Williams, Percy Caldwell, and Sam Levisey. (AHS-VR.)

Six

SCHOOLS

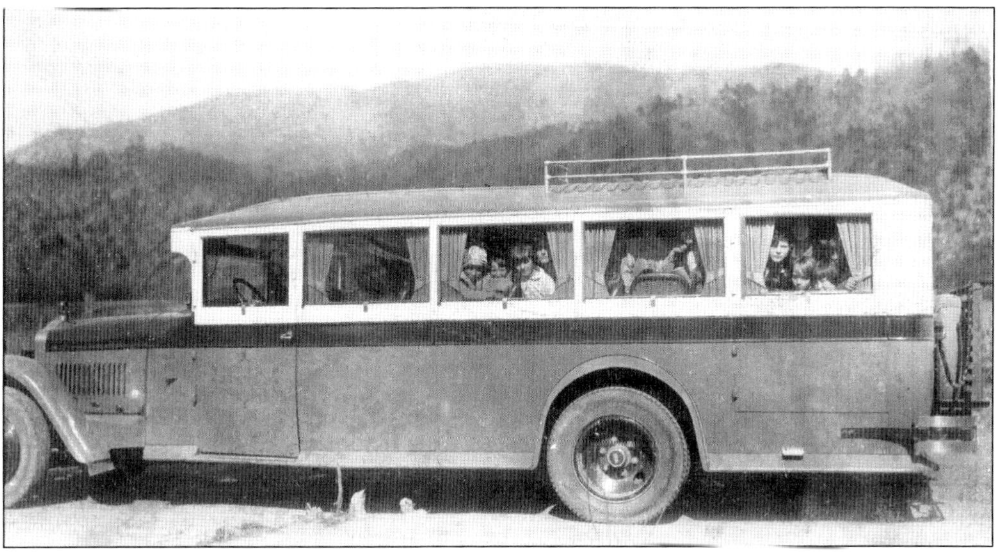

Early schooling in Alleghany County often took place in one- and two-room schoolhouses located in the various communities and attended by students within walking distance of the school. During the 1920s, larger schools were built to provide a more comprehensive educational program and often contained both elementary and high school grades. Transportation was required to ensure that parents complied with compulsory school attendance laws. This photograph shows an early bus that was likely provided by a local operator contracted to the school. (AHS.)

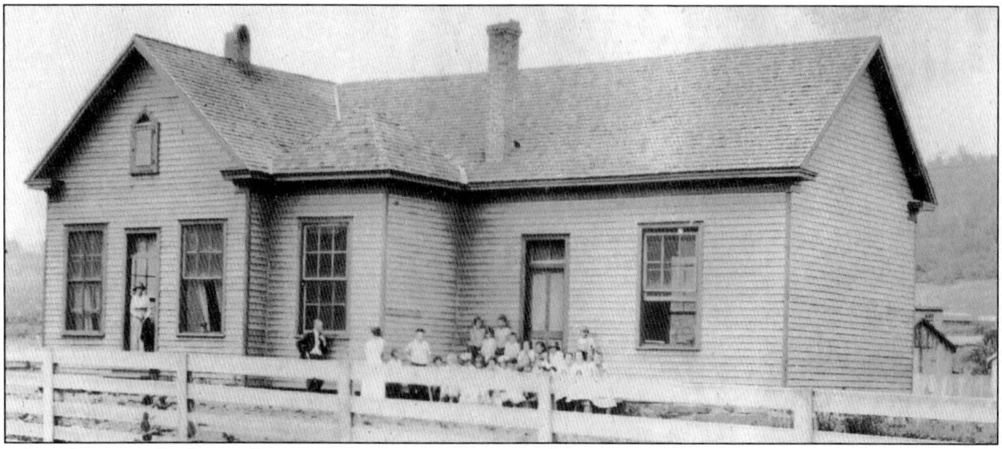

This photograph shows the two-room school in Callaghan built in 1916. It was located on the lower road in the Callaghan community. The present Callaghan school was built in the 1960s on adjacent property and faced the upper road, which was US Route 60 and the Midland Trail. (AHS.)

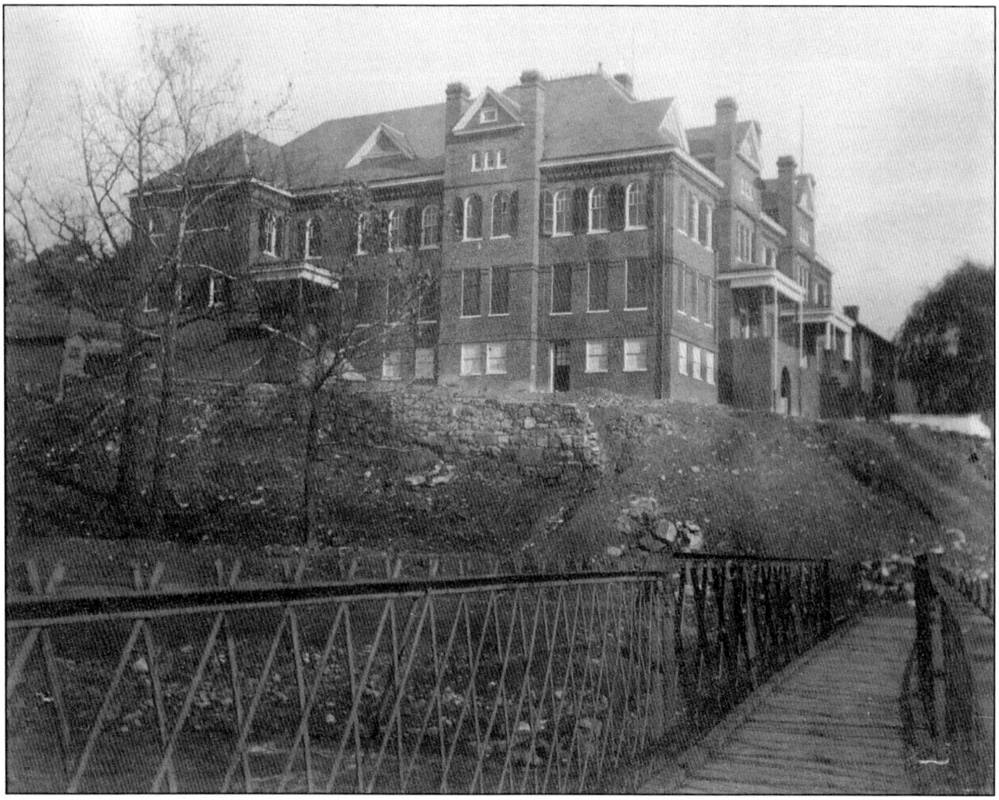

The Moody School in Clifton Forge was originally erected in 1896 as an eight-room brick school building. It was named for Capt. W.C. Moody, who was chairman of the district school board. It was later expanded and went through several additions, demolitions, and reconstructions. The old Clifton Forge West Elementary School is now located at the site and is occupied by the Clifton Forge Department of Social Services. The footbridge across Smith Creek connected Pine Street. (AHS.)

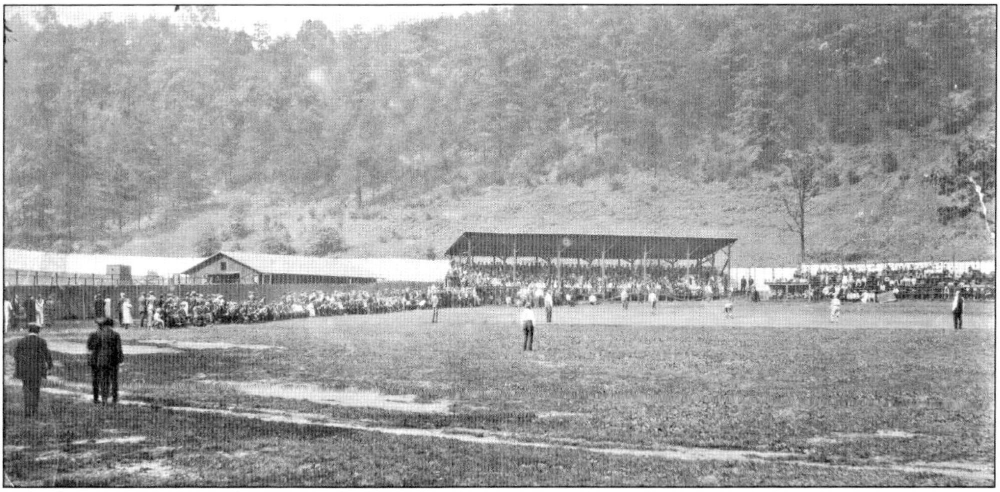

This is an early photograph of Memorial Park in Clifton Forge. While the grandstand and bleachers were mostly full, some fans still preferred to stand along the foul lines. The hill in the background suggests that the orientation of the diamond was where right field is today. (AHS-VR.)

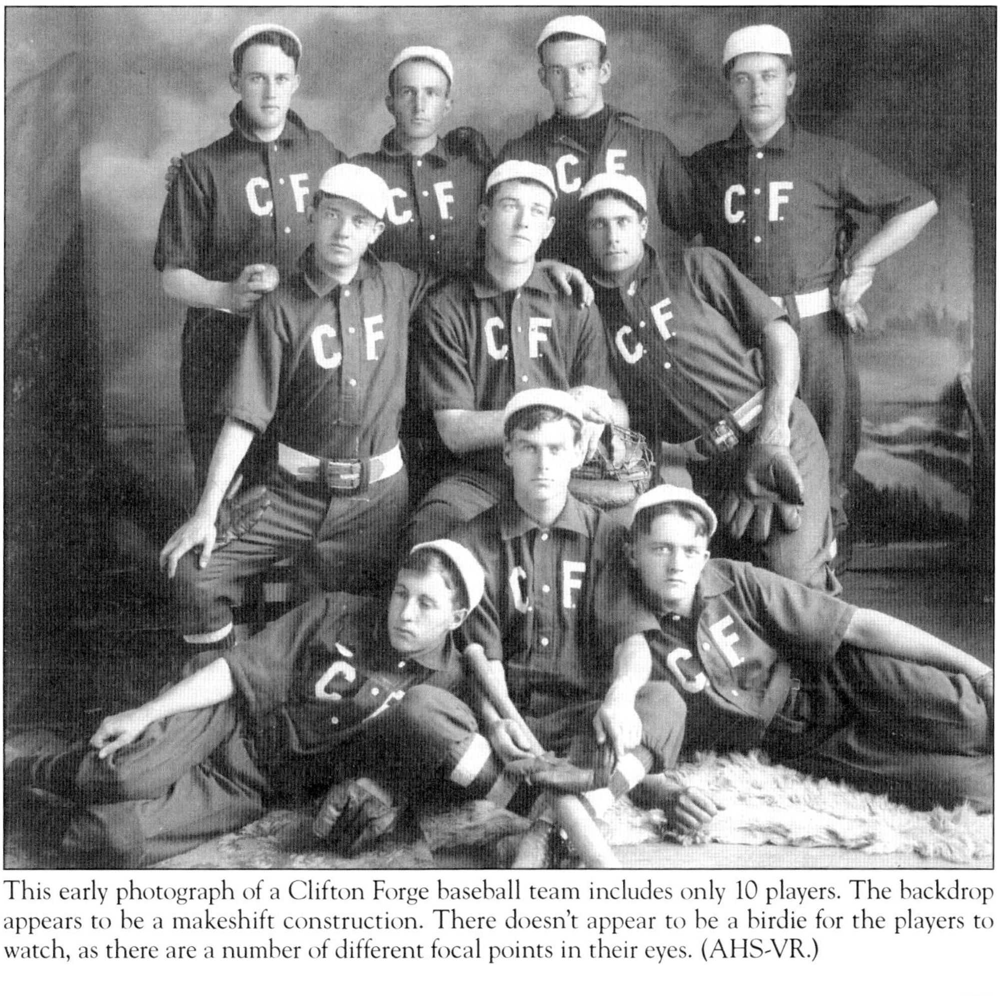

This early photograph of a Clifton Forge baseball team includes only 10 players. The backdrop appears to be a makeshift construction. There doesn't appear to be a birdie for the players to watch, as there are a number of different focal points in their eyes. (AHS-VR.)

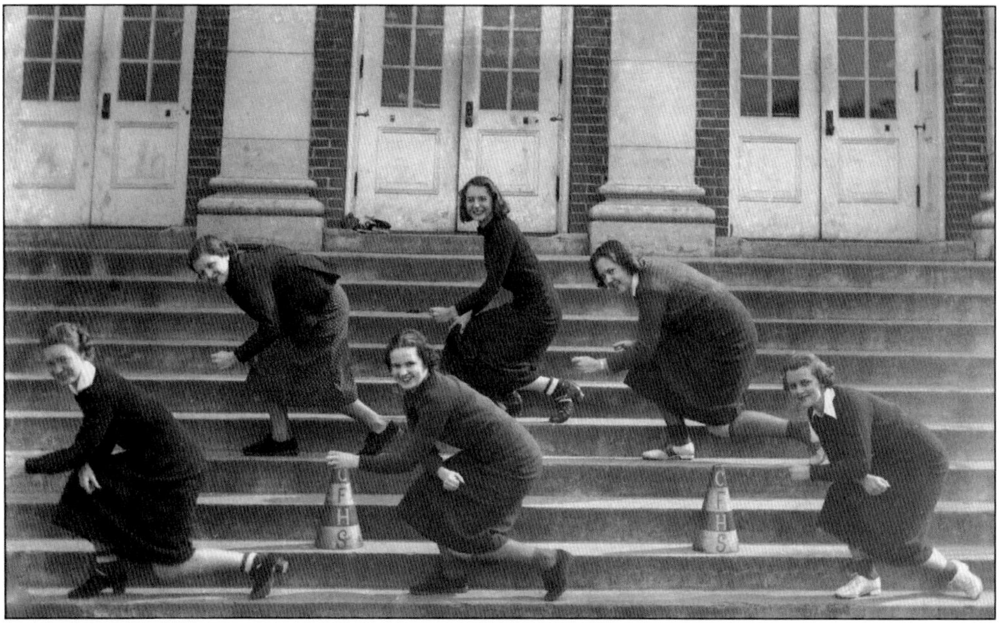

The Clifton Forge High School Mountaineer cheerleaders pose on the front steps of the school. The various dresses suggest that the photograph was taken during school hours and there was no time to change into uniforms. One student's school books are on the top step by the middle entrance doors. (AHS-VR.)

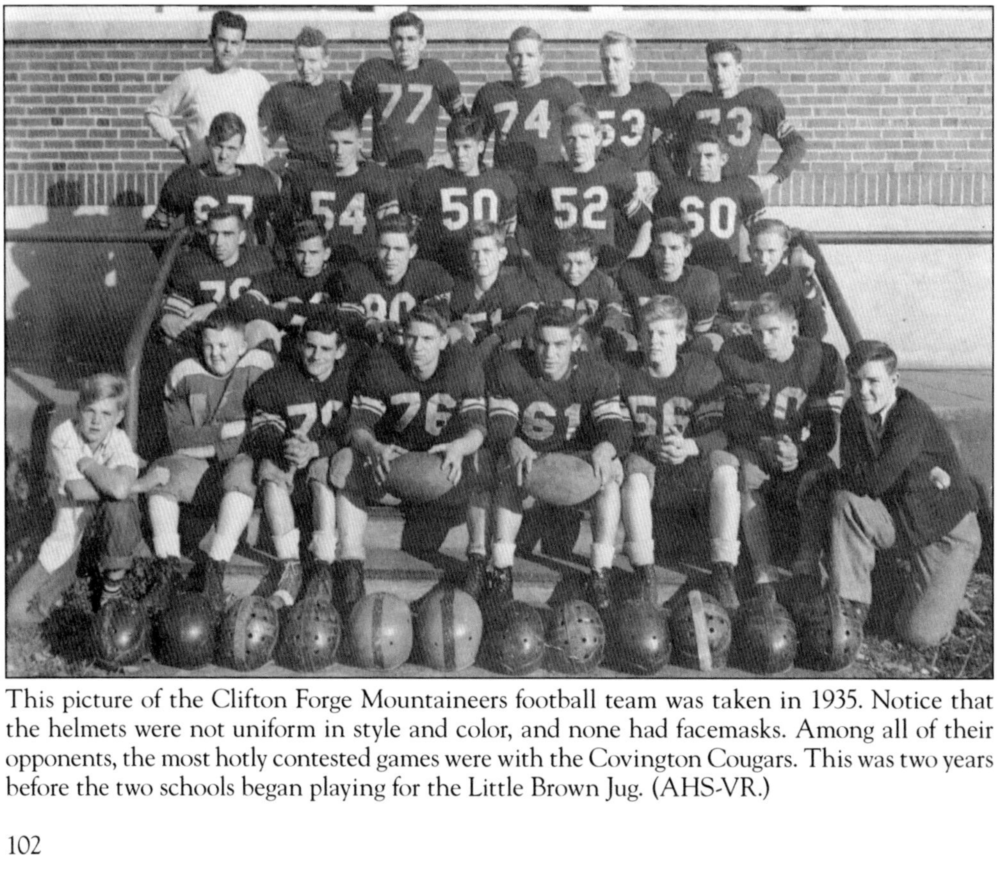

This picture of the Clifton Forge Mountaineers football team was taken in 1935. Notice that the helmets were not uniform in style and color, and none had facemasks. Among all of their opponents, the most hotly contested games were with the Covington Cougars. This was two years before the two schools began playing for the Little Brown Jug. (AHS-VR.)

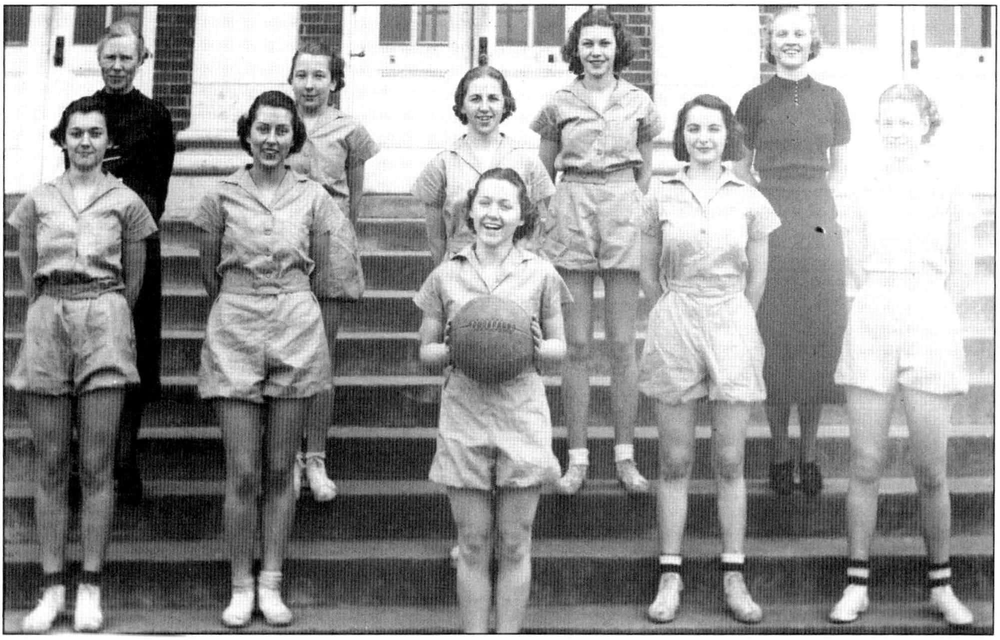

The 1935 girls' basketball team poses on the front steps of Clifton Forge High School. Basketball games were played on the massive stage of the high school auditorium until the new National Guard Armory was built in the front of the school. (AHS-VR.)

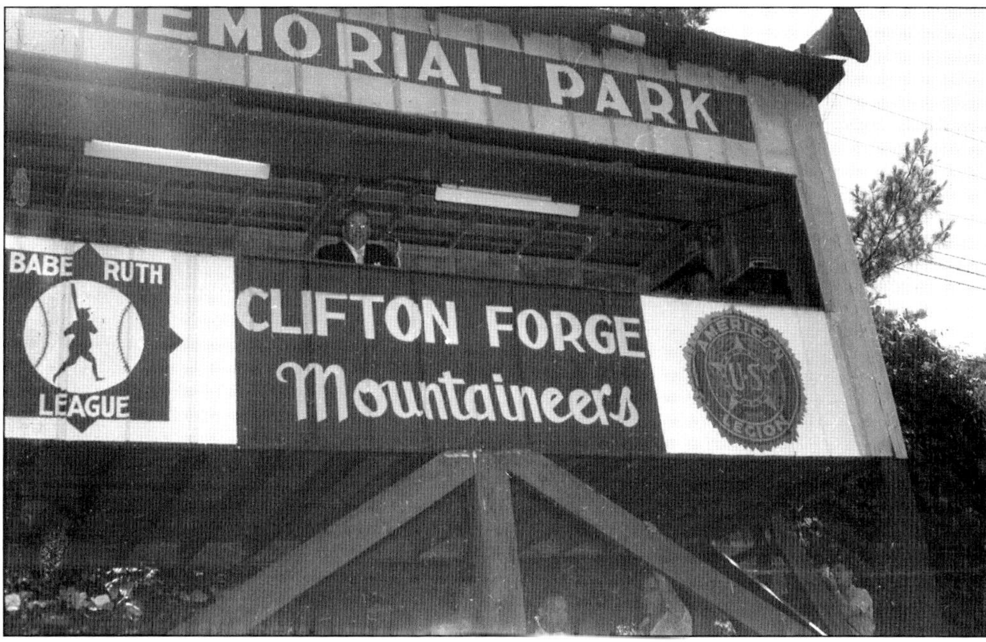

The press box at Memorial Park in Clifton Forge was supported by large posts and strategically located in right field. During football season, the gridiron was located in the outfield, and the press box was behind the sideline bleachers. The field was not only utilized for high school sports, it also hosted Babe Ruth and American Legion baseball games. Local newspapers covered the contests, and radio stations often broadcast the football games. The press box was a necessary fixture for the athletic program. (AHS-VR.)

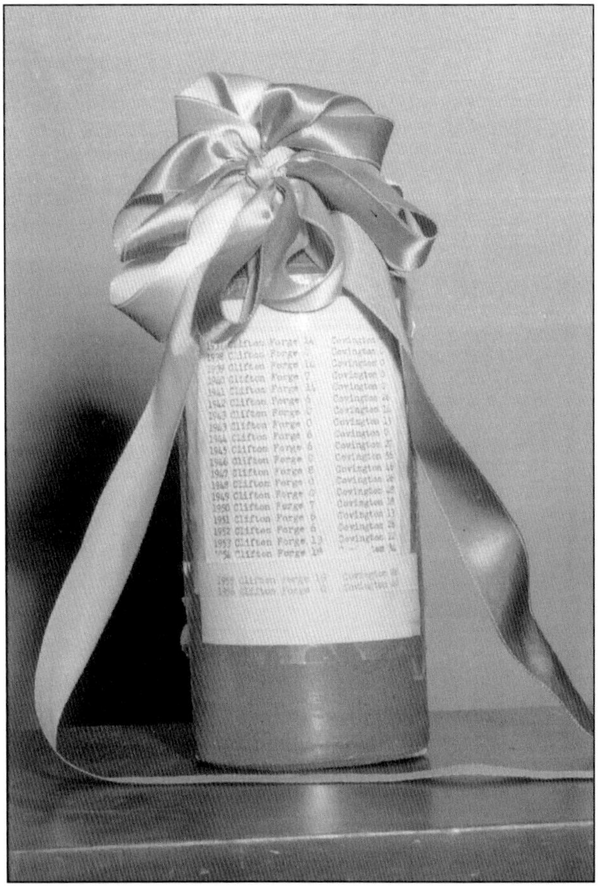

In 1937, the administrators of Clifton Forge and Covington High Schools inaugurated the tradition of awarding the Little Brown Jug to the winner of the schools' annual football game. The piece of pottery was meant to be a symbol for the practice of good sportsmanship. It took Covington six years to record its first victory in the annual contest, and the jug traded hands a number of times over the years. Clifton Forge won the final contest between the schools, held at Casey Field in 1982, prior to its consolidation with Alleghany County Schools. Clifton Forge High School became Clifton Middle School. The trophy is now safely held at Covington High School. (AHS-VR.)

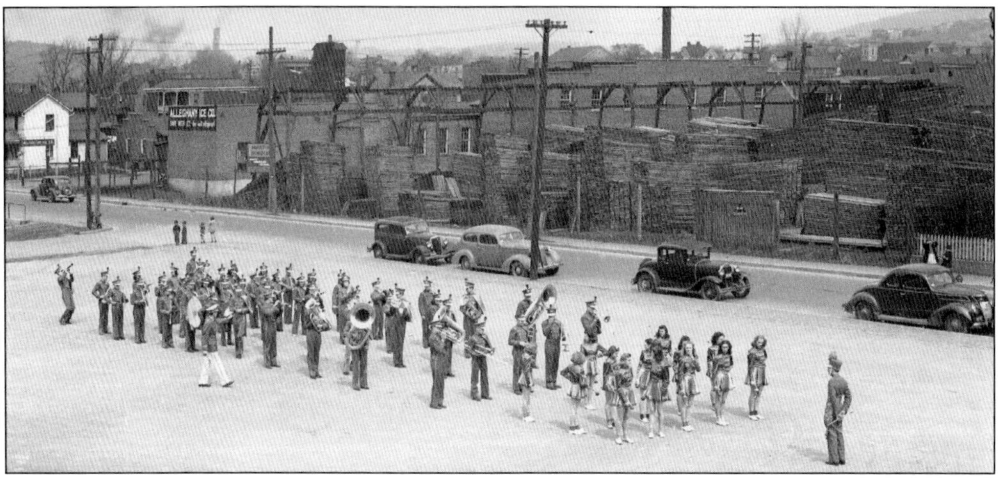

The band was an important extracurricular activity for area high schools. In addition to exposing students to music instruction and appreciation, the band added excitement to athletic contests and local parades. This photograph of the Covington High School Marching Band was taken in the 1940s on the lawn in front of the new building on Lexington Avenue. Across the street is the Nettleton Lumber Yard. The Alleghany Ice Company is on the left in a building now occupied by D.D. Kerns Construction Company. (AHS-VR.)

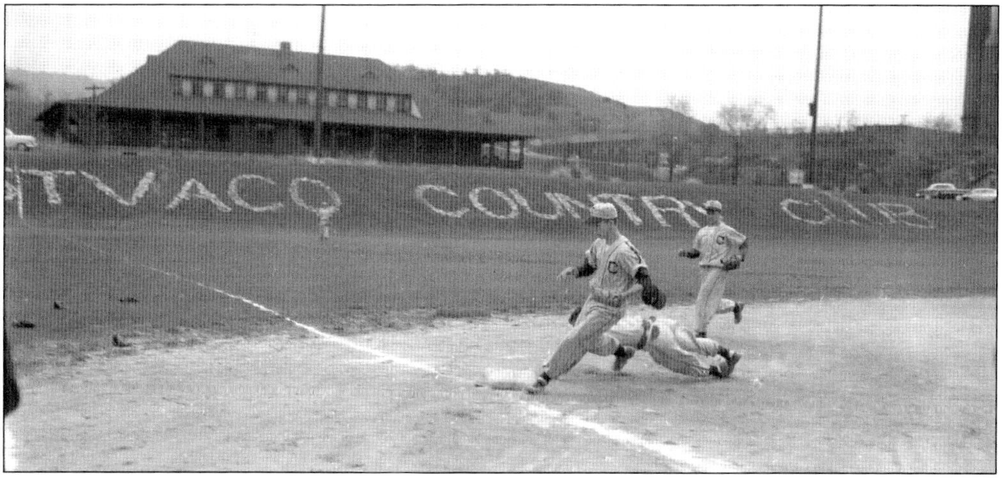

Local manufacturing facilities often invested in the welfare of the community by offering recreational opportunities for the local population. The Westvaco Country Club had a grand clubhouse with a golf course in the rear between the mainline of the C&O Railway and the Dunlap Creek. The baseball field was used by local amateur and semipro teams as well as those from the high school. Prior to the new school on Lexington Avenue, which had its own football field, Covington High School also held contests at the Westvaco Ballfield. (AHS-VR.)

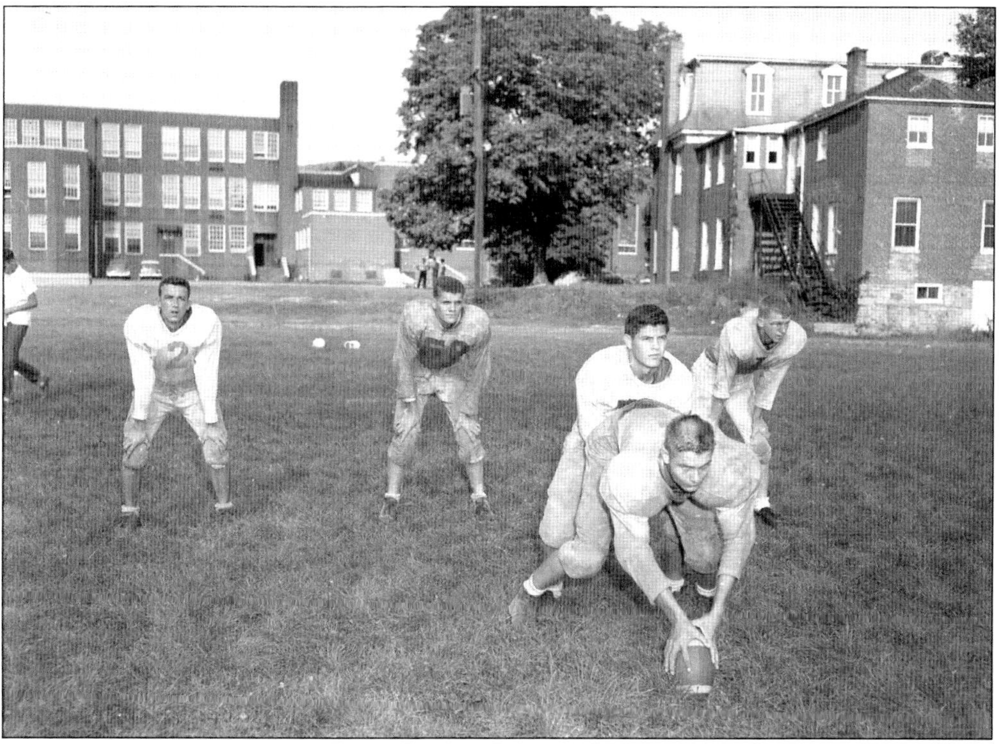

Covington High School played its football games on Burton Field behind the school. Here, the backfield is set to practice a few plays. This photograph was taken before the new addition was built at the back of the school. The stately house on the right was the Sively House, which had once served as the location of Loving Funeral Home. It was used as a home economics cottage for years before being torn down to provide a track facility at the school. (AHS-VR.)

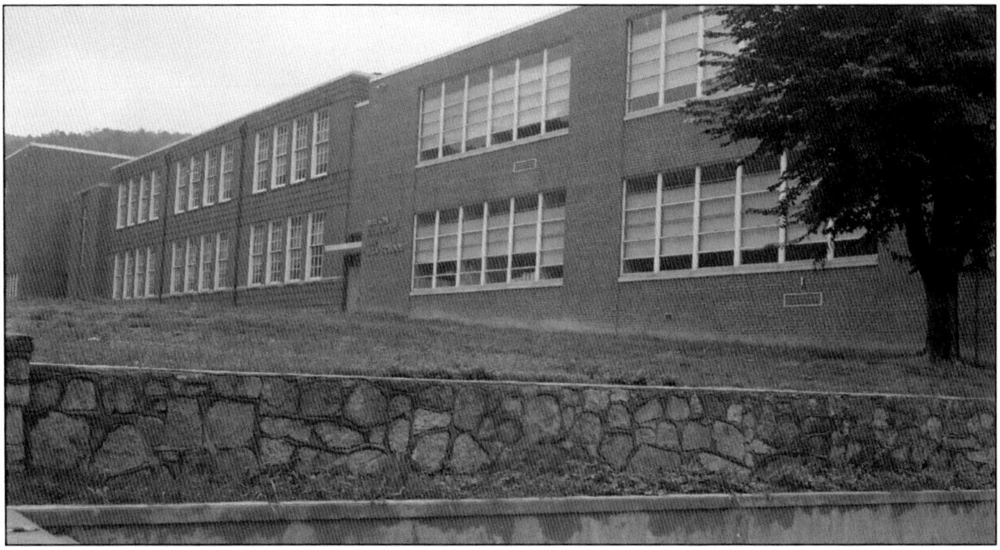

When the Works Progress Administration built the new Covington High School in 1939, it also built a new school for the African American community. The original Watson School housed both elementary and high school grades and served not only Covington but also students from Alleghany and Bath Counties. The middle of the school, with the multi-paned windows, was the structure built in 1939. A gymnasium and cafeteria on the left was a later addition. The classroom addition on the right was constructed in the 1960s. After the total integration of schools in 1966, the school became Jeter-Watson Elementary School. (AHS-VR.)

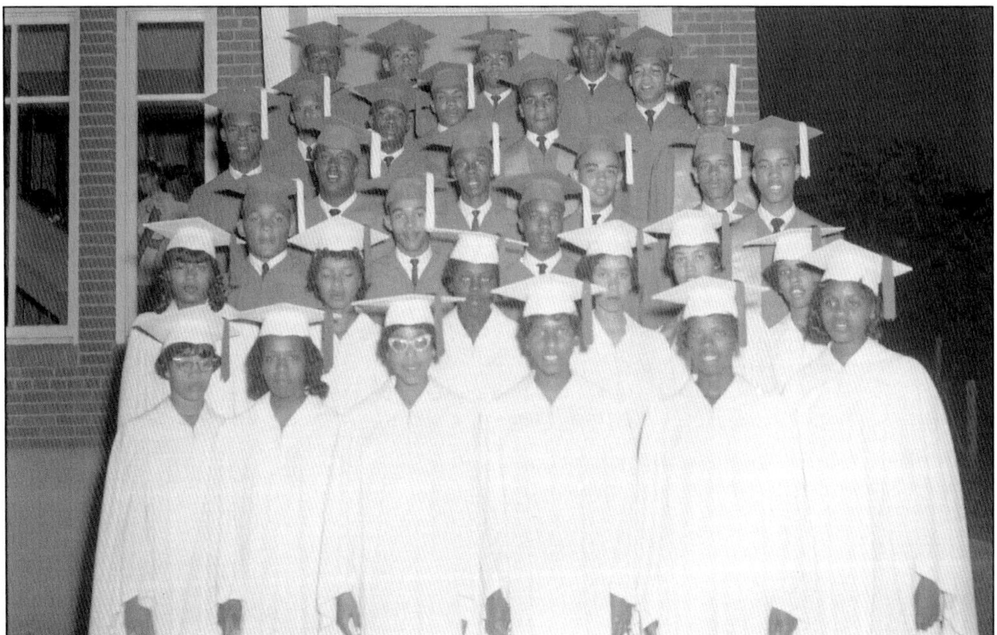

The African American community took great pride in the education of its children and graduated outstanding students who would enter the local workforce or pursue advanced degrees in college. Students were held to a high standard and distinguished themselves in their academic pursuits. This photograph is of the graduating class of 1960. (AHS-VR.)

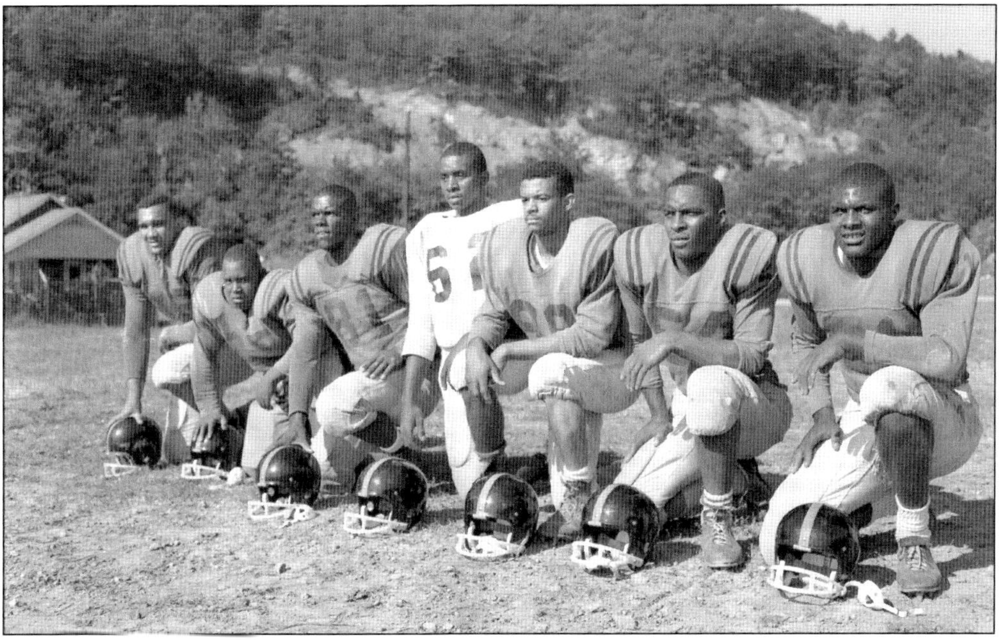

The Watson High School Hornets produced a number of outstanding athletes and athletic teams. The black-and-orange-clad Hornets played under less than ideal conditions but usually had winning seasons as they competed against Jefferson High School of Clifton Forge, Carver of Salem, Lucy Addison of Roanoke, Dunbar of Lynchburg, and a number of other area schools. This photograph was taken in August 1964 during a practice session on the dirt and cinder lot above the school. (AHS-VR.)

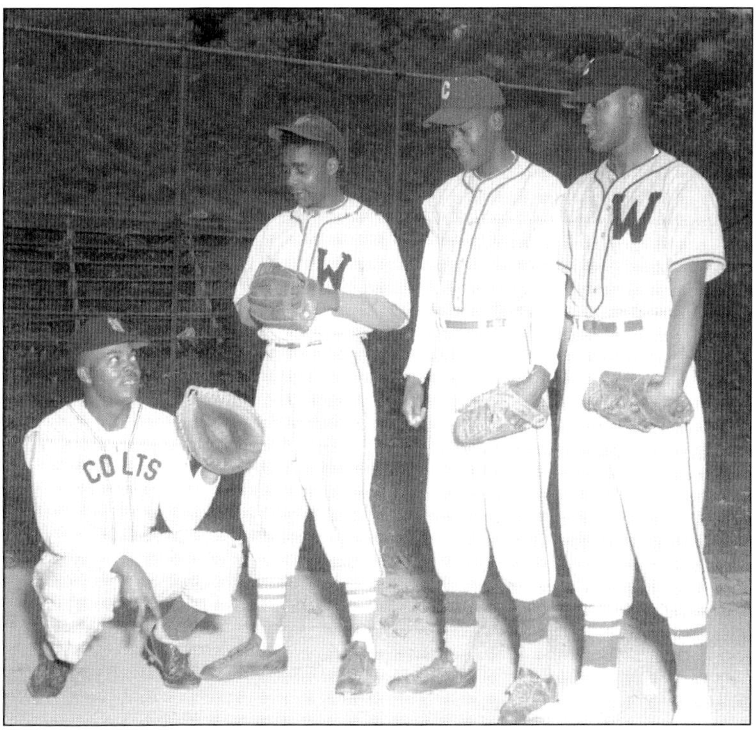

The baseball teams also had success. Watson High School fielded a team, and there was also a local semipro team known as the Covington Colts. They also played games at the Westvaco Ballfield and had Coca-Cola as a sponsor. (AHS-VR.)

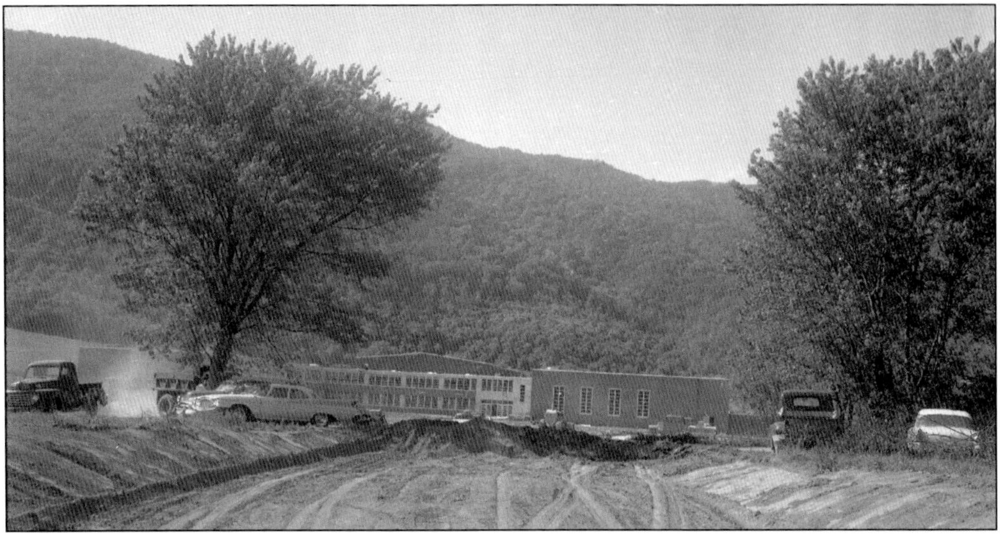

In the early 1960s, the Alleghany County and Covington City Schools agreed to cease their jointly operated school systems. Alleghany County High School was constructed in Valley Ridge and opened its doors in 1963. The new school welcomed more than 1,000 students who had been attending school at Covington, Dunlap, Boiling Spring, or Central High School. (AHS-VR.)

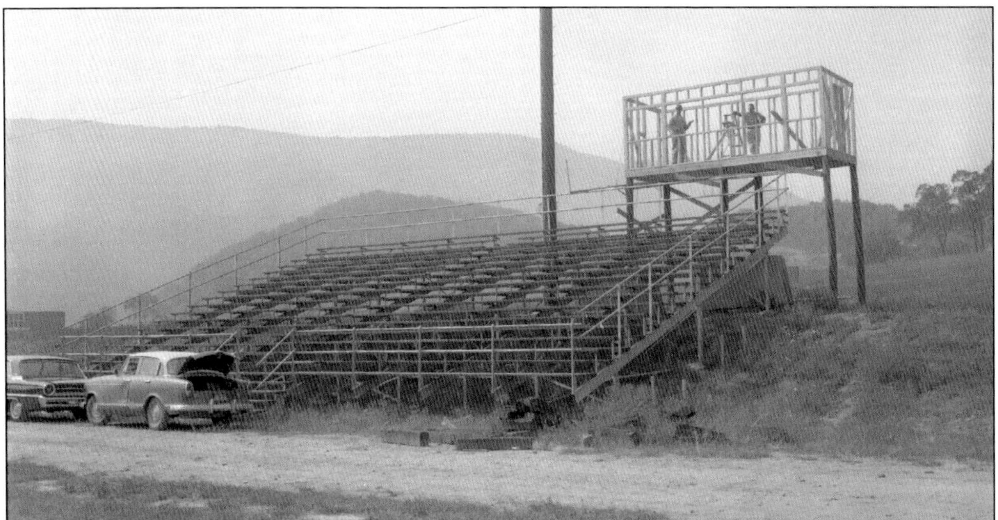

The Alleghany County Colts began their athletic program when the school opened in 1963 and played most of their home games at Memorial Park in Clifton Forge. This September 1964 photograph shows the construction of a new field at the school. As was the case at other football facilities, a press box was required. Utility poles supported the frame construction of the elevated structure. A first-class, three-story, concrete-block structure is now in place to accommodate the press and public address announcer at Alleghany High School. (AHS-VR.)

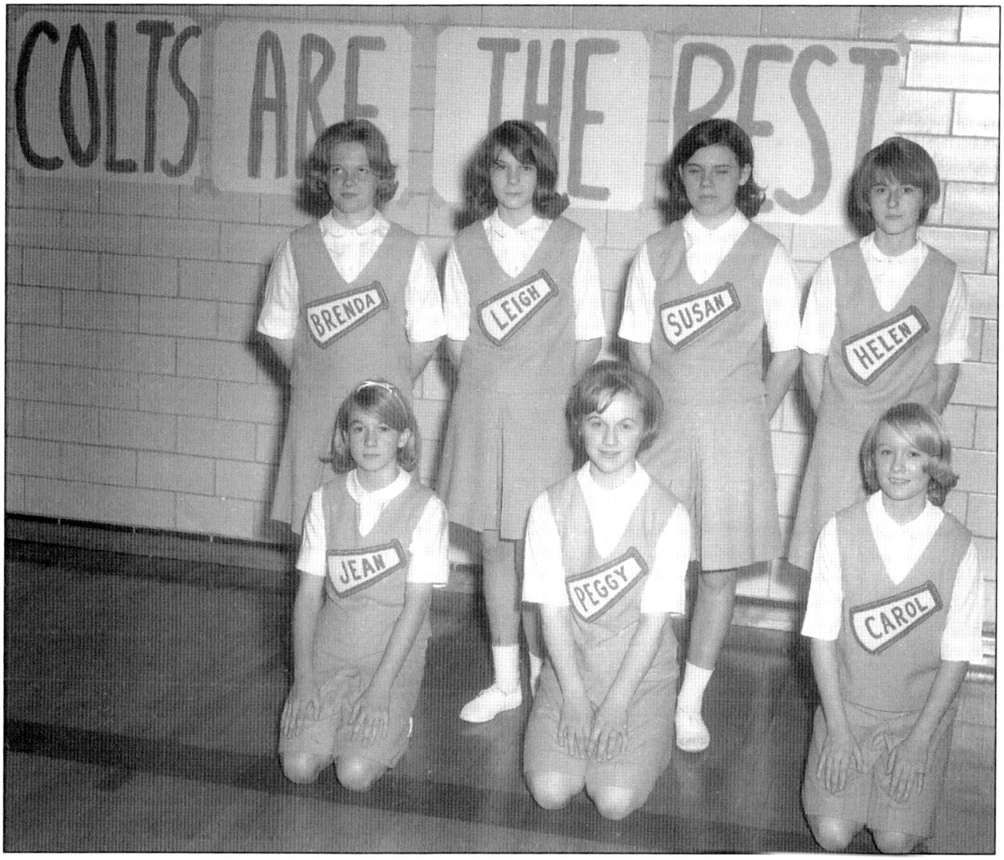

These junior varsity cheerleaders are shown on January 7, 1966, in the gymnasium at Alleghany County High School. From left to right are (first row) Jean Shawver, Peggy Hylton, and Carol Thompson; (second row) Brenda Hayslett, Leigh Thrasher, Susan Persinger, and Helen Bradley. (AHS-VR.)

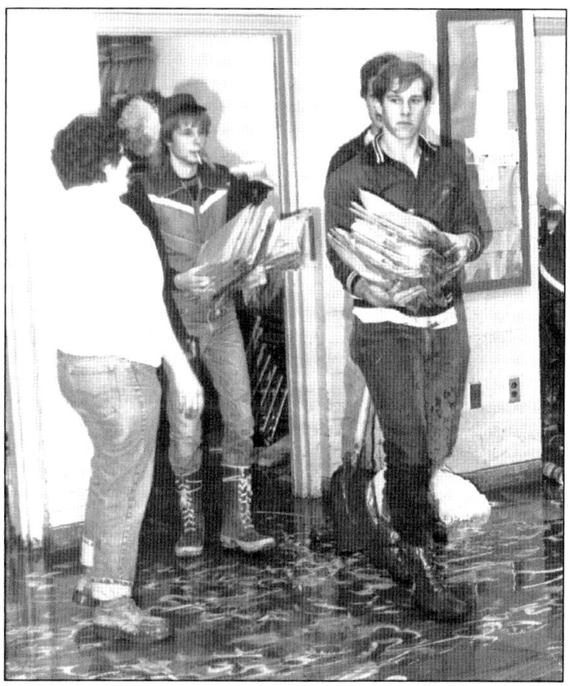

In November 1985, severe flooding in Alleghany County resulted in significant damage to Alleghany High School. Several feet of water filled the lower floors of the building, and the football field was severely damaged. Student, faculty, and community volunteers worked together to quickly clean, sanitize, and repair the building to get school back in session in just over a week's time. The school's final football game of the season was played at the school on the Saturday following the flood. (AHS-VR.)

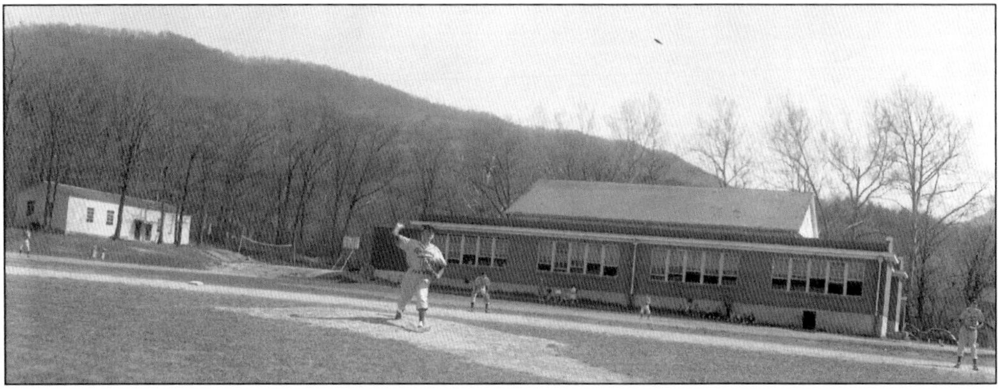

Wade Leech is on the mound for the Covington Cougars in this game played in Low Moor against the Central High School Falcons in 1962. Central housed both elementary and high school classes and utilized the white building at the back and rooms above the old company store of the Low Moor Iron Company, across the street in front of the school, to accommodate its student body. (AHS-VR.)

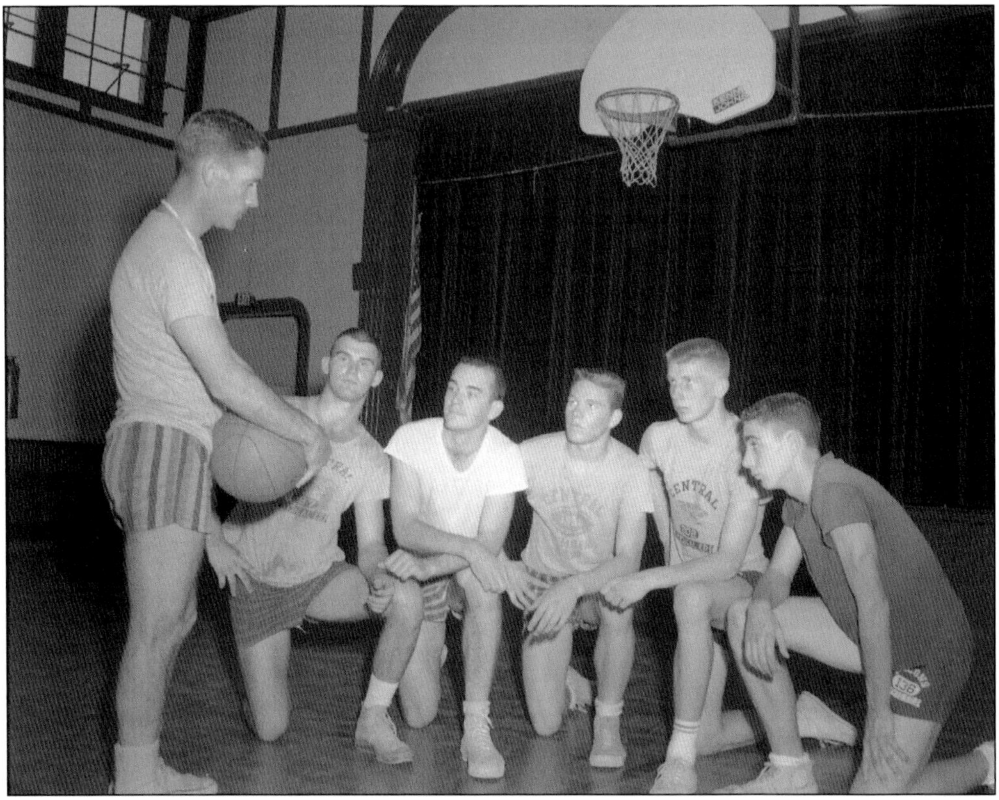

The Central High School gymnasium also served as a school auditorium, with a stage at one end of the basketball court. Classroom doors opened into the gym, making it difficult to conduct physical education while classes were in session. This picture was taken in November 1960. Sneakers or tennis shoes were the athletic shoe of choice, as this was long before the advent of Air Jordans. (AHS-VR.)

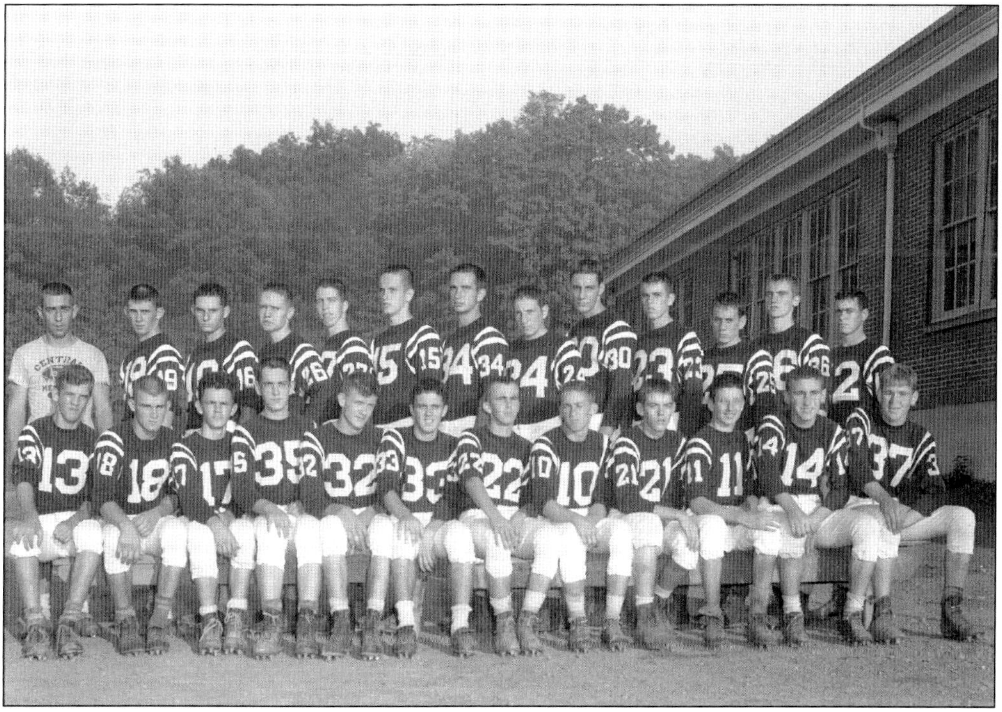

Despite the fact that Central High School was perhaps the smallest school competing in District 5, the football team had a full complement of players. Students from Longdale, Nicelytown, Iron Gate, Selma, Low Moor, and the eastern end of the county came to Central to complete their high school education. (AHS-VR.)

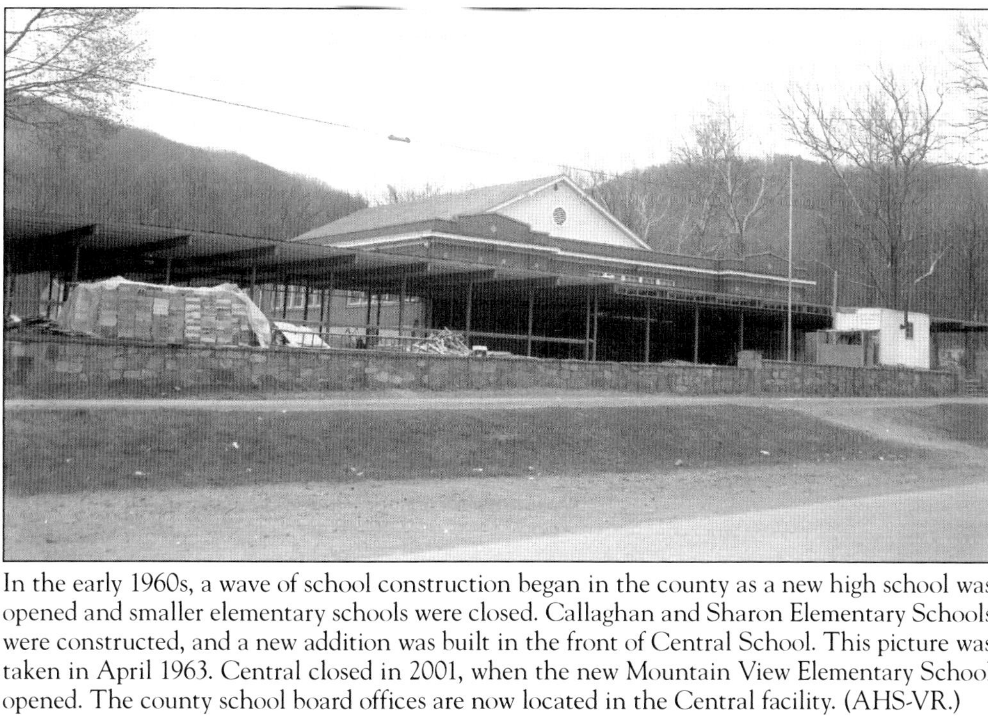

In the early 1960s, a wave of school construction began in the county as a new high school was opened and smaller elementary schools were closed. Callaghan and Sharon Elementary Schools were constructed, and a new addition was built in the front of Central School. This picture was taken in April 1963. Central closed in 2001, when the new Mountain View Elementary School opened. The county school board offices are now located in the Central facility. (AHS-VR.)

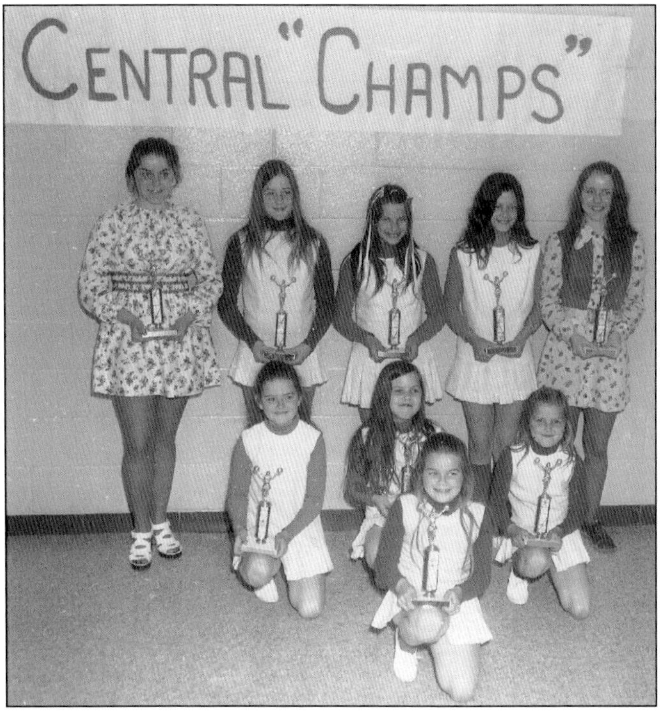

After the high school students left in 1963, the youth athletic league sponsored by the Alleghany County Department of Parks and Recreation continued to give the elementary schools an outlet for competition in sports. These Central "Champs" cheerleaders proudly display their trophies on April 19, 1974. Pictured are Anita Smith (first place), Tracy Averill (second place), Blair Shepard, Lorrie McCoy (third place), sponsor Lisa Paitsel, Sandy Simpson, Tamra Golden, Angela Lipes, and sponsor Vickie McCoy. (AHS-VR.)

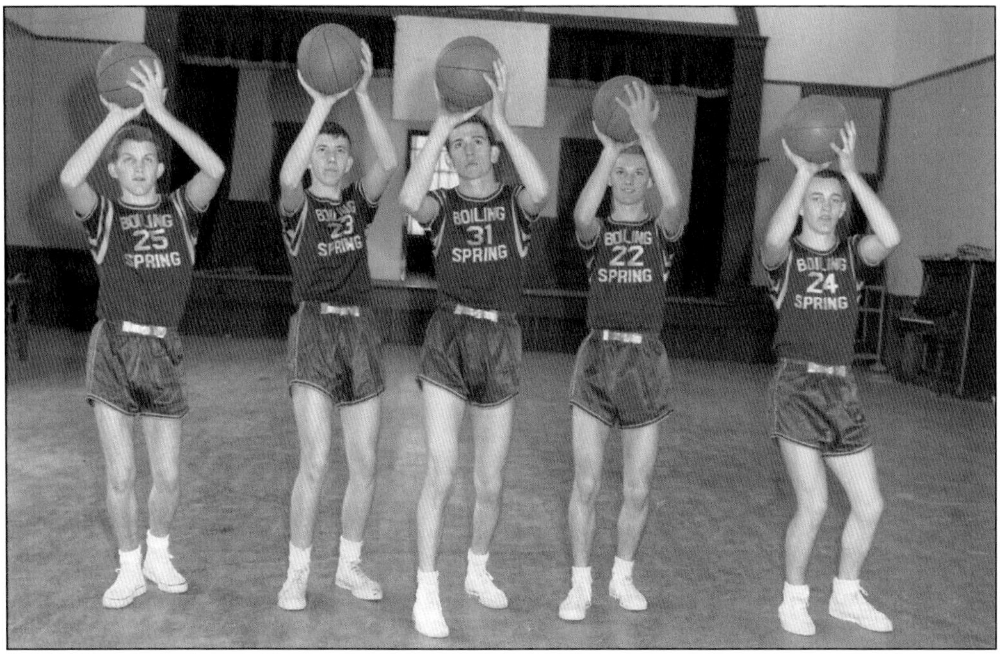

Just like Central, Boiling Spring School also housed elementary and high school grades, with the gymnasium representing the central focus of the school. Players had to be sure to pull up fast to miss the stage when making a layup and also avoid running into the piano on the side. The short length of the court is evident by the fact that the center jump circle is just inches away from the free throw circle. These Boiling Spring Bobcats basketball starters are, from left to right, Autry Gaines, Roy Hall, William Simmons, James Campbell, and Robert Nida (AHS-VR.)

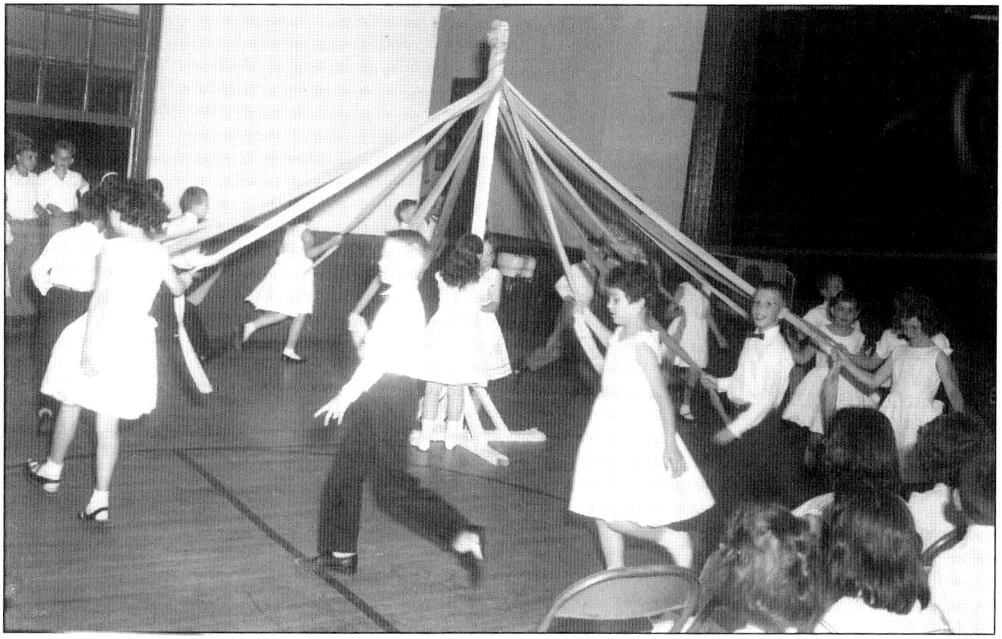

May Day was a special celebration at a number of elementary schools. These third-grade students at Boiling Spring School are dressed in their best Sunday outfits to dance the traditional Maypole dance at the Spring Festival on June 1, 1962. Schools without gyms traditionally held the celebration on the school lawn, which was one of the few times students didn't have to keep off the grass. (AHS-VR.)

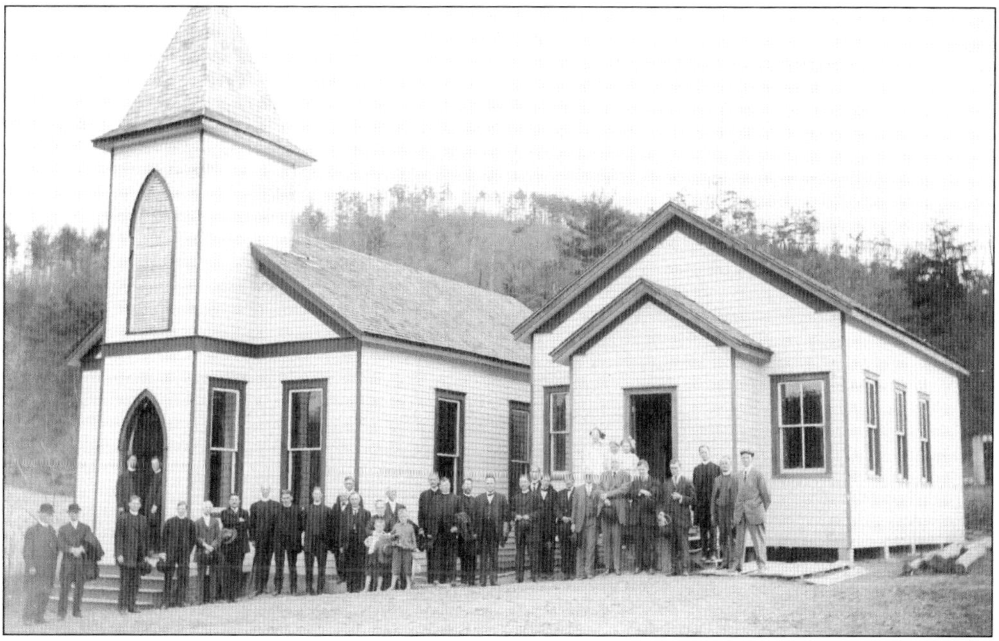

Boys' Home was originally started as a mission and boarding school by the Episcopal Church. The denomination still supports the programs of this home for boys. This photograph shows the chapel on the left and the one-room schoolhouse in the early 1900s. The school originally housed as many as 30 boys. (BH.)

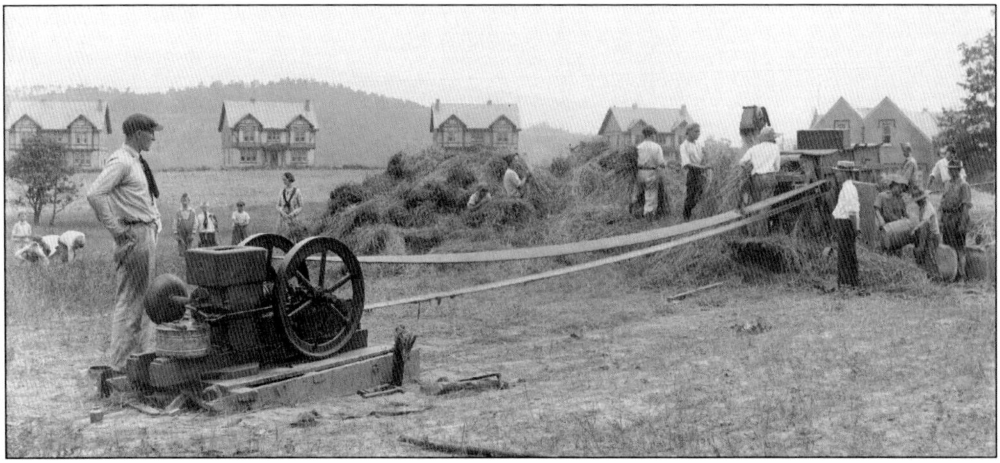

In addition to a safe home in one of the several cottages on the hill, Boys' Home provided a school for the boys and exposed them to both agricultural and industrial pursuits. Here the boys are feeding a threshing machine to extract grain from the crops of the fields of the Boys' Home farm. (BH.)

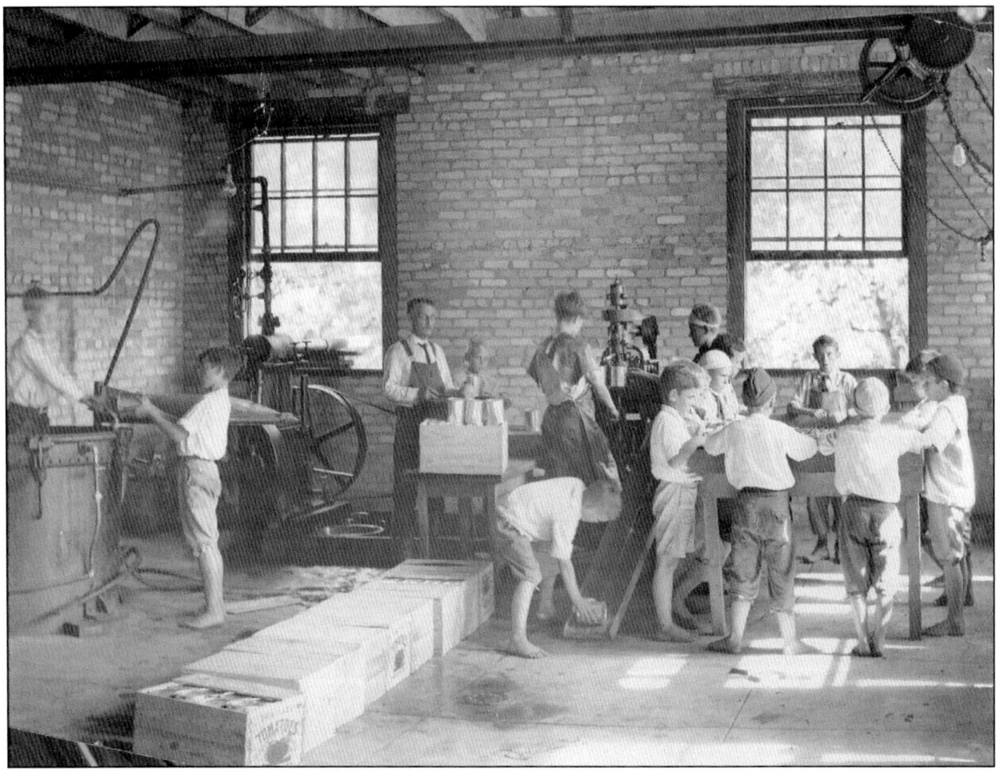

A cannery provided useful skills for the boys and also preserved locally grown vegetables. There was no need to wear shoes, as the open windows reveal that this was a warm day on "The Hill." Instructors and adults at Boys' Home were expected to present a professional appearance and create an atmosphere of respect and good discipline. (BH.)

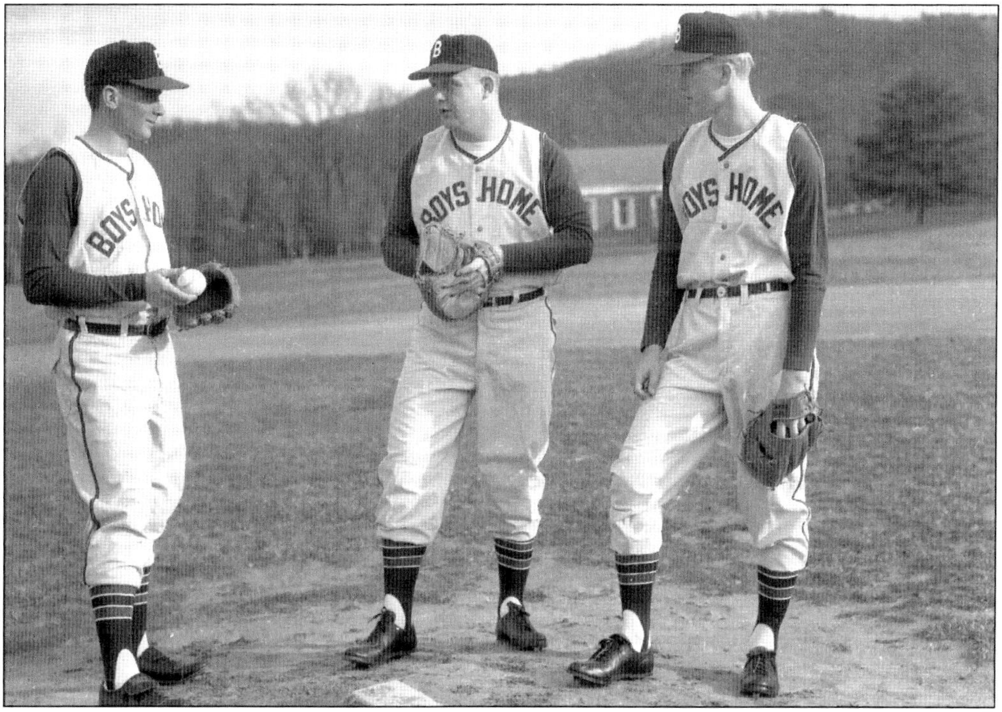

There was more than work for those who called Boys' Home their home. While most attended public schools in Covington and Alleghany County, where they played on the high school football teams, the home had its own basketball and baseball teams. Three of the finest athletes on The Hill are shown here in the early 1960s discussing strategy on the mound. From left to right, Buddy Hobbs, Pete Dimmick, and Mike Nunley provided a strong battery for coach Paul Siple's teams. Buddy and Mike pitched, and Pete caught behind the plate. (AHS-VR.)

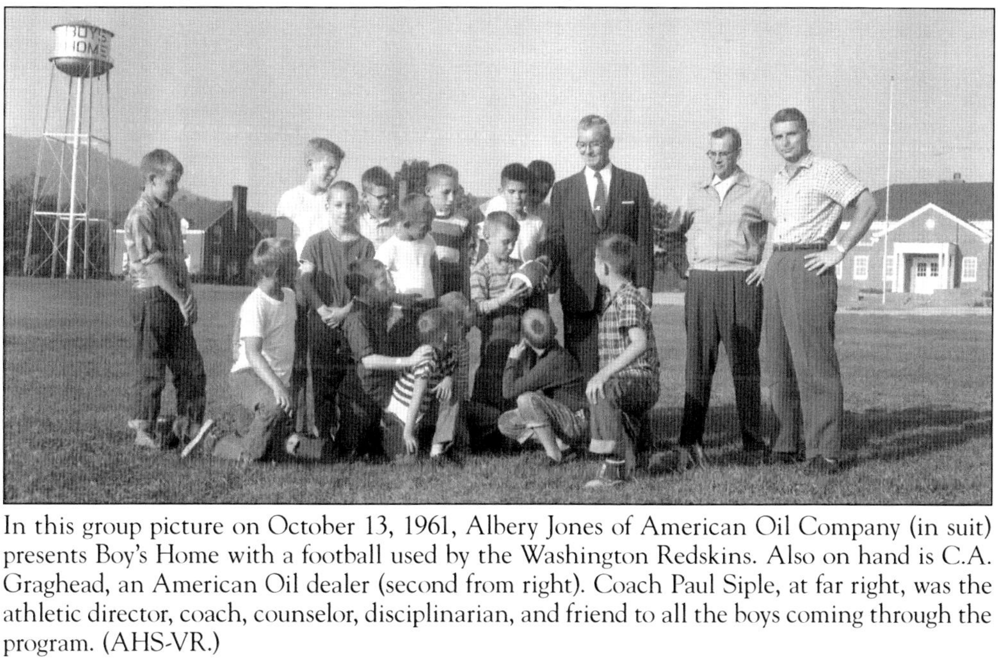

In this group picture on October 13, 1961, Albery Jones of American Oil Company (in suit) presents Boy's Home with a football used by the Washington Redskins. Also on hand is C.A. Graghead, an American Oil dealer (second from right). Coach Paul Siple, at far right, was the athletic director, coach, counselor, disciplinarian, and friend to all the boys coming through the program. (AHS-VR.)

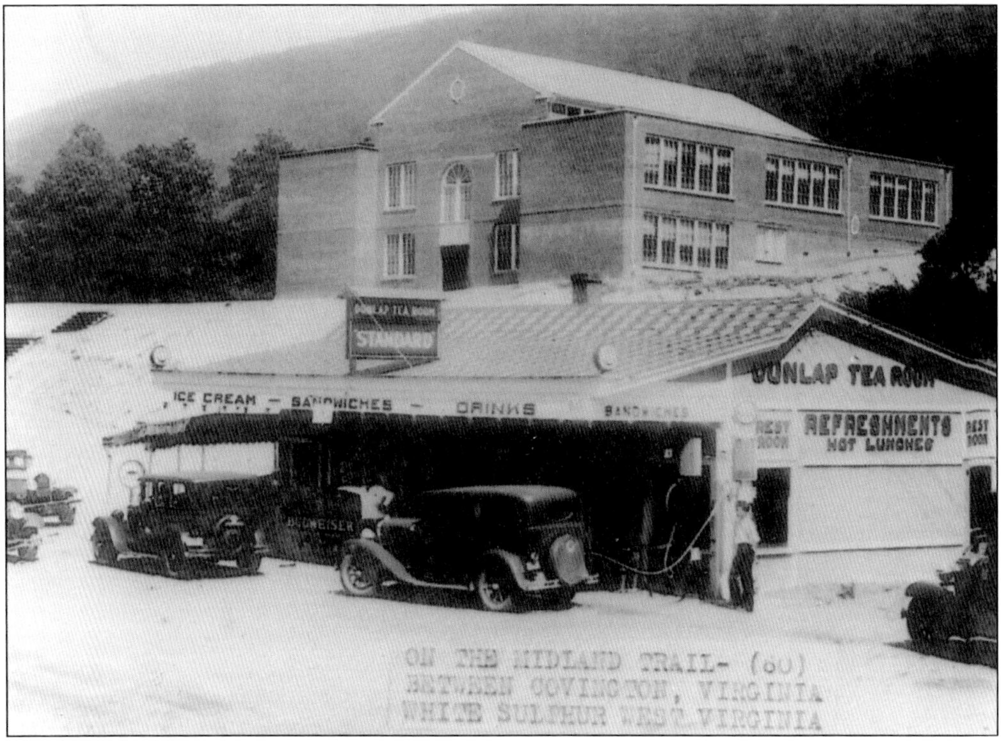

Dunlap School, like Central and Boiling Spring, served all students in the Callaghan, Dunlap, Crows, Hematite, Alleghany, and Sweet Chalybeate sections of the county. The structure was located on the old Midland Trail (US Route 60), and like the other comprehensive schools in the county, a gymnasium/auditorium dominated the central area of the school. The Dunlap Tea Room was a favorite stop on the road between Covington and White Sulphur Springs, West Virginia. (DB.)

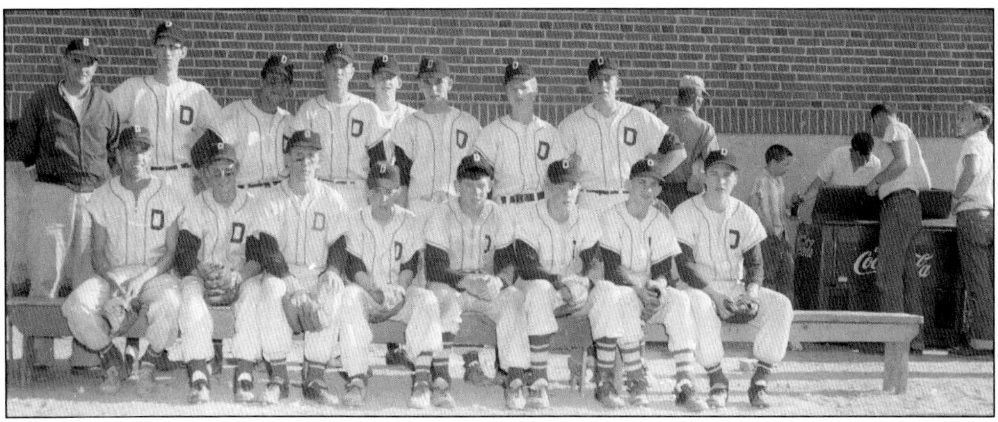

This photograph is of the Dunlap High School baseball team, coached by John Jenkins. This small school competed against similar sized schools, including Valley and Millboro in Bath County, New Castle in Craig County, and the local rivals from Boiling Spring. (AHS-VR.)

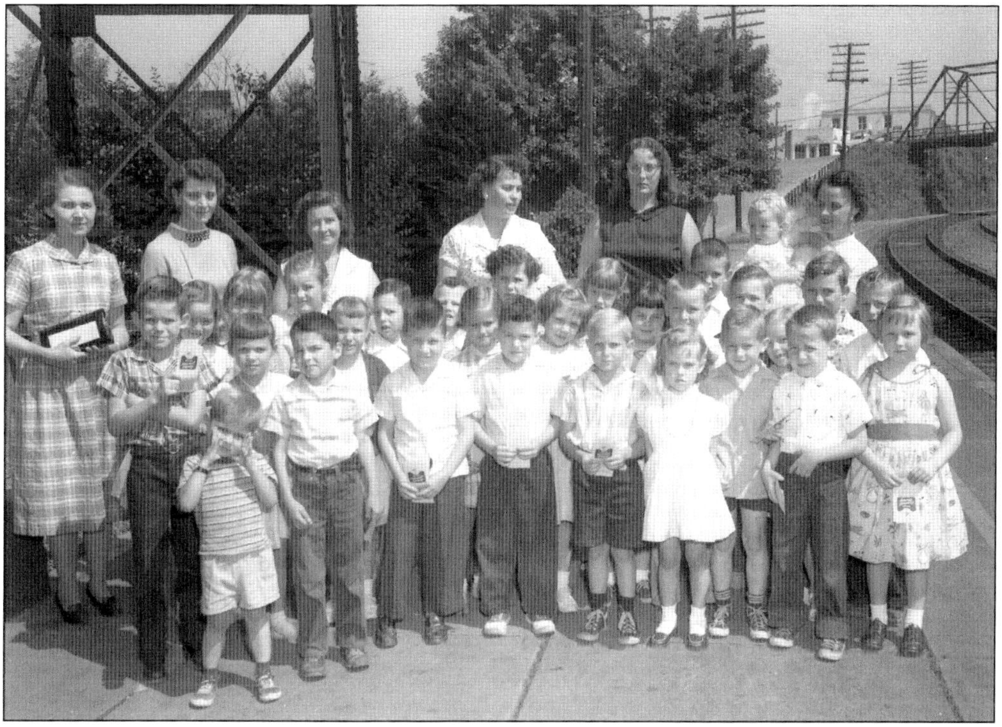

These first-graders from Dunlap rode the train from Covington to Clifton Forge on June 4, 1959. Here they pose for a picture by the Covington Depot. The steel structure to the rear supports the pedestrian bridge. (AHS-VR.)

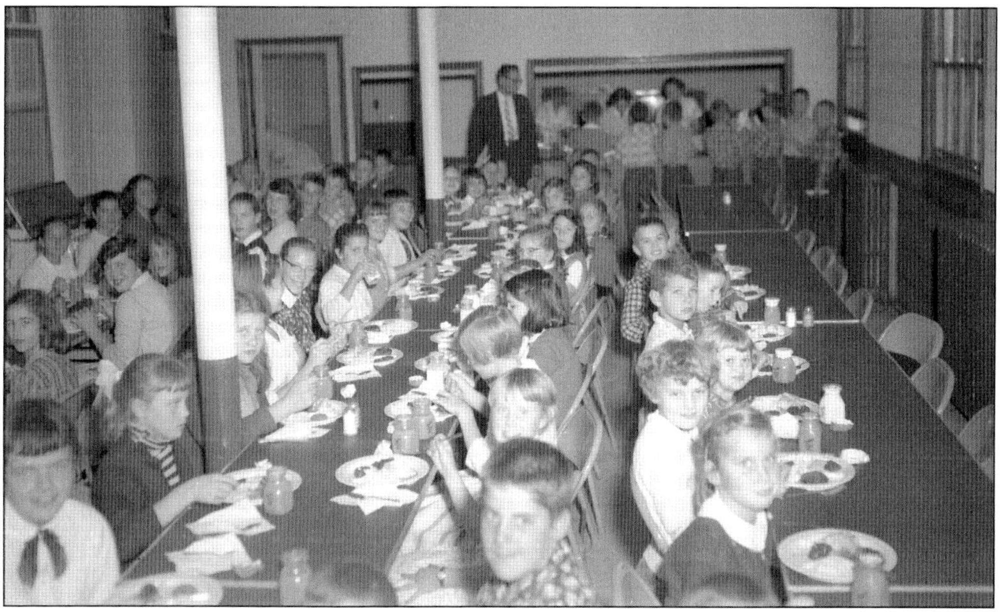

Students are enjoying lunch in the new Falling Spring cafeteria on September 26, 1957. Bill Fleming is the youngster in the bottom center of the photograph. Perhaps readers can identify other students in the photograph. The milk bottles carry the label of the local Peerless Creamery in Covington. (AHS-VR.)

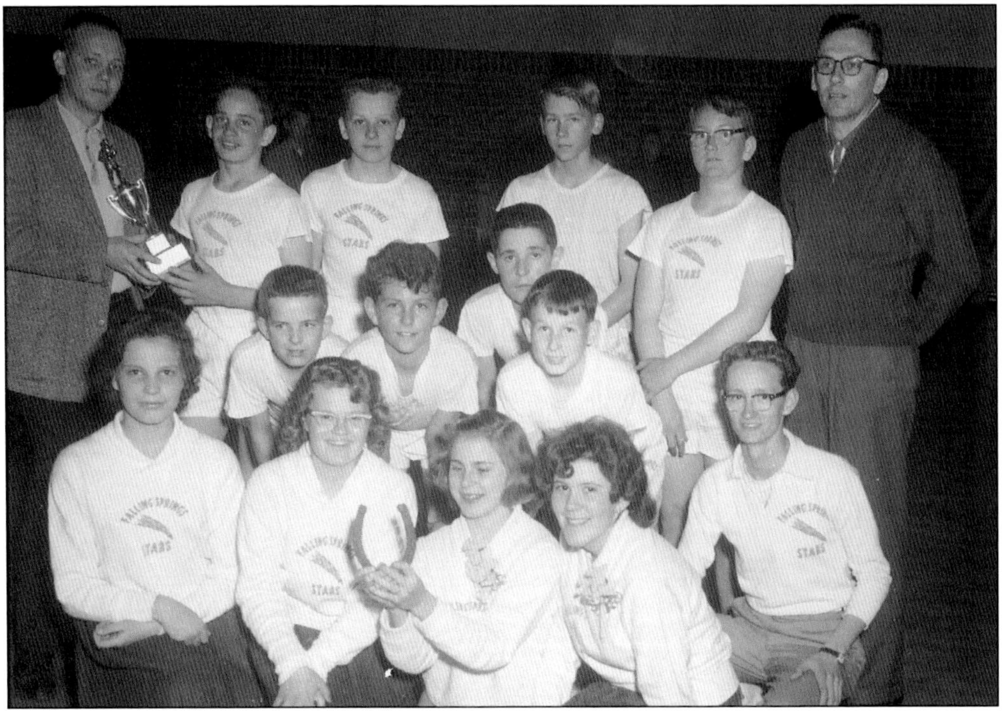

Members of the Falling Spring Stars are shown here accepting their youth league trophy, surely captured due to the good luck provided by the horseshoe. (AHS-VR.)

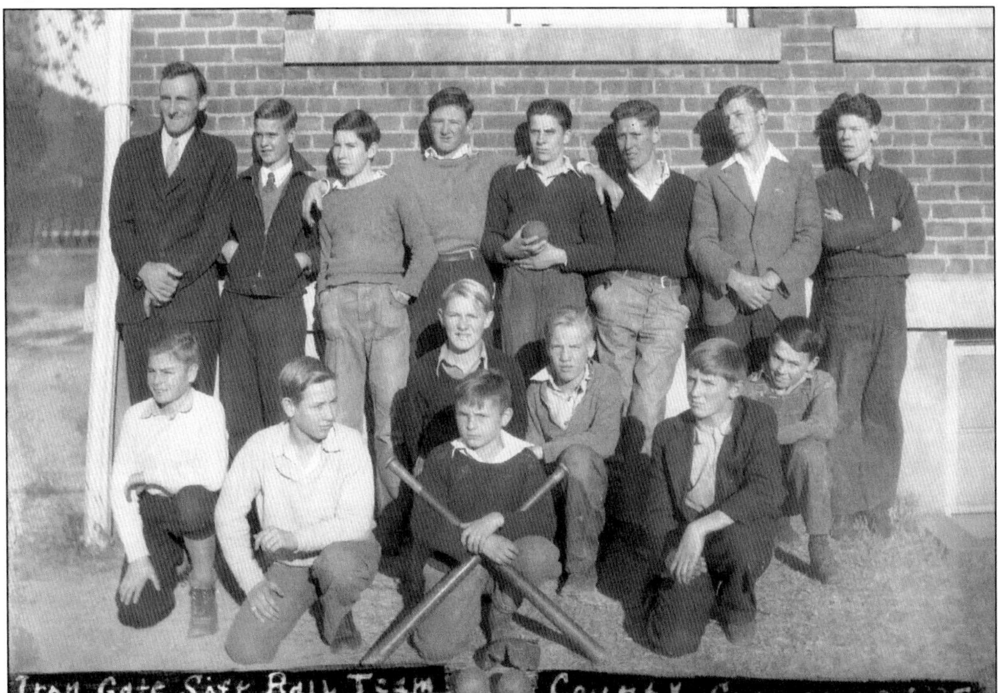

This photograph is of the Iron Gate softball team, county champions in 1935. They are standing in front of the Iron Gate Elementary School. (AHS-VR.)

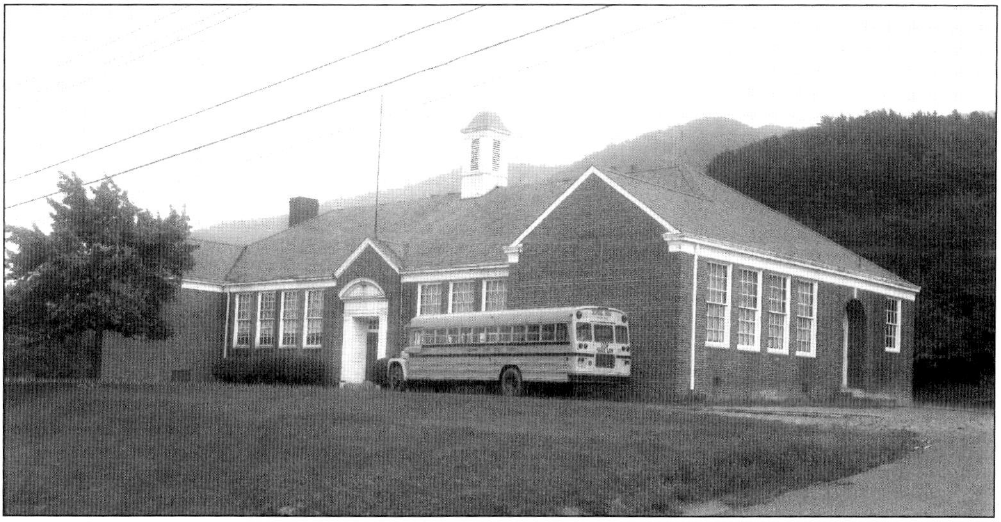

The original Graded School in Selma burned down on November 13, 1935. This six-room school was completed on January 5, 1937. This picture was taken in 1972. It became a satellite of Central School and accommodated third- and fourth-graders. It is now owned by a private individual. (AHS-VR.)

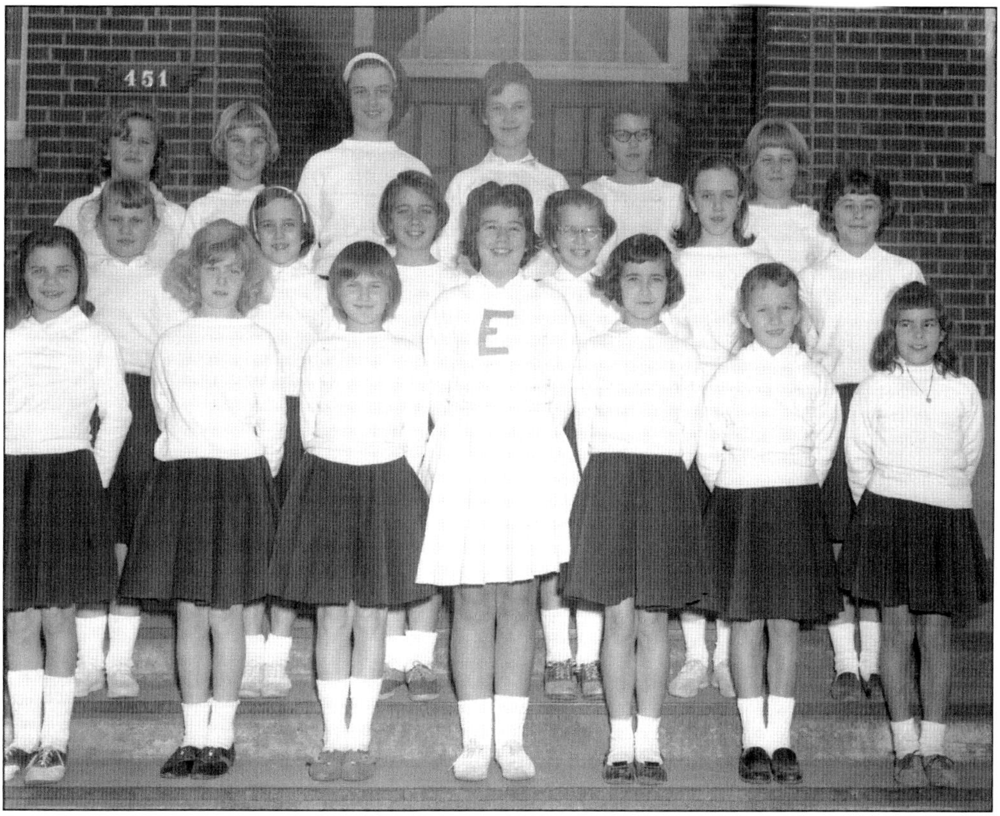

The Edgemont cheerleaders pose on the front steps of the school in the 1960s. Edgemont had been built around 1930 and remained in use until the new Edgemont School was built on Indian Valley Road at the edge of the city. (AHS-VR.)

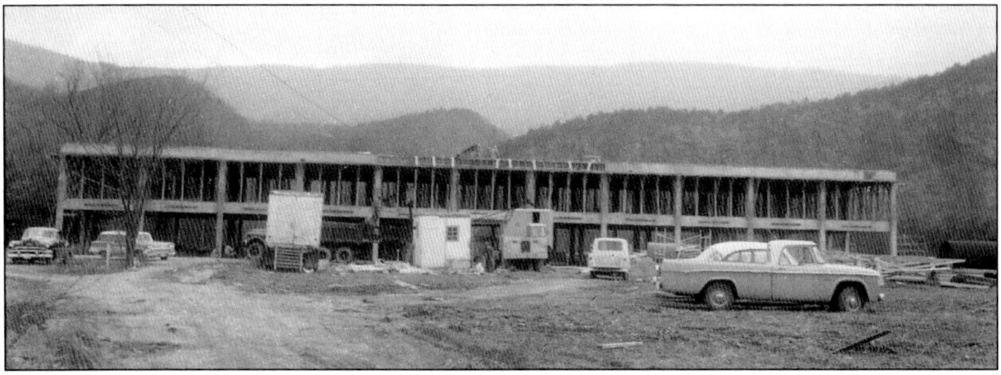

Just west of Clifton Forge, a community college was built in 1964 and was known as the Selma Poly-Tech and Feeder School, a part of Virginia Tech. This photograph was taken while the school was being built in March 1964. (AHS-VR.)

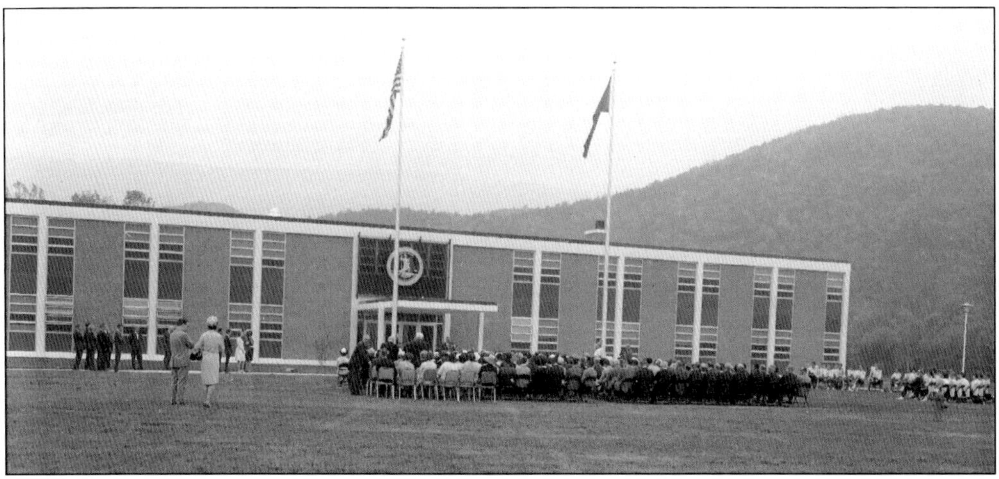

This photograph is of the completed building in May 1965, celebrating its first commencement. The school soon became the Dabney S. Lancaster Community College. The college was built on a site originally owned by James Wooly, who received a land grant for the property from King George III in the 1770s. It was bought by Joseph Haynes in 1789 and sold to the C&O Railway in 1890 by his descendent William Haynes. The C&O once operated a dairy on the site and donated the land for the college in 1963. (AHS-VR.)

Seven

Present and Future

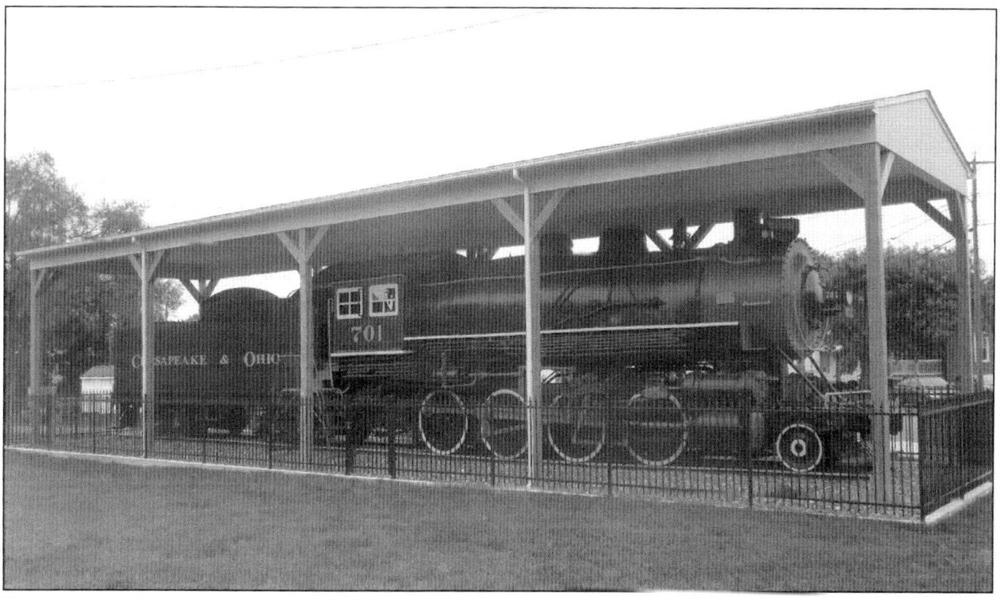

Locomotive 701 of the C&O Railway was built in 1911 in the Richmond Shops of the Baldwin Locomotive Works. The sole locomotive on the Hot Springs branch line, it was known as "the Merry Widow" and made as many as four trips daily, primarily to support the operation of the Homestead Hotel. It was given to Covington in 1954. It was painted and given a new shelter in 2015 through a combined project accomplished with financial and in-kind support from the City of Covington, the Alleghany Foundation, and local businesses. (AHS.)

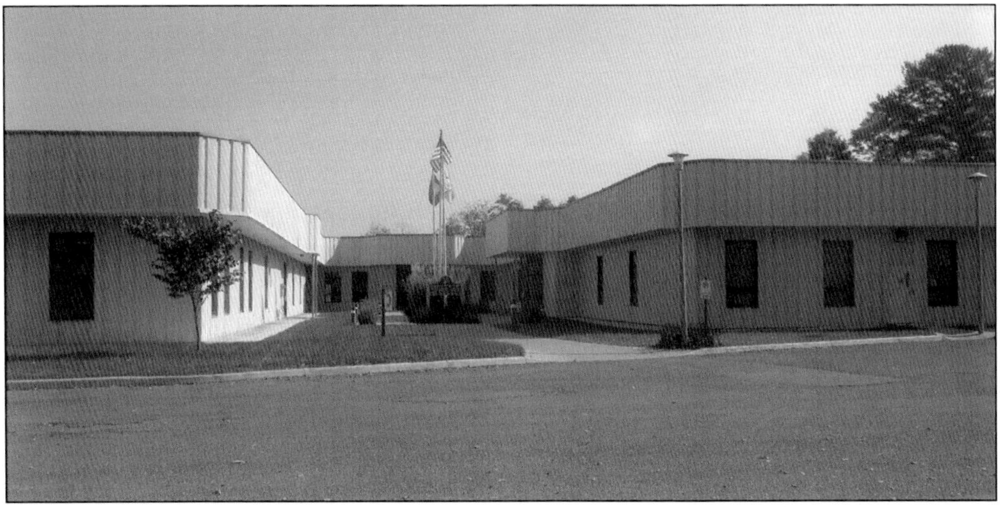

Alleghany County consolidated its central administration in this single facility in Low Moor. The offices of the county administrator, commissioner of the revenue, treasurer, central accounting, public works, and the department of parks and recreation occupy the complex as well as the board room of the Alleghany County Board of Supervisors. (AHS.)

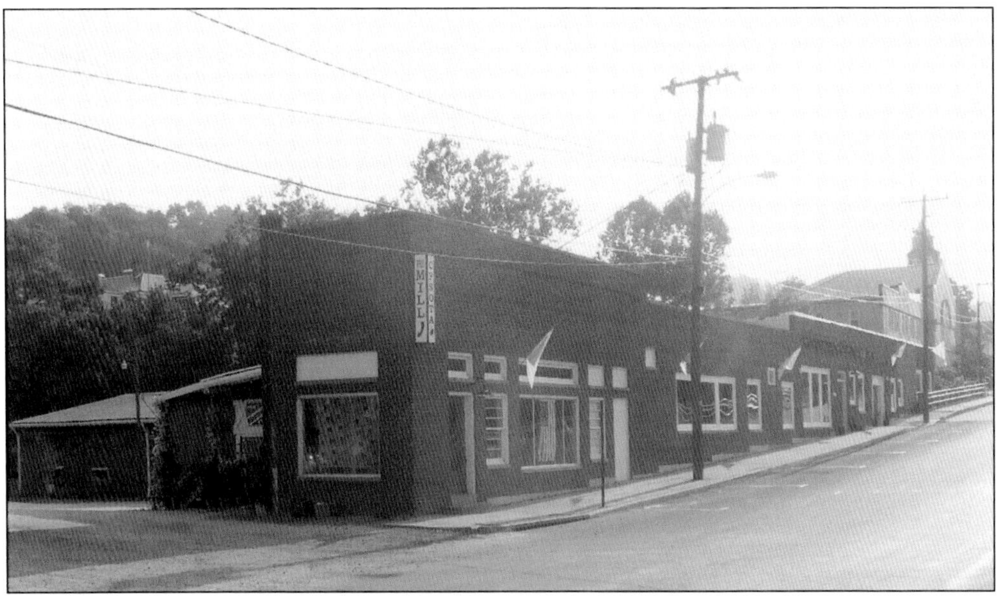

The former Wilson Tire Company was located in these buildings on Church Street that today house the new Clifton Forge School of the Arts. Painting, pottery, photography, blacksmithing, and other artistic classes are provided by the school. The school also houses exhibits and sponsors special events. (AHS.)

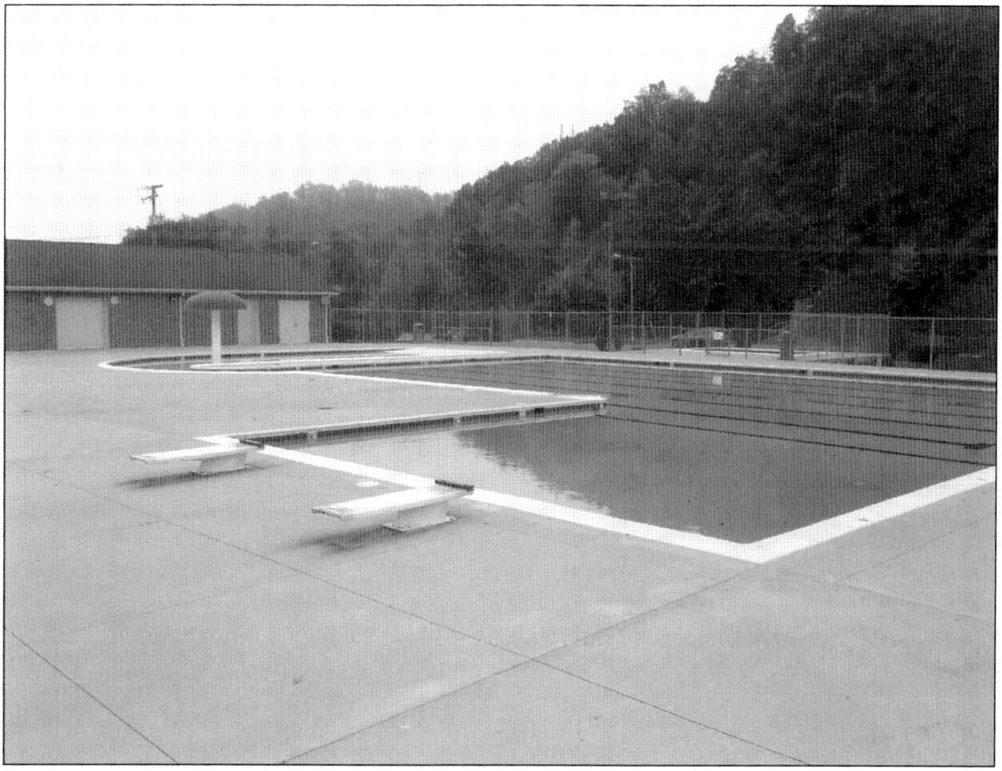

The new Covington City Pool at the Main Street Park not only provides recreational swimming but also teaches classes for beginner and advanced swimmers. The pool is staffed by certified lifeguards and is under the direction of Covington Parks and Recreation. A grant from the Alleghany Foundation helped support the project. (AHS.)

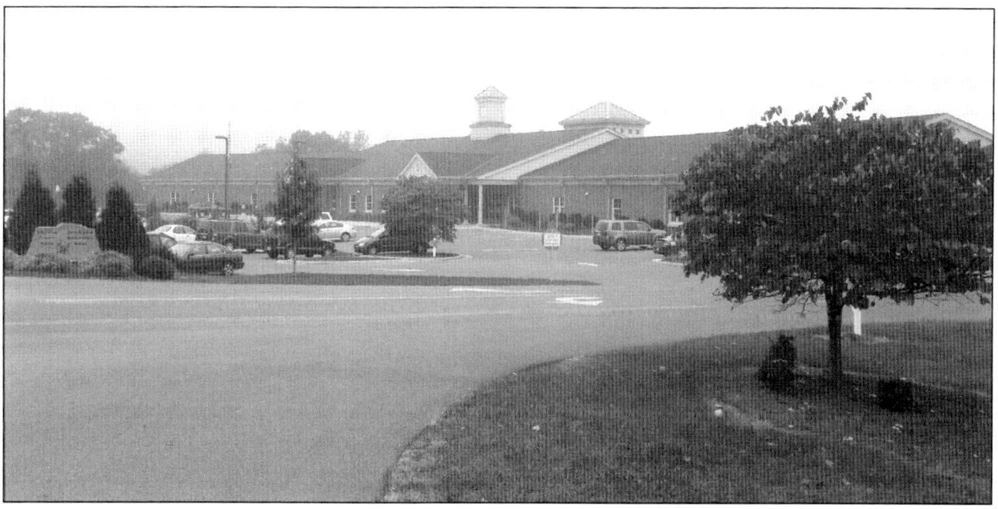

New schools were opened in Covington in 2008. Located on Indian Valley Road, Edgemont Primary School and Jeter-Watson Intermediate School retained the names of the older schools they replaced to maintain the tradition of schooling in Covington. (AHS.)

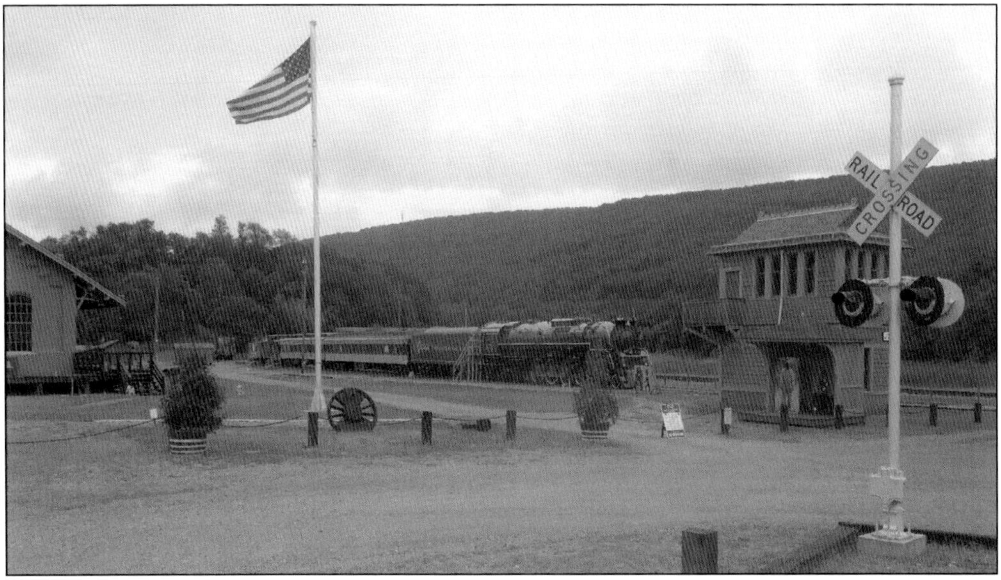

The C&O Railway Heritage Center opened in Clifton Forge in 2010. It is the museum owned and operated by the C&O Historical Society and is housed in the Smith Creek Yard Freight House, where it is open for tours and special events. A replica signal tower and passenger station are located on the grounds as well as vintage locomotives and rolling stock. A miniature train provides rides for children of all ages. The Alleghany Foundation also provided grant funding for portions of this project. (AHS.)

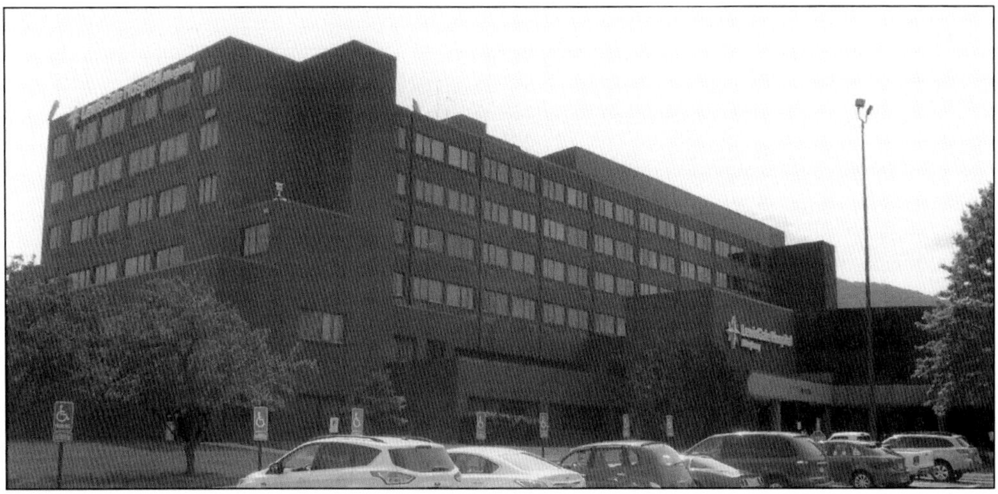

Lewis Gale Hospital–Alleghany was originally opened as Alleghany Regional Hospital on July 17, 1979. It was a consolidation of the Emmett Memorial Hospital in Clifton Forge and the Alleghany Memorial Hospital in Covington. It was first operated as a locally owned nonprofit facility. It was sold on June 30, 1995, to Columbia/Hospital Corporation of America for $35 million. The proceeds were used to establish the Alleghany Foundation, which has provided millions of dollars in grants for worthwhile projects in the development of the Alleghany Highlands. (AHS.)

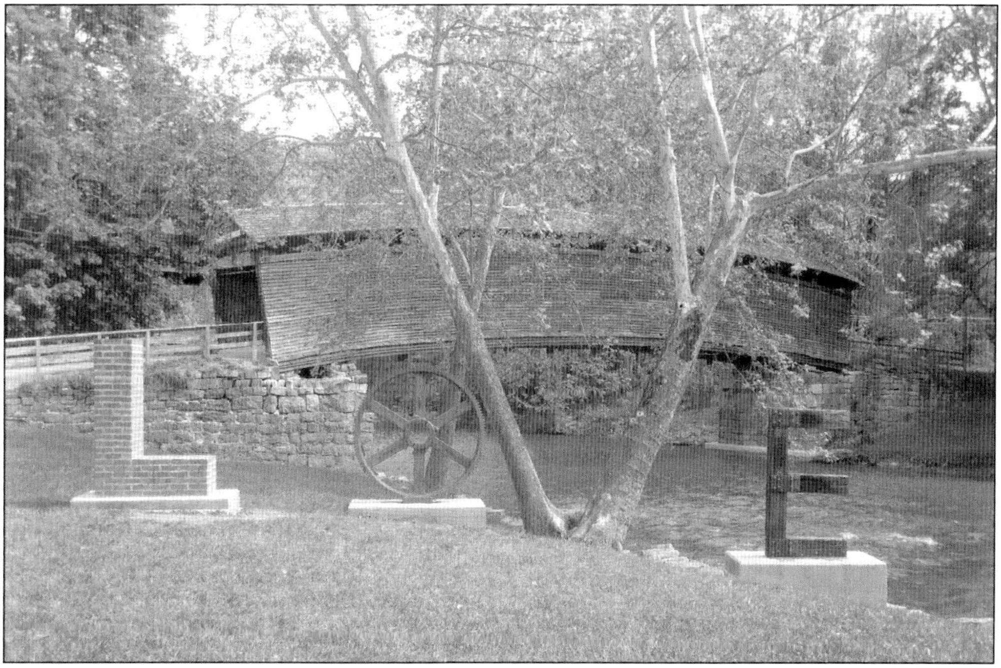

The most familiar and unique structure in Alleghany County is the Humpback Bridge over Dunlap Creek west of Covington. As part of the Virginia is for Lovers campaign, the word "love" was created in the unique fashion shown here. The *L* was constructed from bricks made in the area, the *O* was a machinery wheel used at the Covington paper mill, the *V* is from the natural growth of the trees, and the *E* was created from ties of the C&O Railway. (AHS.)

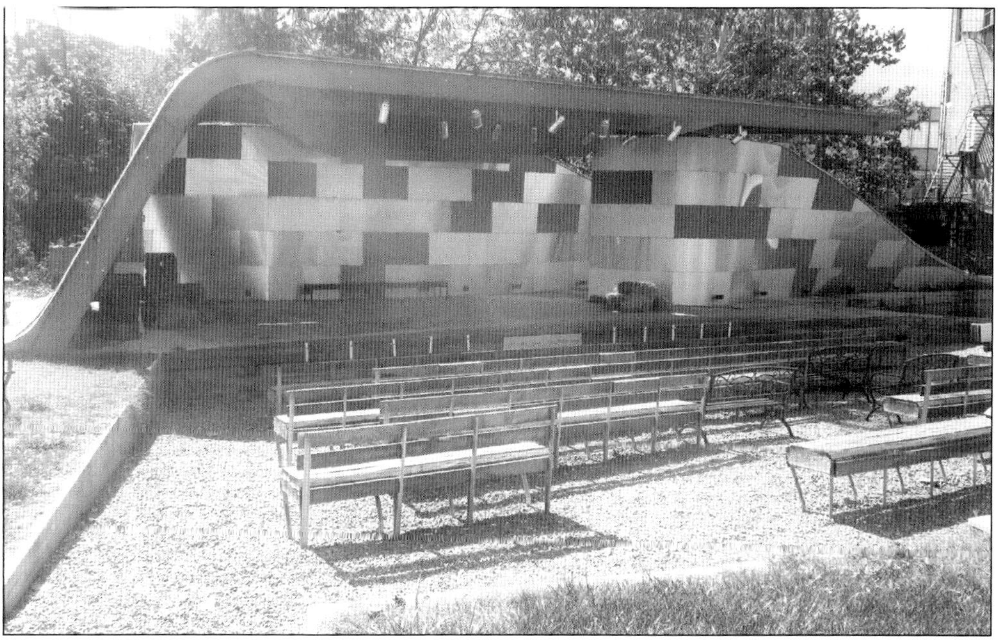

During the restoration of the Historic Masonic Theatre, a grant from the Alleghany Foundation helped fund the construction of this unique amphitheater by architectural students from Virginia Tech. The side of the theater with its fire escapes is shown in the background. (AHS.)

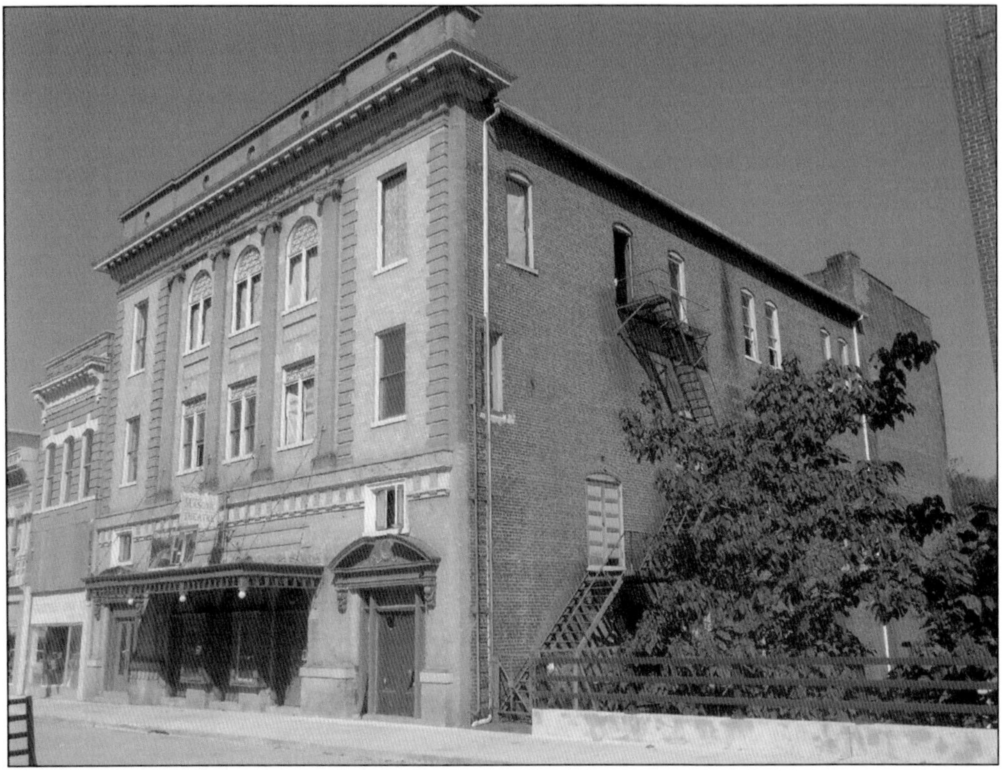

After years of fundraising, planning, and development, the reconstruction of the Historic Masonic Theatre in Clifton Forge was scheduled for completion in July 2016. The Alleghany Foundation, corporate and individual contributions, historic tax credits, and other grants have provided more than $7 million in funding for the restoration. (AHS.)

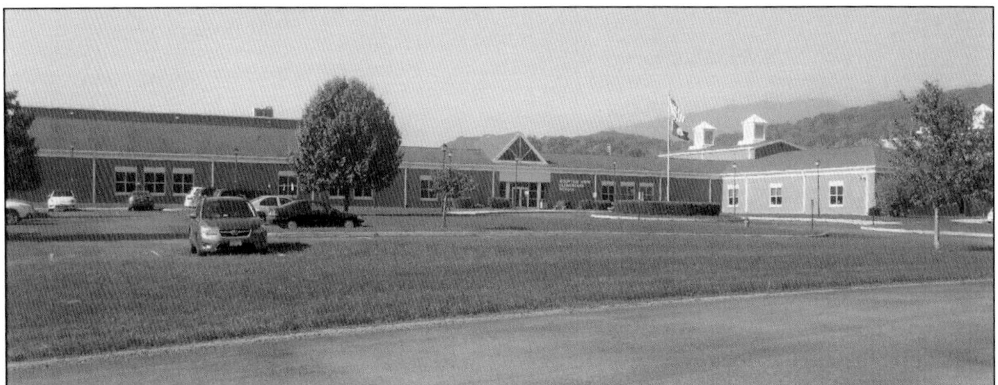

In 2001, two new schools were opened in Low Moor. Pictured is the Mountain View Elementary School, which consolidated Central, Clifton Forge West, and Clifton Forge East Elementary Schools. The land was partially donated by heirs of the Gleason family, who own the Merry Plantation on the property. The other school retained the name of Clifton Middle School and serves all sixth-, seventh-, and eighth-grade students in Alleghany County and Clifton Forge. Grants from the Alleghany Foundation funded the technology infrastructure and athletic complex at the schools. (AHS.)

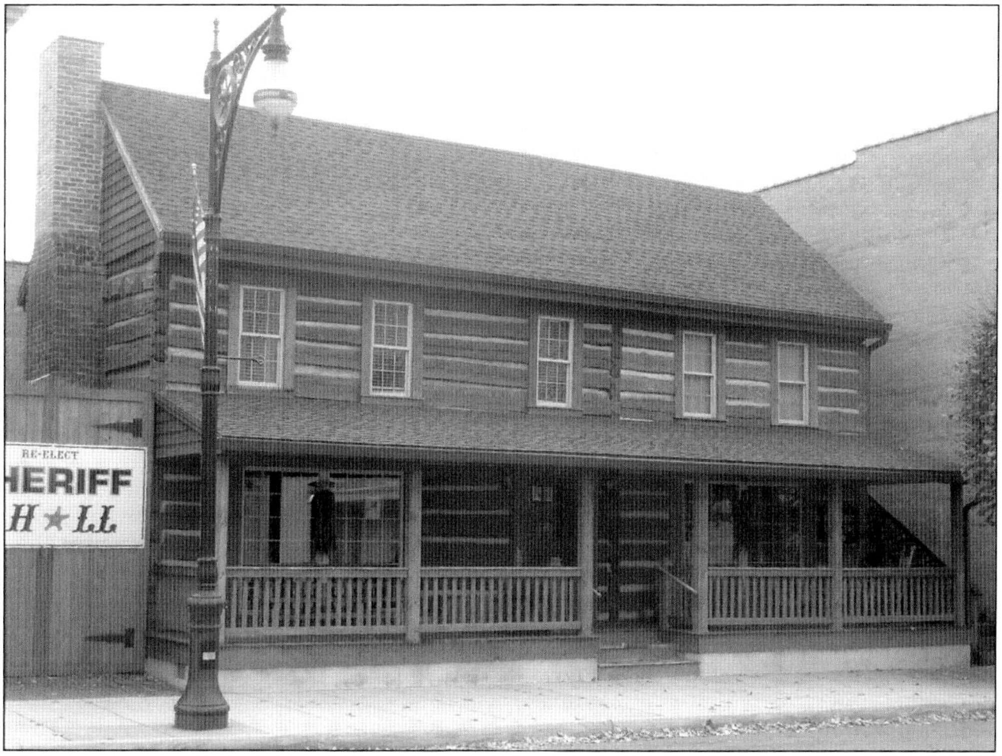

One of the oldest structures on Historic Main Street in Covington is the Scott-Hammond House. It was restored by Warren and Teenie Kegley, owners of Rupert Real Estate. The unique lamp post in front of the building is a replica of those once manufactured by the Covington Machine Shops. This project and other renovations in Olde Town Covington support efforts for the economic revitalization of the downtown. The Kegleys are primary supporters of the Olde Town Covington organization. (AHS.)

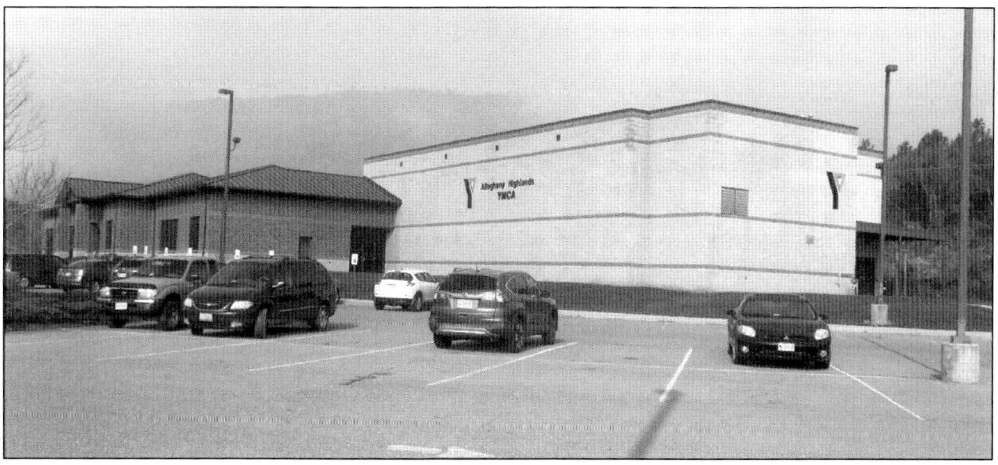

Another project supported by the Alleghany Foundation and corporate and individual contributors was the building of the Alleghany Highlands YMCA in Low Moor. The building provides facilities to enhance fitness and contribute to the recreational opportunities in the area. The Olympic-size swimming pool is used for both therapeutic and competition purposes. The Alleghany Gators swim team represents the area. (AHS.)